NATO, THE WARSAW PACT AND AFRICA

NATO, THE WARSAW PACT AND AFRICA

Christopher Coker

St. Martin's Press   New York

© RUSI 1985

All rights reserved. For information, write:
St. Martin's Press, Inc., 175 Fifth Avenue, New York, NY 10010
Printed in Great Britain
Published in the United Kingdom by The Macmillan Press Ltd.
First published in the United States of America in 1985

ISBN 0–312–56066–4

Library of Congress Cataloging in Publication Data
Coker, Christopher.
NATO, the Warsaw Pact, and Africa.
Bibliography: p.
Includes index.
1. Africa—Strategic aspects. 2. North Atlantic
Treaty Organization. 3. Warsaw Treaty Organization.
4. Europe—Military relations—Africa. 5. North
America—Military relations—Africa. 6. Africa—Military
relations—Europe. 7. Africa—Military relations—North
America. I. Title.
UA855.C64   1985   355′.03306   85–2111
ISBN 0–312–56066–4

Contents

Abbreviations vii

Preface ix

PART I

1 **The Past as Prologue: The Western Alliance and Africa 1949–74**   3
   The Political Dimension   12

2 **The Western Powers and Africa, 1949–74**   19
   United Kingdom   19
   France   29
   United States   40

3 **The North Atlantic Alliance and Southern Africa, 1949–74**   48
   NATO and Portugal: The Policies of Ambiguity   49
   The Anglo–South African Connection   71
   South Africa and SACLANT, 1972–74   82

4 **NATO and Warsaw Pact Intervention, 1970–78**   87
   The Soviet Union and the Defence of Guinea, 1970–74   88
   Soviet Intervention in Angola, 1974–76   92
   Soviet Intervention in the Horn, 1977–78   103

5 **France and Western Security, 1974–83**   113
   Chad and French Unilateralism, 1969–83   116
   Franco–Belgian Intervention in Zaire, 1977–78   122
   French Operations since 1978   129

6 **NATO and South Africa, 1974–83**   134
   South African Intervention in Southern Africa   143

PART II

7 The Warsaw Pact and Africa, 1959–83   **157**
Eastern Europe and Africa's Minerals   158
CMEA Shortages   164

8 The Warsaw Pact and Southern Africa, 1974–83   **172**
Southern Africa: The Looking Glass World   176

9 The Warsaw Pact, East Germany and the Threat of Western Intervention   **190**
   192
GDR and Southern Africa, 1974–78   196
GDR and the Warsaw Pact since 1978   203
Conclusion

PART III

10 Africa, the Western Alliance and the Soviet Challenge, 1961–78   **207**
Bases and Base Rights   212
British Arms Sales to South Africa   222
Africa and Portugal   226
Franco–Belgian Intervention in Shaba, 1978   230
African Attitudes to the Soviet Intervention in Angola   235

11 Conclusion: NATO and the Threat to Africa   **241**
The Alliance or the Allies?   248

Notes and References   255

Bibliography   287

Index   301

LIST OF TABLES

Table 1	Ships and aircraft sold to S. Africa	138
Table 2	Capital stock – resource extraction	164
Table 3	Tonnage and value forecast, 1990	170
Table 4	Estimated value of inverted capital	171
Table 5	Polish seaborne foreign trade	181
Table 6	Oligopolistic firm concentration	186
Table 7	Survey – Reaction towards US proposals to expand Diego Garcia	218
Table 8	Time trend – wars in black Africa	247

Abbreviations

AFLANT	Air Force Atlantic
ANC	African National Congress
CMEA	Council for Mutual Economic Assistance
DPC	Defence Planning Committee
EFTA	European Free Trade Union
EURCOM	US European Command
FAZSOC	French Indian Ocean Fleet
FNLA	National Front for the Liberation of Angola
FREMLIMO	Front for the Liberation of Mozambique
FROLINAT	Chad National Liberation Front
GDR	German Democratic Republic
IBERLANT	Iberian Atlantic Command
MAAG	Military Assistance Advisory Group
MAP	Military Assistance Programme
MIDEASTFOR	US Middle East Command (naval)
MPLA	Popular Movement for the Liberation of Angola
NORAD	North American Air Defense Command
OAU	Organisation of African Unity
OEEC	Organisation for European Economic Co-operation (now: OECD)
PAIGC	African independence party of Guinea and Cape Verde
RDF	Rapid Deployment Force
SACEUR	Supreme Allied Commander Europe
SACLANT	Supreme Allied Command Atlantic
SADCC	Southern African Development Coordination Council
SADF	South African Defence Forces
SAN	South African Navy
SHAPE	Supreme Headquarters Allied Powers Europe

SWAPO	South West African People's Organisation
UKMF	UK Mobile Forces
UKJATFOR	UK Joint Airborne Task Forces
UNITA	National Union for the total Independence of Angola
WEU	Western European Union
ZANU	Zimbabwe African National Union
ZAPU	Zimbabwe African Peoples' Union

Preface

Perhaps, no event generated more criticism of Western intervention in Africa than the parachute drop at Kolwezi (1978); perhaps, no event illustrates better Africa's ambiguous relationship with the Western powers. Calling in Western diplomats a month after the Kolwezi operation, Julius Nyerere, President of Tanzania, deplored what he saw as an attempt to reassert Western domination of the continent under the pretext of defending it against outside intervention. The following month, at the OAU Conference in Khartoum, Lieutenant-General Obasanjo, President of Nigeria, rejected the notion that Africa's collective security could be discussed or determined in Brussels. He conceded that NATO was concerned about the projection of Soviet power, but like many African leaders he considered that its concern was unwarranted. Africa had been colonised by the Western powers, not the Russians. In its struggle for independence, it had looked for support to the Warsaw Pact, not the Atlantic Alliance.

The gloss put on events by Tanzania and Nigeria differed markedly from the priorities which figured most prominently in NATO planning. Obasanjo reiterated that for many countries, his own included, NATO's actions were of more acute concern than those of the Soviet bloc. In view of its extensive interests in Africa the West was much more likely to defend them by force. His concern was prompted largely by historical experience. 'Paratroop drops in the twentieth century', he reminded the OAU, 'are no more acceptable to us than gunboats in the last century were to our ancestors. Convening conferences in Europe and America to decide the fate of Africa (a reference to the NATO summit meeting in Washington in the wake of the Kolwezi operation) raises too many ugly spectres which should best be forgotten both in our own and Europe's interests'.

This analysis of events revealed a profound difference in understanding between Western and African leaders. Most Africans found the alleged Soviet threat somewhat unreal – many suspected it was an invention of the Western Alliance designed to fill the palpable gap between its professed support for self-determination in Southern Africa and its tacit support of the *status quo*. If not entirely oblivious to the extension of Soviet power, most believed that the Russians were dangerous only because they were able to exploit problems for which the West itself was largely responsible.

Compared to Soviet intervention in Angola and the Horn which had the broad support of the majority of OAU members, NATO's alleged intervention in Zaire appeared much more threatening. At no time since the early 1960s had the Alliance been invoked more often, or its policies been discussed at such length. Yet it may well be asked whether Africa has ever fitted into NATO contingency planning, or whether, contrary to popular belief, the Atlantic Alliance has been more sensitive to African opinion and more attentive to African aspirations than its critics have given it credit.

The Zaire operation also produced one of the most trenchant Soviet attacks on NATO. A statement put out by *Pravda* cited the operation on 23 June 1978 as evidence of a NATO offensive aimed at containing recent social and economic changes in the continent which had run against the grain of Western interests:

> ... the forces of imperialism, racism and reaction do not want to come to terms with positive changes in Africa. They want to continue exploiting the African peoples and the continent's natural wealth; they still continue to think in terms of 'spheres of influence' ...
> the example of Zaire demonstrates that the imperialist powers are resorting to direct military action against Africa with the use of their own armed forces, thus reviving the worst times of colonial plunder.

Pravda went on to claim that the military action represented a new and dangerous development – the extension of NATO's out-of-area operations. From the NATO Council meeting in Washington and a conference of the five leading NATO powers in Paris, it was clear that NATO's most recent actions marked a new and dangerous phase in its policy of containing the forces of national liberation. It was a policy with the single aim of directing Africa's development into a neo-colonialist 'partnership' based on 'exploitation and plunder'.

What follows is a study of NATO's involvement in Africa from the date of its inception. This study is intended to lay to rest some of the more doubtful claims of NATO collusion with South Africa and its alleged operations against other African governments. It is also intended to highlight what many African states have identified as a quite different challenge from the Warsaw Pact. That challenge has not been ignored, but it has not been discussed very extensively. It concludes by asking how best to parry that threat and what role if any the Alliance should play in the continent.

This book began life as a research project for a NATO Fellowship. I would like to thank Dr Fernand Welter at the NATO Information Office for his unfailing support and Dr Saul van Campen for his encouragement to embark upon this study. I would also like to thank NATO itself for a generous travel allowance which enabled me to travel extensively in 1981. In the making of this work I have incurred many debts, but particularly to Kurt Campbell and John Chipman at the International Institute for Strategic Studies for drawing my attention to many important sources, and to Dr Alan Smith at the School of Slavonic Studies for his advice on the economic section towards the end of this study. I must not least thank the Royal United Services Institute for providing me with the opportunity to publish my findings and for encouraging me to complete the work.

CHRISTOPHER COKER

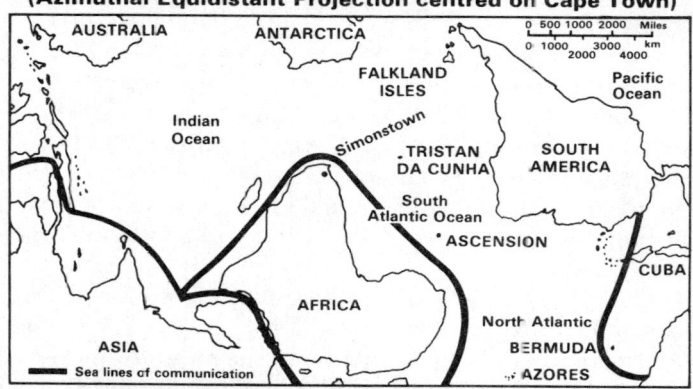
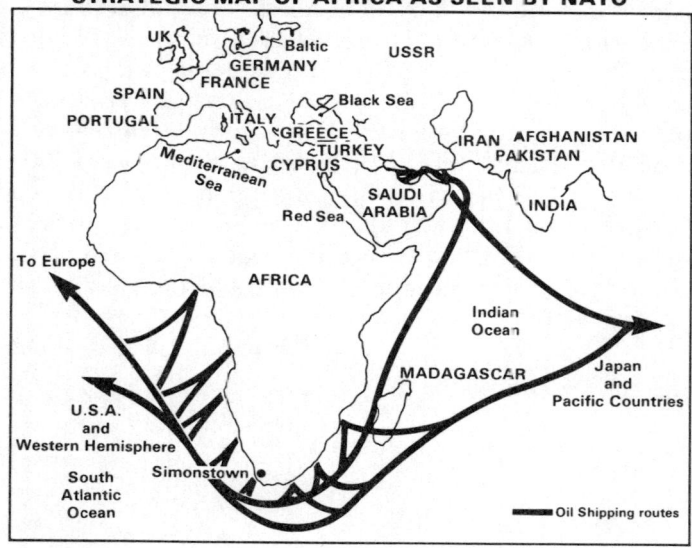

Part I

1 The Past as Prologue: The Western Alliance and Africa, 1949–74

In one form or another, defence against Soviet aggression has been the professed objective of Western policy since World War II. At various times the policy has ranged from confrontation to *détente*, from cold war to peaceful engagement, but whatever the nomenclature or its political content, collective defence has been the keystone of Western strategy. Whatever the West's apparent beliefs and hopes for eventual political reconciliation with the Soviet bloc through trade and other contacts, it has never put its trust entirely in diplomacy.

On the occasion of the signing of the Brussels Treaty on 17 March 1948 between the United Kingdom, France and the BENELUX countries, President Truman told the American Congress that the United States would extend whatever support the situation required. Without American support and the substantial, if diffuse, consensus in Congress that the more threatening Soviet behaviour, the more necessary American participation, the Brussels Treaty would never have been translated into the Atlantic Alliance. After discussions between the Brussels powers and the United States and Canada in the summer, it was decided to invite five other governments to sign the proposed treaty. The Atlantic Pact was eventually signed in Washington on 4 April and came into force on 24 August 1949.

The need to oppose Soviet expansionism had become more and more urgent since 1947. Isolationism, which had proved inadequate in the 1930s, held out no greater promise ten years later. At the same time the Czech *coup* and the Berlin blockade had suggested the wisdom of integrating Western defence more closely. Past experience had shown that individual responses had produced a narrow security outlook and deficient defence. Yet it was only with reluctance that the United States abandoned its dislike of open-ended commitments, a fact borne out by the 16 days which the hearings on the treaty occupied the Senate Foreign Relations Committee and the 12 days which the ratification debate lasted in the Senate itself.

At the time the Europeans put their signatures to the North Atlantic Treaty, the need for an understanding on defence outside Europe as well as within was taken for granted. It should not have been. Although the French argued that any treaty which excluded North Africa would be unacceptable to French public opinion, the BENELUX countries and Canada were doubtful of the wisdom of bringing in North Africa, in part out of concern that Belgium would then insist on bringing in the Congo. The Americans were the most opposed of all – they thought it would be difficult to justify the inclusion of an area which had not been covered by the Brussels Treaty and which did not fall within the geographical scope of the North Atlantic.[1]

The French attempted to elicit a guarantee not only for Algeria but for the whole of North Africa, north of latitude 30°, an area which included the Suez Canal, Tunisia and a large part of Morocco. They even succeeded in getting this proposal incorporated in the draft treaty approved by the Permanent Commission of the Brussels Powers on 26 November 1948. It was the United States which put an end to these hopes by ruling out the inclusion of any African territory. At the ambassadors' committee on 22 December 1948, the Canadian representative objected to the inclusion of any territory which might 'give rise to possible colonial difficulties and introduce a new and complicating factor'.[2]

Even before the formation of NATO, the future of North Africa had taxed the minds of British and American statesmen. At the London Conference in September 1945, the United States had put forward a scheme for a collective trusteeship of Libya. In the years that followed both the Soviet Union and the West changed their positions according to their respective perceptions of security. At one time the Russians favoured returning Libya to Italian control; by 1948 they had come out in support of the original American plan which, by this time, Washington had abandoned. In the end, after an interim administration by the United Nations, Libya

emerged in the vanguard of the new independent African states.
What is interesting about the episode is the views expressed by South Africa's Prime Minister, General Smuts, for whom like Britain the problem of the Italian colonies was inseparably linked with Western security. In September 1945, Smuts had urged the Americans to take Eritrea with the port of Massawa as a strategic base, to complement a comparable British base in Cyrenaica (Libya). From both bases, the Western powers would be able to secure the most important lines of communication between Europe and the Middle East and ensure that the British Commonwealth and the United States would never again have to face the danger they had fought against in 1939.

Perhaps, most interesting of all was Smuts' second reason for Britain to establish a military base in Cyrenaica: the need to overcome a future 'atomic stalemate'. Smuts predicted that when the Soviet Union developed its own nuclear weapons, both Britain and America would be deterred from using their own by the threat of retaliation against their own cities. British control of an atomic base in Libya would:

> ... provide ... the only real answer to any attempted raids by a future rapacious European power, heedless of the consequences; for if the fear of reprisals by densely populated Western European countries should operate against the use of the atomic bomb to their detriment ... no such fear would prevent its use from the deserts of Cyrenaica ...
>
> Only the fear of certain punishment inflicted in the capital and towns of his own country would restrain the aggressor. The remote desert would offer that threat without fear of reprisal ...[3]

Smut's proposal was not entirely disingenuous. The United States did maintain a base in Libya after its independence in 1951 at which B-52 bombers were stationed until the early 1960s. They were even put on nuclear alert at the height of the Cuban missile crisis.

The British and French and, to a lesser extent, their Dutch and Belgian allies, had originally hoped that the NATO Pact would encompass their colonial possessions in Africa, and only agreed not to press the point when they realised that the proposal would never win endorsement in the US Senate. Agreement had to be limited, much to their regret, to Article 4 of the Atlantic Treaty by which the signatories agreed to consult one another:

> if in the opinion of any of them the territorial integrity, political independence or security of any of the parties is threatened.

It was generally understood at the time that the Article did not apply to interests outside Europe. A harassed Dean Acheson explained in secret testimony before Congress that if British or French warships were attacked by Soviet submarines in the Indian Ocean neither the United Kingdom nor France would be able to invoke the Atlantic Treaty.[4] Aware of Congressional sensitivity on the matter, the Truman Administration settled for what it could get. As one memorandum commented at the time:

> ... even the combined military resources of these nations (US, Canada and Brussels Treaty powers) would be inadequate to warrant their assuming hard and fast commitments for the security of a large number of geographically scattered countries. A line must be drawn somewhere. The problem is to devise an arrangement which would best meet the security needs of the nations here represented without over-extending their military capabilities.[5]

The original Brussels Treaty in March 1948 had spoken only of an 'armed attack in Europe' (Article 4). Article 4 of the North Atlantic Treaty went further in defining an armed attack as an attack on North America or Western Europe, including the Algerian departments of France. Although the defence area was defined specifically to exclude the area south of the Tropic of Cancer $22\frac{1}{2}°$ north of the equator, these treaty arrangements did not signify complete agreement among the contracting parties. True to its original intentions, the United Kingdom interpreted the treaty more broadly than America had expected. In the White Paper on 'Events leading up to the signature of the North Atlantic Treaty', the British Government made it quite clear that the united strength of the parties would enable them to defeat any aggession wherever it might occur. Even in those early days, there seemed to be an implicit acceptance of the risk of war in any part of the world which was strategically important in terms of the defence of the

North Atlantic area. A military setback in one area might make the defence of the other untenable.[6]

Indeed, in the early 1950s, the Alliance represented little more than a collection of sovereign states many of which had interests outside Europe which were just as important to the national interest as its commitments in the North Atlantic area. The integration of allied forces was set back on more than one occasion by competing national priorities. The communiqué issued at the end of the NATO ministerial meeting of May 1950 highlighted the fact by agreeing that 'the requirements for national forces which arise out of commitments external to the North Atlantic area'[7] would continue to have priority. As Robert Osgood commented, looking back on the issue ten years later:

> In practice the three NATO countries with the most extensive commitments outside Europe – the United States, Britain and France – followed the principle of balanced national forces as far as pressures towards economy would permit. None felt that the principle of national specialisation called for sacrificing the needs of national policy to those of NATO[8]

As a result, forces were never really rationalised, or the defence burden equitably shared. The French duplicated the contribution made by the British while both duplicated the efforts made by the United States. Perhaps, this would have happened anyway if NATO's defence perimeter had been extended to encompass sub-Saharan Africa and the Indian Ocean. But since geographical limits were imposed, the initiatives for a truly collective European defence and more rational burden sharing in this period were constantly frustrated.

In the first ten years of NATO's existence, there were repeated calls for Africa's inclusion in its contingency planning, if not its formal defence perimeter. In October 1952, one of the NATO standing groups meeting in Paris discussed whether the time was right to redefine the North Atlantic area which had appeared five times in the Brussels treaty. Such questions did not go unanswered. General Livenworth considered that the continent would be a hostage of Europe in the event of war. He regarded it as a useful area for manoeuvring forces, an 'open space' in time of conflict. At the end of the 1950s at a meeting of the Western European Union (WEU), Pierre Messine, the French Minister of

Defence, advocated that colonial bases in Africa should be made an integral part of the defence system of the West. General Norstad, when Supreme Allied Commander Europe (SACEUR), gave much attention to the French West African 'quadrilateral' – bounded by Tunisia in the north, Dakar in the west and Douala in French Equatorial Guinea – which he predicted would play a central role in the Atlantic theatre of operations.

Yet the principle of Africa's strategic value, proclaimed with so much enthusiasm by General Norstad and NATO's Secretary-General Henri Spaak, to whom the Alliance in its present form largely owes its being, did not command unquestioning support. Many commentators who expressed strong views on the subject prepared for the next war by looking to the lessons of the last. Those who did not considered Africa much less important.

During World War II, new developments in air transport had given West Africa strategic significance as a staging post for the transport of war supplies from North America to the North African theatre. Several ports, including Dakar and Freetown and Takoradi and Apapa in Guinea, became stop-over points on the alternative route to the Indian Ocean round the Cape of Good Hope. After the war they remained as a prominent legacy of the fighting. Accra, Apapa and Kano were just a few of the impressive chain of strategic air-bases in West Africa which had played a significant role in anti-submarine operations in the South Atlantic when the war at sea had held in the balance.[9]

Not surprisingly, memories of the war persisted well into the 1950s. In an article in 1955, Admiral Richard Connolly discussed Africa's strategic importance in terms resonant with the themes of the 1940s when the Torch landings in North Africa and the campaign in the Western Desert had given rise to a massive logistics base from which Allied operations in the Mediterranean had largely been directed. For Connolly, the loss of the outer ramparts would be disastrous. With the Europeans in political control of the interior, NATO would not have to contend with enemy operations in Africa itself which might turn its southern flank. Indeed, Connolly characterised the continent as a set of regional 'islands' with no coherent set of communications linked entirely by communications at sea. The 'islands' provided bases at which resources could be located and stored and from which ground and air operations could be projected into the Middle East, or the mainland of Europe. 'The continent', he wrote, 'may be considered in one sense as an aggregate of separate base areas and, in another, in its entirety, as a vast defence complex.'[10]

Evidently, there was a strong similarity between the strategic preoccupations of the allies in the last war and the arguments put forward by the strategists of the 1950s. Both believed that operations outside Europe might be necessary to sustain a European war. Both looked to North Africa as an initial point for air operations and a base from which to mount an effective defence of shipping. Both took as their central canon the belief that operations in the central theatre might turn on the defence of the southern flank. Africa was seen, not as a battleground, but a supply base.

The 1950s was also, of course, a period of decolonisation when the conflict between European rule and African nationalism conspired to sharpen the political antagonism between ruler and ruled within Africa and to restrict the colonial powers' freedom of manoeuvre outside it. In one respect the colonial powers were disposed to give priority to their political relationship with Africa rather than to their strategic relations. In another the transfer of power to politicians who wished to remain neutral or non-aligned did not alter the facts of power. In the short run, the emergence of new countries on the periphery of NATO's defence perimeter threw the base rights and communications network into even greater strategic relief. At a NATO Council meeting in 1957, the United Kingdom and France were urged before handing over power to secure control of key strategic installations, to ensure 'full use' of African territory in the interests of the Alliance as a whole. A number of participants believed that the loss of base rights would inevitably follow if Africa withdrew from the European orbit.

Among the military commanders, some hoped to achieve their objectives by translating political control into economic influence. General Heusinger, for the *Bundeswehr*, proposed taking advantage of Africa's continuing reliance on foreign aid to coerce African countries into cooperating in the military field. Even politicians such as Dean Acheson thought that the West should not bother to disguise what foreign aid would be used for; that it should fulfil all its obligations including the provision of economic assistance in strict conformity with the immediate task of underwriting Western security.

In the event, the relationship between the metropolitan powers

and their dependencies defied precise description in the late
1950s. Britain and France were determined to modernise their
base facilities (for which they won full approval from their allies at
the NATO Council meeting of December 1962), while the
non-colonial powers continued to express interest in right of
access to 'allied strongpoints' on the continent, a request which
was last put forward at the Ottawa meeting of the Council the
following spring in connection with the development of NATO's
multilateral nuclear forces. America's only strategic base in Africa
– Wheelus Field in Libya – was put on an alert during the Cuban
missile crisis and there were plans afoot immediately afterwards
to moor Polaris A-2 submarines in Kenitra, Bizerta and Tripoli.
As late as 1962, the members of the Alliance controlled 17 airbases
in the continent as well as naval bases at Agadir, Mers-el-Kebir,
Bizerta, Djibouti, Mombasa, Simonstown, Lagos, Beira,
Lourenço-Marques and Luanda.

And yet within a matter of years, NATO's strategic decoupling
from the continent had begun in earnest. The 1960s marked a
retreat of Western power, not the strategic reoccupation of the
continent under the pretext of meeting the communist challenge.
For there were in the Alliance two different responses to
decolonisation, the second of which required NATO planners and
member countries alike to recognise the nature of their predicament and to deal with it realistically. The first has just been
discussed: the disposition on the part of many Europeans to pay
almost exclusive attention to European security in the broadest
geographical context contrary to the almost universal preference
for non-alignment on the part of the new countries.

At the same time, many more were attentive to how new sources
of conflict at the margins of NATO's traditional defence perimeter
might affect its future. No less a figure than John Foster Dulles
acknowledged in 1956 that while problems outside the Atlantic
community vitally affecting its interests had not been discussed on
a proper community basis, NATO was not the proper organisation to implement policies which involved the developing world.[11]
Taking up the point, the Committee of Three which had been set
up to look into the problem specifically defended the Alliance
against the charge that it had become an agency which had
permitted the colonial powers to pool their resources in defence of
imperial privileges and racial superiority.[12] The committee
reiterated that NATO was not only concerned with preventing

war, or defending its interests if deterrence failed; it was even more concerned with 'seizing the political and moral initiative to enable all countries to develop in freedom'.

Different though these two responses were they had one thing in common: the conviction that Africa would only ever be a secondary theatre of operations. On the whole, the 1950s saw no major international crises in the continent, no immediate deterioration of international security and few new departures of any significance. The Special NATO Committee which was set up in 1956 to implement measures agreed upon by its members and to coordinate the policies of the colonial and non-colonial powers played an important role in getting Belgium into line during the Congo crisis of 1960.

Throughout the Congo crisis, NATO's chief concern was to maintain Western access to the country's vast economic resources. In the early 1960s, the Congo produced 60 per cent of the world's cobalt, 70 per cent of its industrial diamonds and 10 per cent of its copper. Katanga alone was the fifth largest producer of copper in the world. There was some disagreement between the United States and its NATO allies as to how access to its resources could best be secured: through support for Lumumba's government, or for a secessionist Katanganese administration; but the main objective for both of them was still economic.[13]

Indeed, by the time the NATO Council got round to producing a general set of guidelines on Africa in 1960 to insure greater unanimity among the Europeans as well as between the Europeans and the United States, decolonisation was already far advanced. By 1965 the process was complete for all the NATO powers except Portugal. The pretensions of France and Britain to world power status did not survive into the latter half of the decade.

In retrospect, NATO's decision not to intervene during the Congo crisis, despite the urging of Belgium, marked a turning point in its relations with Africa. The resentment in Brussels occasioned by American policy in the Congo was articulated by Henri Spaak in a private letter to John Kennedy on the occasion of Spaak's resignation as Secretary-General of NATO:

> In the form they were made public American ideas could not be approved by the French, the Belgians or the Portuguese, nor it seems to me, by the English; that is to say, by those who have

the most direct interest in African problems. The so-called American plan was never discussed in NATO. The allies of the United States heard of it at the same time as its enemy . . . Common sense tells us that one cannot be solidary in one part of the world and enemies in another.[14]

Whatever might or might not have been the dictates of common sense, NATO's major powers, including Britain and France, did decide not to intervene in the Congo with consequences that were all too obvious to the more perceptive American observers.

Writing in 1965, Henry Kissinger observed that having shed their colonial possessions, often under American pressure, the Europeans had developed a psychological bloc against running major risks in areas of the world from which they had only just been expelled.[15] It was not complacency with regard to Africa's future which narrowed the Alliance's scope but rather a sense of the overwhelming difficulties the Europeans faced and the burden of their obligations which would bear no extension. The task of maintaining an extra-European role – formidable enough while they remained colonial powers – was further aggravated by the need to spend even more in Europe as defence costs escalated. By the end of the 1960s, it seemed quite unlikely that the Europeans would ever be able to translate their preoccupation with post-war economic recovery into a vision of recovering their pre-war international role.

On the whole, the Alliance survived the era of decolonisation remarkably well. At the end of the 1950s, Raymond Aron found relations between the United States and Europe no worse than at the beginning, and in many respects considerably better. The worst storm had been weathered; the Alliance had come through the Algerian war intact. Even if Portugal elected to leave (and its refusal to decolonise was already causing concern), this would be a failure, Aron concluded, of only secondary importance in a policy which in all other respects had met with unequivocal success.[16]

THE POLITICAL DIMENSION

As we have seen, there was nothing in the history of NATO's relations with Africa in the 1950s to substantiate the commonly prevailing view that the Alliance had extended the scope of its operations: indeed a sharp distinction continued to be drawn between what the allies did on their own account and the missions of the Alliance. Even though French or British policy was often of vital concern to the allies, NATO was not in a position to intervene itself even had its secretariat wished. The smaller European powers combined to scotch British and French attempts to extend the Alliance's responsibilities further afield out of concern that decisions affecting their own security might be made without their participation. The French might be wary of supporting American policies which might well involve them in a crisis outside the European theatre; but equally the smaller European powers felt they ran the risk of being drawn into a conflict in Africa as allies of Britain and France.[17] The smaller members did not encourage those most able to act outside the North Atlantic area from doing so in case they themselves were called upon to shoulder more of the defence burden in Europe.[18]

Consultation between the smaller and larger members of the Alliance and between the United States and its European allies gave rise to problems from the outset. The pledge in Article 4 had little meaning as an affirmation of allied unanimity since there was no agreement on what it encompassed. Was it necessary for all members to agree on what Britain or France did outside Europe regardless of whether they themselves could act or not? Or did agreement merely imply little more than an exchange of information among the major allies, and an abdication of responsibility by the rest?

In the early days, perhaps, it did not matter. The Europeans were still in occupation of most of Africa; it was still unnecessary to consult the Africans themselves, or to take their opinions into account. For most of the 1950s, the Europeans were neither sensitive to African pressures, nor alert to African opinion. Since most of the continent was still divided among the colonial powers, access to its reserves and resources was not under threat. Africa had not yet become the area of instability it is today. Yet as soon as decolonisation began in earnest, the colonial powers found it necessary to consult their allies more often. It was not long, in short, before the political repercussions of military action began to become apparent.

In 1951 the North Atlantic Council reiterated the need to consult on all matters of common concern. More than merely broadening the scope of consultation was at issue; the Council called upon all its members to make consulation an integral part of national decision-making, arguing that it would be unwise to separate by geographical area matters of allied concern from those which were ostensibly outside it.[19] At its meeting in Lisbon the following year, the political committee recommended that the Council itself should enquire into the possibilities of closer consultation. The United States and Britain, anxious to build up the Alliance and its existing institutions, were reluctant to broaden the scope of discussion to include non-European matters.[20] When the Council met again in December, it became clear that the Americans wanted decolonisation to be speeded up and feared that too close cooperation with their European partners would implicate them in their colonial policies. Nothing illustrated more clearly the difficulties of political cooperation within what had become, for better or worse, a purely regional alliance in the face of conflicting allied interests and policies outside it.

The Suez crisis of 1956 forced both sides to treat the matter more seriously. It was the first crisis to arise from the actions of its members in Africa, the first and the last to involve a complete breakdown in communications between the United States, Britain and France. NATO significantly failed to present a common front at the international canal users' conference which met in London in August in the wake of Nasser's nationalisation of the Suez canal. Despite the fact that NATO was heavily dependent on oil from the Middle East, much of which transited the canal on its way to Europe, Greece refused to attend, while the Federal Republic of Germany (FRG) adopted a 'correct line' that was not appreciated by its allies. It was not altogether surprising, therefore, that Britain and France decided on the use of force without consulting their allies, even though the forces used in the operation were largely made up of units assigned to NATO.[21]

At the ministerial meeting in December 1956, the Alliance agreed to press ahead with the recommendations of a report which had already been commissioned from the Foreign Ministers of three of the smaller member states: Gaetano Martino (Italy), Halvard Lange (Norway) and Lester Pearson (Canada). The committee made three recommendations: that changes in the policy of any one of the members should be notified in advance; that views should be exchanged so that each member could take into account the views of its allies; and that decisions on matters of common interest should be taken collectively. They did not define the subjects on which they considered a collective consensus should be sought – indeed, they recognised the difficulty of attempting to specify in advance all the subjects and situations in which consultation might be desirable, let alone to separate by area matters of NATO concern from those of purely national interest. As the heads of government resolved shortly afterwards:

> Our Alliance cannot, therefore, be concerned only with the North Atlantic area or only with military defence. It must also organise its political and economic strength on the principle of interdependence and must take account of developments outside its own area.

Despite reaffirming its belief in consultation as a universal prophylactic, however, very little progress was actually made. Effective consultation rested ultimately on the interest and will of the member governments. It was easy to profess devotion; it was difficult and, in fact, was soon shown to be impossible, if the proper conviction was lacking, to convert the profession into practise. Even at the time the United States pointed out that it could not be expected to consult its Atlantic partners about its own policies outside the North Atlantic area where these involved obligations to countries that were not members of NATO. Implicit in this reservation was the belief, frequently voiced in this period, that the concern of the Alliance was in fact limited to an area defined by treaty,[22] a view not shared either by the smaller European members who were concerned about developments outside it, or by Britain and France after the Suez debacle. Indeed in 1958, the French proposed that, together with the United States and Britain, they should be jointly responsible for formulating policy in the developing world. It was a measure of how seriously they took their international responsibilities that they looked forward not only to setting up a consultative body within the existing treaty organisation, but also to restructuring the Alliance itself. In de Gaulle's opinion, nothing else would allow NATO to remain relevant in the 1960s:

> We think that at least among the world powers of the West something must be organised, as far as the Alliance is

concerned, with regard to the political and occasionally strategic conduct of the Alliance outside Europe, particularly in the Middle East and Africa, where these three powers are constantly involved.[23]

It is clear that de Gaulle hoped that at least two things would come of the scheme – first, that the United States would fall in with French policy in Africa, particularly in Algeria where it had been the subject of sustained criticism; secondly, that France would be given a veto over American involvement in areas peripheral to European interests. The first objective was central to de Gaulle's foreign policy in general and his wish to broaden NATO's traditional scope from its emphasis on Western Europe. Had he not felt that Soviet aggression in Europe was less real than the United States imagined, his preoccupation with Africa might have been less marked.

Both the principles and implications of de Gaulle's plan, however, were out of tune with American aims. The Americans, ever wary of antagonising their other European allies, pointed out that NATO already offered a forum for discussing matters of international security and that France's membership of organisations such as SEATO already offered it an opportunity to collaborate with its allies outside the confines of the North Atlantic. The Eisenhower Administration was quite prepared to broaden the scope of consultation, but not to abandon allied unanimity for the sake of a three power directorate.[24]

It was all the more ironic, therefore, that in the mid-1960s it was the Americans, hard-pressed in Vietnam, conscious of the cost of their ever-burgeoning international responsibilities, who proposed consulting their allies more often. Disturbed by the growing gulf in understanding between the United States and Europe, George Ball, then Under Secretary of State, reached agreement with NATO's Secretary-General, Manlio Brosio, on a procedure for consultation on problems arising outside the European theatre. The proposal, which entailed four additional ministerial meetings a year at the level of deputy foreign minister or above, was intended to supplement the annual meetings between the Foreign Ministers of the Alliance. Three such meetings were actually held in 1965, the first at the request of Belgium, the last two at the request of the United States. But, as Ball later noted, these consultations never progressed beyond the *pro forma* stage of expressing known positions:

> Most governments shied away from the expression of any but the most formal views emphasising that their interests outside Europe were marginal and that each problem discussed was basically one for the United States to deal with it as it saw best. France which had sought in 1958 to create a world directorate ... to develop strategy and concert policy around the globe refused to participate in the discussion at all. Under instructions from his government, the French representative read a statement expressing the view that NATO was not an appropriate forum for considering problems that occurred outside the geographic limits defined by the North Atlantic Treaty.[25]

In 1965, the Americans found to their dismay that European policy-makers did not perceive their international predicament in the same stark terms nor draw the same conclusions. Despite extensive political and economic interests in Africa and its continuing dependence upon non-European trade and lines of communication, Europe's strategic dilemmas shaped and, were in turn, shaped by European defence. The pretensions of France and Britain to world power status did not survive into the 1960s. The task of maintaining an extra-European role, formidable enough while they were colonial powers, was made more demanding by the ever-escalating costs of defence procurement. In addition, they faced two serious challenges – domestic protests in their own societies against military intervention overseas, more muted to be sure in France than in Britain, and the increasing reluctance of their former dependencies to accept without question the authority and style of European leadership. Critical of American policy in Indo-China as the United States had once been critical of European colonialism, their loss of military confidence and demonstrable unwillingness to incur responsibilities outside the area of major concern prompted them increasingly to question the American interpretation of Soviet intentions, to look to other explanations of Africa's endemic instability, whose roots they suspected ran much deeper than Soviet subversion.

This divergence of interests threatened to become more marked in the 1970s. The inability of the Europeans to act outside Europe (even France's African commitments required comparatively small forces) altered the familiar outline of Alliance politics. Although Britain and France, who had so often in the past assumed responsibility for NATO's non-European interests, continued to act in the Alliance's interests, if not its name, in the Gulf and Southern Africa, they did so with increasing reluctance. It was not, as Dr Kissinger maintained, that Europe only had regional interests. It had global interests but only limited means to protect them.

By 1974, the Europeans and Americans were both agreed that the defence of the Middle East and the trade routes south of the Tropic of Cancer were of concern to every member of the Alliance, not only the United States. Indeed, countries such as Britain had already tried to provide some protection for shipping in the southern Indian Ocean though with no great success. But this was not where differences arose; differences arose over the methods of protecting shipping. As Ian Smart noted at the time, it was not the goals of the North Atlantic Treaty that had failed the United States and Europe, but the programmes and methods by which both sides sought to attain them.[26] Differences of approach had often led to disagreements over practical policies among its members, but not disagreements over ends. Genuine conflicts of interest as such have never been very easy to discern at any stage in its history.

These differences were brought into sharp focus after 1974 when Soviet intervention in Southern Africa confronted its members with a security dilemma which was not easily resolved. The Soviet Union succeeded where the United States had failed in concentrating the Europeans' minds on African security. But that is to run ahead of our story. Before turning to events after 1974 we must first discuss how the three most important NATO powers in this period – the United States, Britain and France – acted on their own behalf and that of the Alliance, and how the Africans themselves interpreted their actions.

2 The Western Powers and Africa, 1949–74

The overview of NATO's relationship with Africa which we have just provided is essentially incomplete. It is a descriptive historical account that touches only briefly on the contribution made by individual members. If we were to leave their policies out of account, the question of Africa and the Atlantic Alliance would hardly arise.

While the area of NATO's relations has been ignored by scholars, the same does not hold true for French and British policy in Africa, which has not suffered from similar neglect. Perhaps, because the early focus of attention was on the purely national implications of their policies, it has taken analysts rather a long time to look at the impact of those policies on the Western Alliance. This again is not easy to explain since the line between what was in the national interest and what was in the interest of NATO as an alliance was often remarkably narrow.

Concentration on national policies alone provides a restricted, even distorted picture since their role as colonial, later ex-metropolitan powers and their role as members of an alliance with worldwide responsibilities were not independent of each other. What follows is an attempt to show how the policies of three NATO countries shaped and in turn were shaped by their perceptions of NATO interest.

UNITED KINGDOM

Although Africa entered into the calculations of both British and French defence planners throughout the 1950s, one could be forgiven for thinking, from the evidence of British Defence White

Papers, that Africa itself was not considered strategically important at all. It is noteworthy that while support for a continued British presence came from many quarters – from professional soldiers, politicians, political commentators and diplomats – it was never widespread. The broad consensus which existed in France for *la politique Afrique* had no parallel in the United Kingdom.

The British, ever aware of their global responsibilities, were more concerned with the Far East (their only long term defence agreement with any independent Commonwealth member was with Malaysia), much more inclined to look to their position east of Suez in terms of the East–West conflict (from which Africa was as yet largely isolated). The boundaries of Britain's sphere of responsibility east of Suez, discernible in the wake of decolonisation and the extension of the cold war to the developing world, did not encompass Africa at all. The end of the war in the Mediterranean had signalled a temporary end to any significant British military role in the continent. The onset of nationalism merely confirmed it.

Britain and France between them faced two dilemmas in the period though their answers to them markedly differed. The 'winds of change' which swept them out of Africa in the late 1950s inevitably coloured their attitude to permanent staging posts and garrisons. At one time, both countries had thought of establishing vast military bases across the continent as resupply points for operations further east but the nationalist challenge, which forced them to transfer power earlier than they had planned, forced them to re-evaluate their strategic position. Military positions soon became overseas burdens, strong points became liabilities. A former British minister eventually concluded that the defence of the bases left over from the Empire had become more burdensome than the defence of its earlier unity.[1]

Of the many schemes entertained by military planners in the 1950s, none matched in size or conception the plan to build a vast base complex in Kenya. In one form or another it was discussed every year after 1951. By the time it was finally approved in November 1957, the Soviet threat in the Middle East and the putative threat of penetration in Africa had imported a sense of urgency into government deliberations. The British originally intended to station part of their strategic reserve in Kenya. Within three years, plans were afoot to house three battalions in the old camp at Gilgil and a new air-conditioned barracks in Kahawa. At the same time, the British contracted to built two up-to-date airfields at Eastleigh and Embakasi outside Nairobi, from which troops could be airlifted at short notice. Arguing that correct strategy demanded the concentration of decisive strength at the decisive point at the decisive moment, the British planned to use Kenya as the embarkation base for their strategic reserve.

Nationalist agitation brought these plans to nothing. Kenya eventually obtained independence less than six years after the decision to proceed with the base was first taken, and the last British troops left five years after work on the Kahawa barracks began. British ministers had not envisaged independence for Kenya before the mid-1970s; indeed, until 1961 the War Office still held firmly to the view that the army would remain on until 1969.[2] In the event, the War Office was not consulted at all about the decision to transfer power in 1963. Within ten years of being mooted, the whole idea of a Kenyan base, which had been accepted by the British military and political leadership, was abandoned. The new government in Nairobi eventually agreed to allow the Royal Air Force (RAF) limited staging rights, and limited training facilities for British troops, but the headquarters of the 24th Infantry Brigade Group had to be redeployed in Aden, and the remaining members of the force flown back to Britain. It is within this context, the radically changed climate of strategic opinion produced by the nationalist challenge, that Britain's response to events after 1963 must be assessed.

Britain's strategic decoupling from Africa followed very closely upon its withdrawal from the Middle East. The evacuation of the Suez base in 1954 forced Britain to redeploy 80 000 troops stationed in the canal zone in Libya and the Sudan. Both countries were considered useful staging posts for operations in the Middle East, but by 1964, in the face of Arab protests, the British were forced to waive their right to use the El-Adem airfield in Libya as a transit post for missions against other Arab countries. Similar restrictions applied in the Sudan where the government insisted on being kept informed of the ultimate destination of all flights out of military bases, jealously guarding the right to search all aircraft on arrival.

In a matter of ten years, British strategy, the main principles of which had gone virtually unchallenged since the war, had to be revised fundamentally. Talks between the British and Libyan governments in 1965 over the removal of the British army garrison at Tripoli left intact the right to use El-Adem until 1973, but even before the revolution which brought Colonel Quaddafi to power, the government of King Idris had asked Britain to phase out its base altogether. In August 1967, the British agreed to withdraw all military units at once and to surrender all military installations within six months, leaving only 2000 servicemen in Tobruk and a few airmen in El-Adem. Negotiations on the evacuation of these remaining units began in earnest after the *coup d'etat* in November 1969 with agreement being reached for total withdrawal by the end of March 1970. Britain's obvious reluctance to hold out in Libya illustrates how easily successive British governments convinced themselves that nationalism made it imperative to reduce continental liabilities and relieve the strain on limited resources at home.

Similar problems were encountered on the West coast. The standard air route for the RAF commuting to the Far East was via North Africa. Aircraft of Transport and Bomber Commands regularly flew this course from airfields in Britain to El-Adem, Aden, Gan and the Maldives. The treaty with Libya (1953) and later one with the Sudan (1956) gave Britain overflight rights over their territory. After the Suez crisis, however, the War Office began to look at the alternative West African route and the availability on a permanent basis of air-staging facilities at Kano and Lagos. The British initially hoped that the Nigerian bases would be under their control; in the event, they only managed to negotiate unrestricted overflight and air-staging rights. Nigeria won valuable concessions in return, including the promise to train and assist its armed forces and assure arms supplies. But most of these benefits could have been obtained, as they were after the treaty's cancellation, by less formal Commonwealth arrangements.

The cancellation of the Anglo-Nigerian treaty in 1962 played a major part in determining the pattern of post-independence defence cooperation between Britain and its ex-colonies. Indeed, the next country to become independent, Sierra Leone, decided that 'in the present circumstances' there was no need for a defence agreement with London at all.[3]

The second dilemma the British faced proved to be equally intractable. Neither Britain nor France had resources enough to square the costs of maintaining a significant military presence in

Africa (at a time when the Soviet threat was not very real) with their obligations as signatories of the North Atlantic Treaty. Overseas bases increasingly competed with their priorities in Europe. Nothing suggested in 1963 that the dilemma would be posed any less starkly in the future. But the dilemma was much starker for the British than it was for the French. The French were concerned with security in North Africa which fell within NATO's Tropic of Cancer boundary; the British with a position in East and Southern Africa which fell well outside it.

British bases and staging posts in Africa provided a logistical infrastructure for operations in the Middle East and South-East Asia. Many of the newly independent states resented the presence of British troops precisely because their presence could only be explained in terms of the cold war. It might have been more acceptable if Britain had made known its intention to defend sympathetic governments from internal subversion. French troops were used in the role more often and more convincingly. Francophone Africa's dependence on France and the willingness of many former French dependencies to invite in French troops contrasted markedly with the practice of most Anglophone states who kept Britain at a distance by denying British troops any facilities on the continent. Britain, in fact, entered into remarkably few treaty commitments with African countries – no more than three in the whole period and two of these were with Indian Ocean governments, the Maldives and Mauritius. Agreement with the Maldives in July 1965 provided Britain with restricted access to territorial waters adjacent to the Addu Atoll up to 1 December 1986. A six year defence pact with Mauritius, concluded in March 1968, guaranteed the use of a military airfield and other limited facilities. Kenya, the only country on the mainland to sign a treaty with the British, agreed to make training and naval facilities available at Mombassa.

If Simonstown is omitted, the British maintained nothing that remotely answered the description of a permanent base in any part of Africa. Moreover, apart from Nigeria, with whom the British were formally allied in a defence pact until 1962 and Ghana where British officers were to be found in all important staff posts and battalion commands until 1961, the British kept their hands remarkably free of military entanglements.

By 1968 it seemed reasonable to assume that Britain's presence in Africa was passing rapidly into history with the commitments that sustained it. African entanglements had been inescapable because of colonial sovereignty, but once independence had been granted the presence of British troops seemed neither necessary nor desirable. After returning from East Africa in 1964, the British Defence Secretary, pressed in Parliament to say whether it would be desirable to conclude a comprehensive defence agreement with East Africa, replied that the Africans themselves were quite happy with the agreements which existed.[4] In the light of such statements it is not surprising that the British chose to deal with their security interests in Africa on an *ad hoc* basis, rather than seek security in a comprehensive defence pact which would have left neither party much room for manoeuvre.

However, this was not the whole story. While the British withdrew from Africa they remained east of Suez. As late as 1966, the Royal Navy (RN) had over 70 ships at sea in the Indian Ocean, including two aircraft carriers, one commando ship and at least two guided missile destroyers. Until the late 1960s, the British government fought shy of divesting itself of its overseas responsibilities, or depriving itself of a significant role in the world, still less of creating a dangerous vacuum which neither the United States nor its European allies might be able or willing to fill. Despite reduced circumstances, Britain's contribution in the Indian Ocean was still one that it alone was uniquely equipped to make.

Several years later, Britain's Prime Minister Harold Wilson, admitted that his judgment might have been at fault in clinging to a policy which had met with opposition from within his own cabinet.[5] Yet at the time he had not been alone in holding to the opinion that it would be unwise to pull back from a part of the world where British forces were most needed, in favour of concentrating them in a part of the world where they were needed much less. A thousand men East of Suez appeared a much more attractive proposition than another 1000 men on the Rhine.[6]

As economic difficulties mounted at home, however, the British found it increasingly difficult to find economies in their NATO contribution. The United Kingdom found itself simply underpowered to play a decisive role in Africa and provide a credible contribution to the defence of Europe. The decision to abandon the construction of a new generation of carriers and to replace the cancelled F-111 swing-wing aircraft which had originally been ordered so that the RAF could continue to operate East of Suez in the 1970s seemed to mark the end of a British presence in the Indian Ocean which many commentators and naval pundits had long found unconvincing.

East of Suez Revisited, 1970–74

But for the appearance of a Soviet cruiser, two destroyers and accompanying tankers in the Indian Ocean in 1968, the British might never have reversed their decision. Certainly, the arrival of a Soviet squadron occasioned considerable alarm. Between November 1968 and the following spring, the Soviet Navy visited most of the East African ports including Mogadiscio, Dar-es-Salaam and Mombasa. Between 1967–71 a total of 81 surface warships and submarines and auxiliaries were observed in the region, the number never averaging less than 18 or more than 21 a year, though many more were often listed.

The Conservative government which came to power in June 1970 took the Soviet threat much more seriously than its allies. The government of Edward Heath, impatient of those in NATO who refused to look beyond European security, was unwilling to abandon the Indian Ocean to the Soviet Union. At the Commonwealth Conference in 1971, he informed his colleagues that it was precisely because the Alliance was unwilling to extend its responsibilities south of the Tropic of Cancer that the United Kingdom must. Where it could do so it acted with its allies. At a NATO Defence Ministers conference in 1972, Britain and the Netherlands announced their intention of undertaking joint Indian Ocean patrols.[7] Where it could not act in concert, however, Britain was quite prepared to act alone.

The British acted quickly to re-establish themselves in the Indian Ocean, to deny the Soviet Navy, if not a permanent foothold, at least a preponderant position. In addition to participating in a Five Power Commonwealth Task Force in the Far East, they reactivated the Simonstown agreement and signed an agreement with the United States to build a communications station on the island of Diego Garcia. In December 1970, the British Foreign Secretary, Sir Alec Douglas Home, told the Foreign Press Association in London that unless the Western powers maintained their position in the Indian Ocean, they might soon discover that they had very few policy options left.[8]

These measures represented an attempt to revise, if not entirely reverse, the 1968 decision to pull back British forces. Nevertheless, the arguments that had justified the pullout then were just as compelling three years later. The British believed that they faced a maritime threat which could be contained by maritime methods. The decision to reinforce their presence in the area by a frigate and a submarine was quite inadequate to deal with the Soviet reinforcement of its own squadron, or even to dispute control of the seas with the naval forces already in position.[9]

The only realistic response, if the British really were preoccupied with the Soviet threat, would have been a diplomatic initiative to dissuade the local states from offering the Soviet squadron bunkering facilities which it needed most to expand the scope of its operations. A purely naval response no longer carried conviction for a power of Britain's diminishing resources. Yet many of the states which had attached the highest value and derived the most protection from the RN's presence before 1968 refused to be drawn when sounded out about the matter. From their cool reception to Heath's commitment four months later 'to keep the peace in the Indian Ocean and sustain the countries that are working to develop their economic and social systems in a free and democratic manner,'[10] it was clear that many local powers preferred to put their trust in the demilitarisation of the Indian Ocean for which they had voted at the third conference of the non-aligned movement two months earlier.

For what the British had left in 1968 was not a vacuum of power – but a vacuum of purpose which the limited forces they deployed after 1970 simply could not fill.[11] Britain's ability to reinforce its forces east of Suez was still impressive – during the Ber Satu Padu exercise in June (1970), 2500 men, 20 helicopters and 200 vehicles were airlifted to the Far East within ten days. But the strategy was inordinately expensive – it meant re-equipping RAF Support Command and shifting naval priorities to fixed-wing aircraft at sea – in other words, refitting the Navy's three remaining carriers until the first generation of V/STOL cruisers entered service. Since the government was as opposed as its predecessor to building a new generation of carriers and since it is doubtful whether existing manpower could have met the requirements after the defence cuts of 1968, it must be wondered whether Mr Heath fully understood the implications of his decision to reverse Britain's withdrawal from east of Suez.

The demands of financial retrenchment, coupled with a less

apocalyptic view of Soviet naval power, led the incoming Labour government in 1974 to make substantial cuts in the specialist reinforcement forces which had been assigned to NATO in 1968, though they had never been fully equipped for armoured operations. The cuts in the force levels of the UK Mobile Forces (UKMF) and UK Joint Airborne Task Force (UKJATFOR) substantially reduced Britain's ability to intervene outside Europe as well. One of the commando ships was paid off earlier than planned, the other reallocated to the Alliance as an anti-submarine carrier. Of the two assault ships, only one was kept in immediate operational readiness while the other was kept in refit. Plans to order two purpose built amphibious warships were abandoned.

The government's defence review in 1975 and its decision to reduce the UKMF to an airportable formation, equivalent to a reinforced brigade group, was not entirely prompted by the conviction that Britain's future lay in Europe. There were many who were equally convinced that Britain could not renounce an interest in events outside Europe, that its contribution in future need not be so weak nor its enemies so powerful as they were often portrayed. But the hollowness of Britain's brief redeployment east of Suez after 1970 was apparent to everyone but Britain itself. It was clear from the lukewarm support which it had elicited from the Africans who had thought it more provocative than reassuring. It was especially significant that the defence review of 1971 had hardly figured at all in NATO discussions.

Since the decision in 1968 to concentrate on the north Atlantic area could only have been taken in the context of Britain's NATO commitment, the decision to reverse it could only have been convincingly taken if NATO had agreed to release Britain from its European obligations, or to undertake a review itself of the threat to shipping lanes in the south Atlantic. As it was the decision to stay complete withdrawal was very brief. Mobile and naval forces were not restructured; naval exercises were undertaken for a few years, the largest of all in 1974, but they served only to parade a commitment the British were no longer in a position to meet. The economic facts of life had not changed simply because the situation in the Indian Ocean had changed for the worse.

Conservative party policy had marked a change of emphasis, not substance. Faced with a choice of priorities, the government had deferred making a decision but its eventual choice had never been in doubt. That did not mean that Britain was not in a position to make a contribution. There was still an argument for keeping British carriers in service since they were larger than the two carriers deployed by France and large fleet units had a symbolic importance which through-deck cruisers did not. There was still an argument for extracting a greater return from the expensive refits undertaken in the 1960s, but only in the context of a NATO Task Force, a specialised contribution to Alliance security, not increased defence spending which the British could not afford.[12]

As it was, the defence review of 1971 could have been justified only on the understanding that the United Kingdom intended spending more on defence than the Conservative party had promised in its manifesto. That was not the understanding on which it was made. It could have been defended only on the understanding that the Alliance needed to defend the sealanes round the Cape and that the RN was in the best position to do so. NATO contingency planning, however, was not undertaken until 1972.

The conflict among British defence planners after 1974 was not simply a conflict of political parties and partisan prescriptions. Rather it was a debate over the true nature of NATO's global predicament and the correct response that Britain could make as a member of the Alliance. This was exactly the period when the French began to build up an impressive Indian Ocean presence. The debate in the United Kingdom had been all too reminiscent of the defence debates in the 1950s in which successive governments had been unable or unwilling to come to terms with Britain's reduced role in world affairs. The real debate took place in France. In a speech to the French Defence College in June 1970, the month the Conservative party came to power in Britain, Michel Debré, the Minister of Defence, reminded his audience that:

> Outside Europe, that is to say in the European basin and beyond, where we are at present and where we have interests and commitments, we must keep up our ability to intervene so that we can assert ourselves either in a particular theatre, to a limited extent and of our own accord, or under other conditions *in the context of a joint endeavour*.[13]

An allied endeavour may not have been what many Gaullists had in mind but at least the French were in a position to back up their commitment. Public and private statements bear out that France's professional defence establishment shared Britain's concern over the threat posed by the Soviet presence in the Indian Ocean and had begun to give serious consideration to a collective Western response.

FRANCE

Throughout the 1950s, the French persistently pressed for North Africa's formal inclusion in the North Atlantic Alliance. Their military planners, ever insistent on defence in depth, talked of the two *zones stratégiques* into which Africa was divided. Dakar and Diego Suarez in Madagascar became the main focus of French activity – the central points of an all-Africa defence infrastructure which had no parallel in Anglophone Africa and which found no echo in British defence thinking.

In an article which appeared in *Foreign Affairs* in 1953, General de Monsabert dwelt at length on North Africa's role in Atlantic strategy and:

> its central position at the point where the Mediterranean and African facades of the African and European continent meet. Without North Africa Europe cannot breathe and cannot act unless it be to retreat . . . the real frontier of Europe, then, is the ancient Roman *limes* bordering the Sahara. From Casablanca to Berlin, from Kiel to Gabes everything interlocks and because it does the whole area constitutes a single and indivisible theatre of war.[14]

The strategic concepts which this article discussed were peculiarly French. The more pragmatic British were not prey to the same obsessions. The most striking feature of the French experience in Africa in the 1950s was the enormous disparity between the grand strategic objectives of French policy makers and the actual policies they had to carry out as members of the Western Alliance.

As the 1950s progressed, there were signs that the administrators and defence planners were less prepared than the political leaders for the transfer of power when it eventually came. But their unpreparedness had an immediate result upon which the political leadership was able to capitalise. Unlike the British, the French never maintained separate colonial native forces in Africa. After receiving their training in the *Ecole Militaire* in Dakar, native soldiers were normally transferred to one of two armies – that of French West Africa, based in Senegal, or central Africa, based in the Congo. When the colonies were eventually granted independence few, if any, were able to repatriate enough nationals to form armed forces of their own. They invariably had to ask France for assistance and through a series of bilateral and multilateral defence agreements which became famous under de Gaulle, France duly agreed to continue to meet their defence needs into the 1960s and, if necessary, beyond.[15]

In addition to transferring the soldiers of the *armées coloniales* to their countries of origin, France also agreed to continue training them for both internal and external defence. None of these *accords de cooperation* were ever published and even today their scope remains the subject of much speculation. But through them France managed to maintain 20 000 troops in Africa as late as 1961 (not including those engaged in Algeria), based in Ouakam (Senegal), Port Bonet (Ivory Coast), Niamey (Niger), Fort Lamy (Chad), Bangui (Central African Republic), Libreville (Gabon), and Diego Suarez in Madagascar. Whatever their influence on diplomacy and the form that influence took, the agreements loomed large in French strategy. French military forces were given right of access to local military installations specifically in the context of France's 'worldwide defence obligations'.[16] These arrangements were to figure prominently in the mid-1960s when the French decided to rationalise their network of bases by devising four *zones d'outre mer* and reducing their forces to divisional size at three key points – Dakar, Fort Lamy and Diego Suarez. Thus, although French perceptions of security were still coloured by the belief that its former dependencies would continue to be plagued by internal unrest and destabilisation, Paris no longer considered that their economic and political distress called for French forces to be deployed in West Africa in any large numbers.[17]

That the French saw these cooperation agreements entirely in terms of their own security in the world at large was clear in the military sphere where France wanted the right both to maintain base facilities in Francophone Africa and Madagascar and the right to abstain from despatching forces there if it so chose. The agreements often pointed to the importance of defining defence problems communally. In the accords with Senegal and Gabon, for example, the understanding focused entirely on external defence, while the accord with Madagascar included a stipulation to the effect that a 'system of regional defence and common organisation of defence questions should be established'.[18]

The French planners never lost sight of the primacy of the French position in any of these arrangements. The reason the government demanded that the independent states sign such agreements was to ensure that French bases on the continent remained secure. In a paper written for the *Centre Militaire d'Information et Documentation Outre Mer* in 1961, General Revol argued that it was 'evident that bases are necessary for us . . . first, to go to the aid of those of our African partners who might be in difficulties, but equally to hold on to our place in the world'.[19]

The importance of Africa to France's self-esteem diminished very little at independence. Relations between France and Africa changed in form, but not in substance. While after 1960 any action by Europeans acting in concert, or by France alone, would necessarily be attacked as 'neo-colonialist', there was a sense in which a good deal of French activity in black Africa was taken not only with the compliance, but at the request of African leaders. Indeed, French influence in the region came to be related both to the nature of French power as understood by French leaders, and to the definition given that power by African ones. In the creation of these new relations the old myths of *France–Afrique* and *Eurafrique* played an important role.

Algeria and the Nationalist Struggle

In the main the Western Alliance was fortunate that decolonisation in Africa was achieved quickly and at little cost to the colonial powers. The vexed question of whether to support its members in a crisis for which many might hold its own colonial policies responsible arose only once – in Algeria. In Algeria, the struggle to contain nationalist feeling after 1956 gave point and emphasis to the disquiet evidenced notably by the United States, and to a lesser extent the Scandinavian powers, over any action which might be construed as supportive of European colonialism, and to

NATO's general reluctance to extend its security umbrella to Africa while colonial order still persisted. Throughout the crisis, the Eisenhower Administration continually reiterated America's desire to enter into a period of greater strategic consensus with its European allies in order to contain more effectively the Soviet Union's growing military capabilities in the developing world. In meeting the challenge of Soviet communism, the United States did not consider that France's presence in Algeria served any useful purpose. Indeed, it was here that the line between strategic and political questions became increasingly ambiguous as the war against French rule brought France into conflict with the principle of self-determination to which as a signatory of the North Atlantic Treaty it was in principle committed.

Algeria's progress towards independence took a very different course from the rest of Francophone Africa. Only after an eight year struggle which almost plunged France itself into civil war was independence finally granted. A million French settlers put up a stubborn opposition with the backing from the outset of the French Army in Algeria which consistently claimed that, as a department of France, it should on no account be handed over to the indigenous Moslem population. The army's best attempts, however, failed to eliminate Moslem discontent, or its open expression. Partial reforms failed to improve the position significantly, while fundamental reform, which might have promised autonomy while stopping short of complete independence, was not contemplated for fear of the political consequences among the settler population.

Algeria, a dubious strategic asset for the Alliance (the naval base at Mers-el-Kebir was the home port of the French Mediterranean fleet), fast became a political liability. Despite its concern, NATO did not advocate complete French withdrawal: to have done so might have prompted France to leave the Alliance; it did advocate, however, a political solution as France attempted to deal with growing political difficulties at home and the possibility of something like a political revolution in the early 1960s.

As far as the Europeans were concerned, France was too important a partner to antagonise. Britain and Belgium both had colonies of their own. On the whole, it fell to the United States to express the reservations which many held, but which few were willing to express.

Developments in Algeria must be seen against a background of overall NATO commitments which were already straining America's resources when the Algerian war broke out. The French withdrew an army division from the front line in Germany without consulting their allies, a move not taken kindly by the United States which quickly responded by refusing to allow French forces in Algeria to use the helicopters they had been lent in Indo-China.[20] This show of American resolve effectively disguised the fact that the Americans were already providing military equipment under the Military Assistance Programme (MAP) on a scale large enough to help France avoid a run on its foreign exchange reserves.[21] On the one hand, the Americans wished to avoid antagonising France completely; on the other, they wished to prevent the Africans from shopping for arms in the Communist bloc. In consequence, American policy was confused and confusing.

Although the United States repeatedly expressed its support for Algerian nationalism, the American delegation at the United Nations supported France with remarkable consistency from the time Algeria was first debated in the General Assembly. Of 13 key resolutions which were put to the vote between 1951–57, the United States abstained once, voted with France on ten separate occasions and for the anti-colonial majority only twice (and then only after more militant motions had been soundly defeated).

America's dilemma, of course, was a political one and the question it raised so insistently was whether France would continue to remain a member of an alliance in which it had lost the sympathy and support of its principal ally. The Americans had a choice, either to side with the African bloc, with no certainty that France would retreat, and none at all that American criticism would make the problem any more susceptible to solution, or to stand by the French in public while making very strong representations behind the scenes. For most of the 1950s the United States simply drifted, letting France slip beyond recall. In the event, de Gaulle helped the French find a role in the world more consistent with their limited resources. But by that time, the Atlantic Alliance had lost a good deal of ground politically which in a sense it was never to make up.

The Algerian war tended to bear out the forecasts of those in the United States who had foreseen that its obligations to NATO might one day conflict with its attitude to developments outside the North Atlantic area. A factor which weighed heavily with the Eisenhower Administration, and no less heavily with the Europeans, was that too public a disavowal of French policy in Algeria might prompt the French government to withdraw its grudging support for the complete integration of German forces in NATO. The forward strategy of defence on the Rhine which had been originally adopted at a NATO Council meeting in September 1950 had been held up for almost five years by French objections – during which disputes between the protecting power and Morocco (where the Americans had already invested $500m in a network of bases) had become the focus of international concern. American reticence on later incidents between France and Tunisia (which became independent in 1956), hot pursuit raids against Algerian nationalists, the bombing of Sakiet (which the French claimed to be a rebel base) and an incident in 1961 when 1200 Tunisians were killed while trying to storm the French base at Bizerte, was undoubtedly explained by its unwillingness to jeopardise French cooperation in NATO.

The upshot of all this was that the United States viewed Africa as the French wanted – moreover, it allowed itself to be blackmailed into withholding arms from states whose future sympathy for the West might have been every bit as important as French control of Algeria, and considerably less embarrassing. Two examples must suffice. Because of French objections America refused to sell arms to Tunisia in 1958, putting pay to President Bourguiba's scheme for a North African federation associated with, though not a member of, the North Atlantic Alliance.[22] Its refusal to sell arms to Guinea following French protests that the sale would represent a threat to the French West African Community provoked Seke Touré, President of Guinea, into turning to Czechoslovakia. Later Touré complained of the poor relations between the two countries, for which he held the Franco–American understanding entirely responsible.[23]

From the strategic point of view, the understanding was already becoming intolerable by 1958 and John Kennedy, then a young Senator, was not alone in expressing concern that if the US proved lukewarm in its support for African nationalism, the Africans themselves might one day eject America from the bases it already maintained in the continent. In a speech in June 1959, Kennedy claimed that Eisenhower's support for the French in Algeria had 'endangered the continuation of some of our most strategic airbases and threatened our geographical advantages over the Communist orbit'. The Africans, he added, could no longer be treated as 'pawns in the cold war'; the United States could no longer afford to think of the continent entirely as an appendage of Europe.[24]

Once in office, however, Kennedy himself found that he had no answer either. The issue of American support for its European allies was not resolved and was to remain a major source of conflict between the Pentagon and the State Department. It was impossible for the United States to defend Africa alone as it had tried to defend the Middle East through the Eisenhower Doctrine since the very existence of dependent territories made a unilateral declaration of principle all but impossible; and in any case such a declaration would have had little value since the United States and the countries which had already won independence could not agree as to what power or combination of powers constituted a clearly defined threat to their security. For many Africans NATO represented a more immediate danger than the Warsaw Pact. In the end, the Kennedy Administration deferred to its European partners. When the newly appointed American ambassador to Guinea arrived to take up his post, he was informed by a fellow diplomat that American policy was still 'to tailor our actions in Africa to the wishes of our often short-sighted NATO partners'.[25]

France, Africa and the Indian Ocean, 1965–74

After 1965, from Senegal in the west to Djibouti in the east, the French military presence began to decline. By the end of the 1960s, the departure of the last French soldier was confidently predicted. What accounted for this change, in the first instance, was the number of occasions on which the French felt obliged to intervene to prop up friendly governments, or in some instances reinstate rulers who had been toppled from power in military *coups*. In time French intervention became a byword of neo-colonialism in West Africa. After the first wave of *coups*, it soon became clear that the French would increasingly be called upon to intervene in local politics. The crunch came in Gabon in 1964 when French forces intervened, not at the request of the government but against the regime that had overthrown the government of Leon M'ba 42 hours earlier. France justified its intervention by citing the terms of the 1961 treaty of mutual defence, but the terms seemed incidental when it was recalled that France had intervened on ten other occasions in Africa in the past three years.

After 1965 the failure of collective security, the estrangement of many African states, friends and enemies alike, left a permanent mark on the French perception of its security interests in Africa, and with them those of the Atlantic Alliance.

At the same time, the onset of *détente* between East and West made it possible to justify a partial military disengagement. In accordance with the idea that power should exist, but not be flaunted, French troops in Africa were reduced from 58 500 to 21 300 in two years (1962–64) and again from 21 300 to 6420 from 1965–70.[26] The French did not intervene in Africa at all between 1964–68.

From 1962 onwards, French military power in Africa was based on three levels. First, the immediate defence of its allies in the continent rested on the *Armeés Nationales* of the countries concerned which were largely trained and equipped with French assistance. Secondly, the African based French *Forces d'Outre Mer* stationed at several points in the continent which had been singled out in the cooperation agreements as French military posts, were intended to provide further cover if required. In the mid-1960s, these forces consisted of French parachute units at Dakar, Ivato and Brazzaville; Foreign Legion regiments at Diego Suarez and Djibouti and further army garrisons at Thies and Bouar. Finally, the *Force d'Intervention Interarmées* stationed in the south of France provided reinforcements for the *Forces d'Outre-Mer* in the event of a crisis. Together, explained one military writer, this two tier French system of forces would serve as a deterrent to any aggression in Africa inimical to Western interests:

> deterrence has found in contemporary military vocabulary a new life; the possibility of rapid and massive intervention at great remove has enabled us to reduce our external forces.[27]

This conventional deterrent force, though owing its evolution to political considerations, soon became part of a graduated system of defence.

The value of this graduated system of defence became even clearer under Georges Pompidou who wished to make France's military presence less obvious while ensuring that Western interests were preserved. The value of the *Force d'Intervention* was, in Michel Debré's new formulation, that it served the more general aims of French defence policy:

> ... we cannot consider that our deterrence policy against attack on our territory is credible if we stay passive in the face of menaces which, though they weigh heavily on lands and peoples outside our frontiers, still touch us directly.[28]

If the French were seen to be evidently indifferent to threats to Africa, their policy of deterrence against the Soviet Union might no longer be very convincing.

Debré went on to argue in even more strident terms that the defence of Western interests in Africa was a French duty:

> Concerning Africa it is certain that in upholding the independence (of countries) to which we have granted it, by cooperation, if necessary of a military kind, it will often happen that we will find ourselves opposing movements of subversion whose origins may often be far removed from Africa itself. This is a positive contribution to Western unity.[29]

But at African insistence relations between France and its Francophone allies were soon to change. In 1972 Congo-Brazzaville withdrew from the quadrapartite agreements it had signed and Niger made an official request to have its agreement revised. The revision of the military terms of these agreements had diverse effects. There were still references to collective defence, but the facilities granted French troops in many instances no longer allowed for the defence of African states. More troops were withdrawn, and those which remained served merely to support the continuing French policy of having a military presence on the African continent. In some cases, this was very much to Paris' advantage in emphasising the role such a presence played in defence of the West. The revised accord with Gabon, for example, in allowing French troops to be stationed in the territory, while explicitly rejecting the notion that they were required for national defence, implicitly acknowledged France's geopolitical demand for an African presence that was unrelated to the defence of any particular African country.[30]

These troop reductions continued unabated. In the Sahara, the fulcrum of defence in the 1950s, small units were left in position at two small staging posts, Bousfer and Reggane, to secure communications with the south. By the early 1970s, a spate of successful *coups* which swept French clients out of Niger, the Central African Republic and finally Chad prompted the remaining Francophone leaders to question whether the presence of French troops served any useful purpose.

The evacuation of more than 2000 troops from Chad was followed closely by the evacuation of French forces from Madagascar (1973). At the same time, such previously stalwart allies as Benin and Congo-Brazzaville terminated their defence agreements, while Senegal and Cameroun insisted on defining the obligations more precisely. By 1974, only one company of marines remained in Gabon, and about 1000 troops in the whole of central Africa. By then, the preoccupation of French politicians was not with events on the mainland but with the growth of Soviet naval power in the Indian Ocean. This latter perception brought a meeting of minds with the British at the very time that they were themselves trying to reactivate a presence east of Suez, and when NATO itself was about to undertake contingency planning for the protection of shipping round the Cape. It is not altogether surprising, therefore, that it was in the Indian Ocean, not Africa, that the French concentrated their attention, or that at one time (1976) the French navy, using the rather questionable measurement of shipdays per nation, briefly became the primary naval power in the area.

In June 1973, the navy created a new naval command in the Indian Ocean around a fleet tanker which had been converted into a flag ship and renamed *La Charente*. By the end of the year, the French fleet numbered three frigates and three coastal patrol boats and some additional assault craft based in Djibouti.[31] The headquarters of the independent Indian Ocean command established in September on Réunion had an airfield and a radio relay station linked into similar stations on the islands of Crozet and Kerfuelen to the south. Its possession of Réunion, which was a department of France, and Mayotte, which had consistently refused to join the neighbouring Comoros Republic, enabled France, ever anxious to court African support, to endorse the non-aligned movement's call for the complete demilitarisation of the Indian Ocean. As an indigenous power in its own right, the French did not expect to be bound by restrictions which applied only to external powers, Britain and the United States among them.

Independent though the Indian Ocean command was, however, the ocean itself was still only a secondary, if important, theatre of operations. The French became increasingly aware in the 1970s that the opportunity to devise strategic and political options was limited by their inability to deploy more than half the number of ships they needed outside home waters. At most, they were only able to maintain token forces reinforced occasionally by units (usually two destroyers) from duties in the Mediterranean or Atlantic. By 1972, the year that the French and British navies undertook joint manouevres in the Indian Ocean for the first time, Michel Debré told reporters during a visit to the Malagasy Republic that France was quite unable to protect the shipping lanes on her own.[32]

The French presence in the area had been based from the beginning on a concept popular with the military under de Gaulle – that of the *coup d'arret* – the decisive application of force in a crisis, applied early enough to ensure the achievement of objectives before the situation deteriorated to the point where only the deployment of sizeable forces would be decisive. The prepositioning of forces overseas was a signal to a potential belligerent of French resolve to defend its national interests and deter aggression. Where forces were permanently deployed they did not have to be large enough to inflict decisive defeat; only convincing enough to signal that reinforcement would follow if deterrence failed. Initially, of course, whereas the United Kingdom had reacted strongly to Soviet expansion, France appeared to be relatively unperturbed. Michel Debré expressed the view that the Soviet Union's presence in the Indian Ocean was of the kind to be expected of a great power and should occasion neither fear nor surprise.[33] Within a few years, however, his tone had markedly changed.

By 1972, it had become clear that the French presence in the Indian Ocean was not large enough to deter anybody, least of all the Russians. The French could not undertake the defence of the sealanes without allied assistance. But it had also become clear that they were now confident that a threat to one member would represent a threat to all, regardless of the nationality of the shipping interdicted. The Anglo-French exercises underlined the fact that the interests involved were vital not only to French security, but also that of the Alliance of which it was still a member even though it had withdrawn from the integrated military command. The Soviet Union was left in no doubt that the Alliance would defend its interests, if necessary by force.[34] In 1972 Debré still thought that allied cooperation though important was unlikely for the moment to figure very prominently on NATO's agenda. It was not long, however, before the Western powers, led principally by the United States, began to give serious consideration to the Soviet presence in the area and the threat it posed to NATO's lines of communication.

UNITED STATES

As the principal power in NATO, with security interests which extended far beyond the area defined by treaty in 1949, the United States took a strangely ambivalent attitude to its defence interests in Africa. Apart from negotiating right of access to three strategic air command bases in Morocco in 1950 (when France was still the protecting power), and Wheelus Field in Libya, the Americans fought shy of concluding any mutual security pacts in Africa. So little were they concerned about an external threat to the continent that Section 508 of the Foreign Assistance Act forbade the extension of any military assistance, including the transfer of arms and equipment, for purposes other than internal security.

Several factors explain America's indifference to Africa in the 1950s. To begin with, no-one expected that most territories would be independent until the late 1970s. Henry Byroade, the Assistant Secretary of State for the Near East, warned in 1953 that premature independence would be dangerous, retrogressive and destructive. He called for a 'frank recognition that American security was linked to the strength and stability' of the colonial powers.[35] Such lack of foresight was not uncommon. A UN delegation to Tanganyika in 1955 returned with the impression that it would take 25 years to prepare for independence. In the event, the country achieved independence within six years.

America's initial objection to incorporating Africa into NATO had been predicated, at least in part, on a reluctance to extend defence responsibilities to an area of the world that was not in the front line of the struggle against international Communism. In 1949, the orthodox consensus in Washington was that Africa would remain a strategic backwater for some time to come; that the continent, in the words of one State Department official, was one of the few areas of the world 'relatively stable and secure'; 'where – in the broadest sense – no crisis exists'.[36]

Ironically, the United States was one of the last countries to wake up to the fact that decolonisation was now inevitable; that Africa would for the most part, be independent by the early 1960s and able to choose whether to remain non-aligned or not. As the historian Rupert Emerson recounts:

> the intensification of African nationalism and the growing readiness of Britain, France and Belgium to yield to it, forced the United States to catch up with a procession which it would have liked to believe it was leading.[37]

By then its main concern was to maintain some form of military presence in Africa, to retain, if possible, access to the 16 port facilities to which it had negotiated access with the colonial powers for the refuel and servicing of USN ships. As a report produced by the House subcommittee on African Affairs advised:

> should any nations in Africa have racial disorders, these might result in the loss of the use of these bases by the United States or other free Western forces. It is in the American interest that the peoples in the areas where the bases are located have a peaceful government friendly to the United States and its interests.

One of their reasons for not drawing the continent or any part of it into a collective security pact – in sharp contrast to the Near East and South-East Asia – was the wish to emphasise the scope of European responsibility.[39] Instead of taking upon itself the burden of defence, the United States chose to stress a strategy of 'regional partnership' – encouraging its European allies, and especially Britain and France, to take the lead in military operations. For the most part, the Americans hoped that their partners in NATO would be able to provide a stabilising military presence in Africa until such time as the Africans themselves could develop viable political institutions, or arrangements which would allow them to undertake their own defence.

Although Africa was considered a fast route to the Middle East, American bases there were not considered essential to American security. By the time agreement was reached with Morocco in 1959 to phase out its three airbases over the next four years, Strategic Air Command no longer attached much importance to the forward deployment of B-52 bombers outside the continental United States.

The same held true of its only other air base Wheelus Field, which was closed at the request of the revolutionary government in Libya in 1970. Such was the underlying strategic logic behind these decisions that America came to terms with African nationalism much earlier than Britain or France. This was even true of the communications base at Kagnew in Ethiopia. Initially, American rights at Kagnew were purchased in exchange for support for the Ethiopian claim to Eritrea at the United Nations, and in fact America preferred to provide diplomatic support rather than actually provide the Ethiopians with arms while the British were still involved in the area. Ethiopia's desire for arms provided the United States with some residual leverage which enabled the Pentagon to acquire significant concessions. Not only was Ethiopian Emperor Haile Selassie forced to accept a long term, 25 year lease, but the Americans refused to provide a specific commitment to defend the base if it came under attack. But what eventually induced the United States to aid Ethiopia was Haile Selassie's convincing manipulation of Dulles' notion of a 'northern tier' of defence which had been expressed in the Baghdad Pact of 1955.[40] By proposing that Ethiopia form part of a 'southern tier' of defence against communist influence in the Middle East, Haile Selassie made American interest in the security of the area as great as his own. Some years after his retirement, a former American ambassador to Ethiopia described the importance which the United States had attached to the base:

> The US interest in Ethiopia was simple, then, for Washington. The government defined it as 'the unhampered use of Kagnew'. This facility was deemed then to be 'strategically vital' to the United States, the only such military installation in black Africa. We had 1800 officers, men and civilians working there plus 800 dependents; a total of 2500 with plans already well advanced during my brief period to raise that number to 3500 within a year, . . .[41]

By 1970, however, Kagnew was no longer so important.

Developments in satellite communications had reduced its usefulness. So too had the decision to construct a complementary station on Diego Garcia under American control. The base was run down from a peak of 3000 in 1971 to 35 personnel in 1976. With the decision to phase out the base in October 1973 Ethiopia, and with it Africa, was relegated by clear implication to the outer perimeter of America's defence.[42]

It was during this period that the main American interest began to centre on Diego Garcia, a 17 square mile atoll lying 1174 miles to the south-west of Mauritius, of which it had once been part until it had been detached by the British in 1965 to form the centrepiece of the British Indian Ocean Territory. The island derived its importance from its unique geography and from the changing balance of power at sea after the appearance of the Soviet fleet in 1968. Negotiations for America's use of the island had begun the following year – two years before the arrival of the Soviet Navy. America's interest in the region, in fact, predated Britain's retreat from East of Suez and had it not been for the pressure on resources imposed by the conflict in Vietnam, the USN might well have appeared in the Ocean in force before Britain took its own decision to withdraw.

The proposal to build a communications station on Diego Garcia first emerged from discussions in the Pentagon in the summer of 1967. Although it was accompanied by a comprehensive survey prepared by the Joint Chiefs of Staff of the possible contingencies with which the USN could only deal if it had access to airfields and other facilities on the island, the main intention at this time was to construct an oiling station so that carrier task forces could refuel *en route* from Norfolk (Virginia) to Vietnam. The Office of Systems Analysis succeeded in demonstrating that it would not only cost more to refuel at Diego Garcia than out of the Persian Gulf, but that facilities on the island would be useless in dealing with any of the two dozen contingencies mentioned in the Chief of Staff's report. Working on the assumption that a country under attack would offer the USN access to its own ports, airfields and staging posts, it drew the conclusion that Diego Garcia would be an unnecessary expense.

Nevertheless, concern about the future availability of facilities on the mainland prompted the navy to revive the proposal the following year. This time the Chiefs of Staff presented their case in a different form: proposing that the island could be used as a communications station. The Pentagon subsequently approved this 'austere' facility despite the renewed objections of the Office of Systems Analysis which continued to maintain that political crises in the future, even if amenable to American intervention, could be handled at much lower cost by the temporary deployment of units of the Seventh Fleet based permanently in the Pacific. By the time the 20 year agreement with Britain was made public the construction of a communications station was already well under way.

In public discussions on Diego Garcia, US government spokesmen tended to stress the value of having a base on an uninhabited island where the Navy would not have to worry about nationalist protests. Indeed, the decision to press ahead with the base seems to have gone hand in hand with America's general disengagement from its existing bases on the mainland at the end of the 1950s. The most telling argument of all was that the United States would no longer have to worry about the kind of political developments which had so often resulted in the past in extortion of exorbitant rental or user rights payments.[43]

When asked about the advantages of Diego Garcia in 1974, the Deputy Assistant Secretary for Defence replied that the use of the facility would not require 'abrasive discussions or potentially abrasive discussions involving the sensitivities of littoral states when a requirement comes to use it'. An American admiral reminded the sub-committee on the Near East how important it was to have facilities in the area which could be used by the USN without agreement each time on a case by case basis. The Chief of Naval Operations added his endorsement by predicting that many ports on the east African littoral which were presently available to American warships might no longer be so in the future once the Soviet Union began to seek bunkering facilities for its own fleet.[44] The architects and initiators of the Diego Garcia policy were in fact those leading bureaucrats and military planners who had learned from first hand experience in the 1960s that military agreements with African countries could not always be relied upon.[45]

On the other hand, even a cursory analysis of the formulation of American policy in this period will show that the United States government did not intend Diego Garcia to be the forerunner of a permanent presence in the area. America's response to the Soviet presence in the Indian Ocean was marked by restraint. The

United States believed that its security commitments need not be extensive. In the event of war, the Indian Ocean would be a highly improbable theatre of operations. The Atlantic and Mediterranean were accorded much higher priority. Many officials refused to be impressed by narrow shipday comparisons. If the Soviet squadron had quadrupled in as many years, concluded the chairman of the Joint Chiefs of Staff, any increase beginning from zero would in the nature of things appear more dramatic than a sustained reduction such as Britain's own retreat from east of Suez after 1968.[46]

The United States had originally planned to send more warships to the Indian Ocean in 1965, but had had to defer the plans because of the Vietnam commitment. Although Secretary for Defence Melvin Laird agreed to extend the scope of the Seventh Fleet's operations once it had been released from combat duty in the south China sea, the State Department saw no necessity for the USN to control any part of the Indian Ocean.[47] Indeed, the Defence Secretary preferred to rely on periodic visits by units of the Seventh Fleet rather than incur the expense of maintaining a permanent task force in the area. Although the Arab–Israeli war of 1973 increased the frequency of such visits and prompted the Americans to send an aircraft carrier to the Gulf for the first time in 25 years, not one of the eight Task Forces despatched between 1973–76 sailed south of the Gulf of Aden.

The Arab–Israeli war, however, marked a turning point. The difficulties associated with operating America's only standing force in the area – MIDEASTFOR – from a base in an Arab nation (Bahrain threatened to cancel the lease in 1974) sent the defence planners back to the plans drawn up by the National Security Council (NSC) in 1970, and a study prepared by the Chief of Naval Operations the same year.[48] For the first time the USN had to consider the possibility of combat operations in the Middle East. The pre-planned routine deployment of carrier task forces for non-combat missions in time of peace provided no test of a crisis when carriers and their destroyer escorts would be expected to travel long distances, 4000 miles from the nearest naval base at Subic Bay, 5000 from Guam. Nor did it test the capability of aircraft using large quantities of special low flash-point fuel to mount combat operations over a long period. Studies made of fuel needs for fast crisis response which were undertaken by the USN's Indian Ocean Study Group and subsequently approved by the Chief of Naval Operations in 1968 had highlighted the importance of Diego Garcia as a base for refuelling both ships and aircraft.

It was not altogether surprising, therefore, that it was only in 1974 that the Americans augmented MIDEASTFOR Task Force despite six Soviet naval visits to the Gulf since 1970. For it was not until 1974 that the USN concluded that its principal mission in time of peace was the protection of shipping on the route at which it appeared most at risk – from the Gulf via the Cape into the South Atlantic.[49] In this respect, it was perhaps fortunate for the Western Alliance that the United States took the lead since by this time, the British had already shown that they lacked the resources to undertake the task themselves.

Only two years earlier America's principal concern had been the security of Western Europe's oil supply rather than its own. Gradually it became aware of its own dependence on the energy resources of the Gulf and especially its inability to supply Western Europe with its own stocks as it had during the two previous Middle East crises of 1956 and 1967. This was a dramatic change from the 1960s when its consumption of oil from the Middle East had actually dropped by 50 per cent. Even had the British remained in the Gulf until 1976 as they had originally envisaged, it would have been inappropriate for the United States to have relied exclusively on a British guarantee. It was not altogether surprising, therefore, that the naval base at Jufair (Bahrain) became the first facility that the British had evacuated that the Americans took over themselves.

The United States could derive some security from the interests and capabilities of its European allies in the area but increasingly less as the threat of Soviet interdiction loomed larger. With the Chiefs of Staff predicting that 60 per cent of all oil consumed by the US would be routed along the Cape by the mid-1980s few doubted that the most likely point of interdiction in the Indian Ocean would be at its two western bottlenecks: Suez and the Cape. It did not seem coincidental that two of the Soviet 'bases' identified by President Ford were located at the mouths of the straits through which the oil tankers sailed on their way to Europe.[50]

Beyond the horizon in 1974, a new threat was beginning to loom which was to make the task of keeping the sealanes open more complicated and eventually to lead to calls for a more concerted Western response. Of 40 raw materials imported by the United States after 1970, more than half came from African states on the Indian Ocean littoral. The collapse of the Portuguese empire in Southern Africa threw America's dependence into even greater relief. After 1973 the USN's focus of concern shifted briefly from the Gulf to Southern Africa and the threat of disruption in the mines.[51] It was not long before the Deputy Secretary for Defence began to call upon NATO itself to draw up contingency plans for the protection of non-renewable resources other than oil.[52] From then on it was only a matter of time before the security bill began to include such items as arms transfers to local clients, construction of better facilities on the mainland, and the expansion of the existing facilities on Diego Garcia.

But in one respect, the answers to many of the questions raised in these years had already been provided by the events of 1973–74 when the oil boycott and the appearance of the Soviet Navy in the Indian Ocean had turned American minds to the oil routes and the protection of shipping and had sent the USN looking for bunkering and replenishment facilities on the East African coast. Faced with the depressing fact that it had the right of access to only three ports in sub-Saharan Africa – Dakar, Monrovia and Mombasa – it began to consider more active cooperation with the Europeans. Confronted by the real or imagined threat of Soviet interdiction, America's defence planners began to recognise that the security of the Cape route had become a matter of concern for the whole Alliance, not merely the United States.

3 The North Atlantic Alliance and Southern Africa, 1949–74

From the time the nationalist revolt broke out in Angola (1961), Portugal's refusal to transfer power in its African colonies and NATO's apparent reluctance to stand firm on the issue combined to give credence to Soviet claims that the Portuguese were members of an 'aggressively imperialist' alliance.[1] Britain's 'collusion' with South Africa helped contribute to the picture. Events in Southern Africa lost NATO the friendship of many African states and won it the respect of none.

To the great majority of Africans, the lip-service NATO paid to the principle of majority rule and its reliance on diplomacy to advance it (which stopped short of suspending arms shipments to Portugal, still less of expelling Portugal from the Alliance), was evidence of Western hypocrisy. Its efforts seemed self-serving at worst, self-deceiving at best. Indeed, NATO itself was seen by many to be an obstacle to the change that its own political leaders professed to want.

As a result, hopes for change in Southern Africa were seen increasingly to depend on internal developments (primarily guerrilla warfare) and external assistance – principally in the shape of arms shipments from the Warsaw Pact. Within NATO itself, the cumulative impact of such criticism was to produce a broad consensus that Portugal's continued membership was a matter of grave embarrassment to the Alliance. Britain's links with South Africa were marginally less so. To what extent can such criticism be substantiated? It enjoyed wide currency, but is it supported by the evidence? Ten years afterwards, we know much more about Portuguese policy. Its conduct of the war, political conflicts at home, the economic crisis produced by the demand on material and human resources have all been analysed and reported in detail. But we still know little about NATO's role. Why the Alliance acted with such circumspection, what Portugal's membership meant to its members, what it meant to Portugal itself – these are matters of understanding. They are no less matters of controversy.

NATO AND PORTUGAL: THE POLICIES OF AMBIGUITY

Although the North Atlantic Area was mentioned five times in the text of the Treaty, from the beginning its signatories talked of a North Atlantic community, whose values as much as the territory of its members were under threat from the Soviet Union. Those who acceded in 1949 were vetted for the soundness of their democratic principles which had inspired them to come together in the first place. The proposal put forward by the Canadian Prime Minister, Louis St Laurent, for a global system straddling all continents and embracing all members of the free world, whether democratic or not, found little favour with his colleagues. The North Atlantic community existed in the imagination as well as on paper; it was a political community as much as a military alliance. The collective security of its members was deemed to depend on the coherence of their democratic principles as much as the coherence of their military doctrine.

It was only when the defence debate began to turn on the threat to NATO's southern flank that the Alliance began to discuss the accession of states, notably Greece and Turkey, who were not themselves democratic. Several of the original signatories, Denmark and Norway among them, expressly opposed the accession of countries who were neither able nor willing to conform with the principles enshrined in the NATO Treaty, but to little effect, largely because the notion of a distinct political community did not exist.

Only Canada raised objections to Portugal's membership. One of the members of the Canadian team which negotiated the Atlantic Pact opined that its members should be bound together 'not merely by their common opposition to totalitarian Communism, but also by a common belief . . . in the principles of democracy, personal freedom and political liberty'. To invite Lisbon to become a member of the Alliance would seriously weaken its effectiveness as a basis for mobilising 'a spiritual counterforce against Soviet aggression'.[2]

In the early 1950s, however, NATO was only as strong as the United States and this at a time when the Americans were more interested in recruiting as many allies as possible to the common cause without worrying too much about their democratic credentials.

Portugal was the only one of the original signatories which did not have a democratic government in 1949. Its Prime Minister, Antonio Salazar, was intolerant of the democratic ideals of the NATO Treaty. Membership of the Alliance, he explained to the National Assembly, would not bind Portugal to political principles which had long been suppressed in Portugal itself:

> The definition of this ideology is obviously unfortunate . . . and suffers from vacuousness and imprecision of certain formulae that are already worn out and disturbing because they are employed everywhere in the most diverse interpretations . . . . We feel ourselves bound by the obligations of the Pact and by its general ends, not by doctrinaire assertions tending to regiment political systems about whose virtues we, in our country, are sufficiently aware.[3]

Salazar's address was illuminating precisely because it revealed the palpable gap between what the Portuguese professed to believe in and what they actually did. In general, most of its allies had a vested interest in its membership of NATO and gave little thought to the regime in Lisbon, even less to that in its African colonies. For that matter, colonial powers such as Britain paid little regard to the Treaty's preamble 'to safeguard the freedom, common heritage and civilisation of their peoples founded on the principles of democracy, individual liberty and the rule of law' when its principles were deemed to conflict with colonial rule. Only later did they appreciate that the doctrine of self-determination which they themselves were to profess so avidly by the end of the 1950s had been from the very beginning at variance with the regime which prevailed in Portugal itself.

Whether Portugal's membership was worth the political embarrassment is another question. From the first the Portuguese showed little interest in making any contribution to the defence of Europe, and actually held out for more than a year before finally agreeing to hold their forces in readiness for the defence of the Iberian peninsula. Indeed, had it not been for their increasing doubts about the long term future of their colonial possessions, they might never have joined the Alliance.

Salazar tried hard to get the African territories admitted into the NATO area, beginning with Cape Verde which fell just outside it. The drift towards decolonisation in the mid-1950s decisively changed the map of Africa, significantly altered the balance of forces and introduced a measure of instability into a continent that had hitherto been isolated from the cold war. Faced with a threat posed in large part by international forces it was too small to contain, Portugal took up the NATO option in earnest. Choosing to administer its colonies on the basis of coercion – repression too weak to root out opposition, but provocative enough to incite it – its new found interest in NATO took two forms. The first, and least convincing, was an attempt to win support for its own contention that the Alliance's southern flank could well be turned if the Soviet Union were ever to gain access to the vast strategic area stretching from the Azores to Cape Verde with its airfield on Sal, and from Guinea to Angola with the natural harbours along its 1800 km coastline.

Its second ploy was to increase its contribution to Europe in the hope of making itself an indispensable ally. Towards the end of 1956, the lines of the new strategy became clearly drawn when the government put at the disposal of the Alliance two airfields at Espinho and Montijo and assigned a third division in addition to the two already assigned to Supreme Allied Command Atlantic (SACLANT).

The growing violence in its African colonies largely nullified its commitment. The nationalist revolt in Angola in 1961, in which 300 000 blacks may have died, was followed three years later by a similar, though less bloody, rebellion in Mozambique. Within a few years, the rising had assumed the proportions of a full scale war which continued to rage until 1974 when its repercussions on the morale of the armed forces precipitated a military coup. At its height, the campaign in southern Africa called for the deployment of over 100 000 troops, including most of the units originally earmarked for NATO.

At a ministerial meeting in Oslo in May 1961, NATO agreed to

allow Portugal to transfer the divisions it had assigned to the
Alliance. The need to contain African nationalism combined with
a long term strategic perspective in which the colonies figured
prominently made perfect sense of the compromise in the eyes of
the Portuguese government. As its Foreign Minister, Franco
Nogueira, observed, if France had been allowed to redeploy its
forces in Algeria so should Portugal; what applied to one member
must in fairness apply to all.[4]

The Alliance remained unconvinced. As the Algerian war had
shown, there were strict limits to what France's allies would
stomach; colonial retrenchment was the first requirement of the
times. The French campaign in North Africa appeared to mark,
even in 1961, the last chapter of its colonial past; Portugal's
response to the Angolan revolt looked like the beginning of a new
and bitter chapter in its 400 year old colonial history. In July, a
mission headed by Admiral Evans visited Lisbon to discover to
what degree the rebellion was likely to detract from Portugal's
contribution to NATO. Clearly, having survived the controversy
generated by Algeria, NATO was not enthralled by the prospect
of an intensified guerrilla struggle in which another member was
about to become involved. The upshot of his discussions are not
known, but Salazar himself admitted that as long as Portuguese
forces were engaged in the defence of its national territory
overseas they could not be expected to defend Western Europe or
West Berlin.[5]

In view of Salazar's frankness, it is perhaps all the more
surprising that the Alliance should have muffled its criticism as
time went on. Indeed, despite Salazar's complaint that Portugal
was fighting in Africa 'not without alliances but without allies',[6]
the allies continued to provide expressions of support. The new
NATO Secretary-General, Dirk Stikker, flew to Lisbon to
reassure the government that the allies still placed faith in its
membership, adding rather gratuitously that the Alliance must
stand together in the face of the communist threat.[7] Two years
later the SACEUR, General Limnitzer, spoke of his admiration
for Portuguese troops in the overseas territories where they were
fighting not only for freedom but also for the raw materials and
bases which were indispensable to Western security.

Not for the first time, however, the Alliance ignored what was
obvious not only to contemporary observers but also to the
Portuguese – that Portugal's lateral connections with NATO

were becoming fewer every year. By 1968, all but a few units of the Portuguese army were stationed overseas; and even these were 50 per cent below the average manning requirement. Apart from a Neptune anti-submarine squadron assigned to Europe, the rest of the air force spent its time flying combat missions in Africa or ferrying reinforcements from Europe. When NATO's first command in Portugal (INTERLANT) was established in February 1967 (controlling the air defence of the Atlantic west and south of Lisbon), the Defence Minister insisted that Portugal's first priority would continue to be the defence of southern Africa.

NATO obligations were rarely if ever mentioned in defence white papers. Although Portugal was then spending over 40 per cent of its national budget on defence, the highest proportion of any member except the United States, the expenditure figured hardly at all in NATO calculations. Indeed, so marginal was its contribution that Dr Henry Kissinger omitted to mention it altogether in his survey of NATO – *The Troubled Partnership* – in 1965.[8] As General Paiva, one of Portugal's most senior commanders, admitted in 1969, the country could not fulfil its NATO commitments and continue fighting in Southern Africa at the same time, although only its NATO partners seemed unaware of the fact.[9]

Thus from 1965, two themes were to persist in the often strained relations between Portugal and its partners and between the Alliance and Africa. Portugal, for its part, safely ensconced behind the Alliance shield, tried to persuade its allies that far from shirking its obligations the front line had shifted from central Europe to Southern Africa. If the allies would not help it directly, they might, at least, turn a blind eye to the use of NATO weapons in the area despite the explicit assurances that were given that they would only be used in Europe.[10] For their part, the Africans persistently criticised NATO for failing to chase up the many breaches of the agreement that came to their attention in the hope that it would eventually begin to question the value of having a politically broken-backed and hence politically unstable country as a member. They had, perhaps, some reason to expect that the political embarrassment in Africa it faced whilst Portuguese rule persisted might succeed where moral arguments had conspicuously failed.

Far from wishing to withdraw from NATO and its political and military entanglements, Portugal wished to extend them. In

October 1968 at a meeting of the North Atlantic Treaty Organisation in Lisbon, the Portuguese Foreign Minister expressed a view long held in the Foreign Ministry that:

> the NATO Alliance should not be indifferent to the preservation for the West of vital strategic positions. We have never understood, for example, how one can separate the north Atlantic from the south Atlantic or how one can ensure the security of one without taking into account the security of the other.[11]

During a NATO ministerial meeting in Lisbon two years later, the Portuguese defence minister offered his colleagues 'territories and bases outside the NATO zone' from which they could control the South Atlantic and the Western approaches.[12]

Clearly Portugal hoped that NATO would eventually see the sense of securing its lifelines in the southern oceans. The *Diario de Noticias*, taking up this theme, reported that the country had already been approached by its allies for naval bases in São Tomé and Cape Verde, a request, that if met, would enable Portugal to 'acquire an important position within the Western defence that far surpasses its military potential... in NATO'. The Portuguese constantly referred to the role that their colonial territories could play in the defence of the sealanes at the two most vulnerable points of interdiction: the Mozambique Channel and the waters off the West African coast. Not surprisingly there were those among NATO's critics who suspected that when authorising SACLANT to look into contingency plans for the defence of allied shipping in 1972, the NATO defence chiefs had been most interested in taking an option on the naval bases in Angola and Portuguese Guinea.[13]

Behind the rhetoric lay very real considerations of strategic interest which weighed heavily with NATO commanders in this period. Naval reconnaissance aircraft could survey the southeastern Atlantic and western Indian Oceans much more effectively from bases in Cape Verde, São Tomé and Nacala than from Diego Garcia or the Azores. On its own, Portugal had neither the naval nor air resources to turn this fact to good advantage, only the bases to put at the disposal of its allies. The airbase at Sal on Cape Verde was the only facility of its kind in the area. Even more impressive was the naval base at Nacala in Mozambique which was built deliberately to American specifications so that it could service, if necessary, all but the very largest units of the American Seventh Fleet. In 1974, Lisbon suggested to the United States that it might reduce its defence costs substantially by using the base instead of expanding its austere facility on Diego Garcia.

Late in 1968, Foreign Minister Franco Nogueira had intimated that Portugal would try to enlist allied support for its mission in Africa by offering the use of bases on the African mainland.[14] The Alliance could perhaps be forgiven for looking into the matter in the years immediately prior to the collapse of Portuguese rule. Faced with the build-up of Soviet naval power and the risk that this posed to allied shipping, many NATO planners believed that Portugal's position in the Indian and South Atlantic oceans might hold the key to the problem. They knew that the use of such bases would be politically unwise and that as the situation in Southern Africa deteriorated an allied presence in the area would make nonsense of the concept of limited liability. Since most defence ministers, however, were entirely opposed to the provision of a NATO task force, or a substantial increase in military spending, it was not altogether surprising that the NATO Assembly approved a report in 1972 which asked Portugal

> to make available its facilities on the Azores, the Cape Verde islands, Madeira and Sao Tomé *and to contribute on the African continent* to the protection of the Cape route if NATO should request it.[15]

NATO seemed to stand condemned by association every time one of its commanders expressed an opinion. In March 1972, Admiral Charles K Duncan, SACLANT made several remarks in the course of Congressional hearings that seemed to imply support for the Portuguese position.[16] The timing was especially unfortunate since the North Atlantic Council had met in Lisbon the previous summer for the first time since 1952. In the same year Rear Admiral Eugene Fluckey, Commander Iberian Atlantic Command, argued that with the expansion of Soviet naval power 'the southern flank (of NATO) has now become a front'.[17] Speaking to a visiting Congressional mission in Lisbon, Fluckey noted that NATO was 'well on the way to hardening the Achilles heel that has existed in this Iberlant area'.[18] He left no doubt that he was in favour of a more flexible position on NATO operations south of the Tropic of Cancer. Most interestingly of all, the State

Department admitted for the first time in December 1974 that Portuguese Africa had figured prominently in NATO contingency planning, an admission which went far beyond the NATO Secretariat's earlier declaration that only the security of areas outside its immediate defence perimeter had been the subject of discussion.[19]

Nevertheless, even the Americans saw no need to hold *points d'appui* on the African littoral under Portuguese control. Their representative on the Committee of 24 reminded its members that NATO had never been interested in colonial bases. Indeed, the contention that foreign military bases had ever been a serious impediment to independence could be disproved by looking at the long list of countries which had become independent in the last two decades. Most foreign bases were located in independent countries as a result of the mutuality of defence and security interests which had survived independence.[20] Most NATO ministers, as opposed perhaps, to defence planners in SHAPE, believed that the bases would be available to the Portuguese provided they transferred power in time.[21] And although the Portuguese persuaded many people that the African challenge to their rule was part of an international communist conspiracy, they never persuaded their partners that access to bases in Southern Africa would help to contain the threat of international communism. It was one thing to agree upon general principles, quite another to act upon them.[22]

Portugal and the Invasion of Guinea (1970)

Perhaps NATO's most embarrassing moment in Africa came in November 1970 when the Portuguese government chose to invade the West African state of Guinea. Trapped in a predicament of its own making Lisbon appeared to be caught between two opposing claims on its allegiance: its colonial mission on the one hand, its NATO obligations on the other. After 1970, it was frequently seen as a self-willed power prepared to intervene in Africa without regard to NATO's real interests, or proper understanding of its own.

The main nationalist movement in Portuguese Guinea, the African Party for the independence of Guinea and Cape Verde (PAIGC), had turned to guerrilla warfare in 1959 after the shooting of 50 striking dock workers by Portuguese police. With the blessing of the President of Guinea, Seke Touré, the PAIGC began to use neighbouring Guinea as a base for operations, and even conventional military missions. In these it had the support of the Guinean army which often shelled Portuguese positions from across the border.

In 1969, the Portuguese army began a vigorous campaign to eliminate all oppostion. Portuguese incursions into Guinea and Senegal grew increasingly frequent, and a number of protests were lodged with the United Nations by both African states.[23] In 1970, Guinea became the victim of a mercenary raid. Three hundred and fifty Portuguese commandos landed at various points along the Conakry coast. The raid which attempted but failed to dislodge Seke Touré left 300 Guineans dead and 100 Portuguese wounded. Subsequent interrogation ascertained that the operation had been planned by the Portuguese government in an effort to replace Seke Touré's government with a regime more pliable to Lisbon's influence.[24]

Seke Touré's reaction to the raid was to request the Security Council for immediate military assistance. The Council's decision to despatch a fact finding mission instead of a task force was a severe disappointment to the government. The United Nations' muted response was all the more contentious in the light of subsequent events, including a second incursion by 200 Portuguese soldiers at Kondura, the principal PAIGC base. The raid was an open challenge to the authority of the United Nations coming as it did while the investigating team was still in Conakry. It was this second incident which prompted the government to request military assistance from both the Soviet Union and the United States.

America's failure to respond opened the door to the Soviet Union. But it is as well to look at the West's response in a little more detail if only because its collective and individual reaction probably went some way to deterring similar actions in the future. It is not, of course, surprising that NATO found itself implicated in the 1970 raid. At an emergency meeting of the OAU in December, 41 foreign ministers unanimously agreed to condemn 'those states, particularly the NATO powers, who sustain Portugal in her colonial aggression by their continued assistance to her'. They were prompted to do so not so much by NATO's failure to punish Portugal, but by the veto which both the United Kingdom and the United States had exercised the previous

March on a motion calling on Britain to apply military force against the white government in Rhodesia.

In the eyes of most Africans, the West's failure to intervene against white supremacist regimes ensured that situations similar to the Conakry raid would continue to arise in the future. It was not very surprising, therefore, that during the UN debate on Guinea the NATO powers found themselves pilloried almost as much as Lisbon. Even such pro-Western states as Ethiopia and Liberia called upon Portugal's allies to expel her from NATO, or at least, impose economic sanctions to prevent such actions in the future.

In fact, the NATO powers did intervene behind the scenes despite their public diffidence. The United States gave Seke Touré a private assurance that it would do what it could to ensure that the 'grave and criminal aggression' by Portugal did not reoccur. When this message was later leaked by Conakry to the world press, the US ambassador had it read into the record of the Security Council debate. During the debate, the delegates of the United States and Britain refused to defend Portugal against the charges levelled against her.[25] The British and French ambassadors openly acknowledged the veracity of the Council's investigative report and publicly admitted the whole affair was damaging to NATO's international reputation.[26] Even when the Soviet Union despatched a West Africa squadron into Guinean waters at Seke Touré's request, the United States accepted its presence without complaint as a necessary guarantee against future Portuguese incursions.

Behind the scenes, NATO pressure ensured that there would be no repetition of these events. It is still difficult to point out such pressures as they were never publicly referred to either by Portugal or its allies. There is no doubt also that Lisbon was inhibited from intervening again by the presence of the Soviet squadron. Nevertheless, it is possible to infer from the eliptical comments of the Portuguese government that NATO also exercised some restraint.

In spring 1971, the Portuguese Foreign Minister, Rui Patricio, denied that his country received any moral support from its allies:

> It is not true. We are complaining to our NATO allies that they don't give us any support. They won't even give us *political* support in Africa.[27]

An American journalist who visited Portuguese Guiné in the aftermath of the raid quoted Portuguese officers as highly disillusioned at the little support they received from their NATO friends.[28] Even the threat of sanctions was hinted at by one high ranking Portuguese official in 1971:

> We can't afford to internationalise these conflicts any more than they already are. It would be more dangerous for us in the long run. Most of our trouble now comes from *outside involvement* in Portuguese problems.[29]

These oblique references to NATO pressures are interesting, precisely because they appear so often. Lisbon probably took them seriously. Indeed, there is even some evidence that its allies went so far as to warn her that if her forces intervened again and the Soviet Union responded, she would face the Soviet Union alone.[30]

Arms Transfers and Other Matters

The fact that strategic planning was not translated into public policy appears most clearly from the evidence of our second theme: the sale of arms. Between persistent African demands for a complete embargo on the one hand and Portuguese complaints about existing restrictions on the other, the Alliance negotiated uneasily. But there was never any question of supplying Portugal with arms for operations in Africa itself. In the eyes of all but the most reactionary, the priorities were right – NATO's future lay not with Portugal, but with Africa. Claims that NATO tacitly supported Portuguese colonialism are misleading. They are misleading in their suggestion of conscious purpose, and their confusion of expediency with moral approval. They are still more misleading in their neglect of the criticism of Portugal within the Alliance which continued to be made until 1974 with little reference to strategic planning. The genuine dismay with which the smaller allies looked upon Portuguese policy eliminated many doubts and divided counsels.

In March 1961, the Norwegian Foreign Minister, Halvard Lange, informed NATO that in view of his country's support for self-determination it felt obliged to refuse to license in future the sale of any arms or equipment to Portugal. Britain suspended licenses for the export of military equipment at the same time, but confined the embargo to Africa. Indeed, both Britain and France acted as they did largely to head off a proposal for a comprehensive embargo which might have put in jeopardy Portugal's continuing NATO membership.[31] Thereafter, the ultimate destination of arms sold by its partners was monitored only by a system of written pledges. But as African criticism mounted, as its complaints became well documented, its charges more specific, it became increasingly difficult to ignore the evidence of abuse. What remained true from first to last is that the Portuguese never had any intention of honouring their obligations.

NATO weapons as such, of course, did not exist. The North Atlantic Treaty merely provided a facility by which its members could supply one another with weapons, leaving its individual members free to state the conditions, if any, attached to the sale. American arms sales to Portugal were covered by the mutual defence assistance agreement of 1951 which was still in force ten years later. This treaty dealt primarily with their obligations as NATO allies including

> use of assistance received pursuant to para 1 of this article (a) for the purpose of promoting an integrated defence of the North Atlantic area and for facilitating the development plans under Article 9 of the North Atlantic Treaty and (b) in accordance with defence plans formulated by NATO recommended by the North Atlantic Treaty Defence Committee and agreed to by the two governments.

Any extension of those obligations outside Europe clearly put Portugal in breach of the agreement. But the military assistance provided by the United States was also governed by a series of treaties signed in 1960 including an agreement which related to weapons production, the interchange of patent rights and the exchange of information for purposes of defence. All three were negotiated at a time when security interests in the colonies were uppermost in Lisbon's mind. As the Portuguese Minister of Marine remarked in December, the treaties his country had negotiated with the United States would help to facilitate the defence of its colonies from communist subversion.[32]

It must be said that even though many arms did slip through the net in the 1960s, even though the staff of the American consulate in Luanda who were supposed to chase up breaches of the embargo in conjunction with the 25-man Military Assistance Advisory Group stationed in Lisbon often fell down on the job, the US Military Assistance Programme (MAP) averaged only $1m a year, an amount which represented less than 0.25 per cent of Portugal's military spending at the height of the wars. Any resources, therefore, which were freed by MAP were marginal in its calculation whether to press ahead with the war or not. Moreover, from the American side the matter was greatly complicated by the concern that, in its absence, Portugal's contribution to NATO would probably suffer.[33]

But it was not just American arms that slipped through the net. West Germany was heavily criticised for much of the period, especially after signing a defence treaty with Portugal in 1963 by which in return for a military base abroad (Beja) and a training centre for the Bundeswehr at Santa Margarida, it provided the Portuguese government with $3m in military assistance.[34] Assurances that equipment would not be used in Africa were duly demanded and given, but Portugal made no distinction between the defence of the homeland and the defence of the overseas provinces. As a Foreign Ministry spokesman explained in 1965, replying to criticism that Fiat G-91 jets purchased from Germany had been used in Angola:

> The transaction was agreed within the spirit of the North Atlantic Pact. It was agreed that the planes would be used only for defensive purposes within Portuguese territory. Portuguese territory extends to Africa – Angola, Mozambique and Portuguese Guinea.[35]

Although interest in the use of Beja eventually waned, the Defence Committee of the Bundestag recommended as late as 1968 that the supply of military equipment should continue 'despite problems as to the ultimate destination of those supplies'.[36]

It was not surprising, therefore, that conflicting reports about what NATO had agreed to in principle and how its members had behaved in practise, led many Africans to conclude that Portugal and the Alliance had come to share a common interest in containing the nationalist struggle. The reasons for NATO's failure to chase up breaches in its own embargo were to be found in the political relationship between the defence ministries of the various members, in the blinkered response of defence salesmen and a reluctance to face the fact that as long as arms and equipment remained in Portuguese hands they would be used in Africa regardless of assurances to the contrary.

Arms supplied by the United States and West Germany were supplied under the NATO Treaty. This was not true of arms transfers from Britain and France. Arms from America, as we have seen, were sold under a military assistance programme which applied specifically to NATO members, a fact which was also true of Germany. Indeed, this was never denied by the West German government, least of all by the government of Willie Brandt which was more sensitive to the issue than the Christian Democratic administration which had preceded it. By contrast, the sale by Britain and France of the Puma helicopter surprisingly provoked less criticism than the sale of far less sophisticated German and American weapons despite the fact that the helicopter was specifically designed to NATO specifications (The Belgian and Italian contractors being responsible for the delivery of spare parts). Even more surprisingly, the designers from the factory in France where it had been assembled were present when it first went into action in Angola.[37] Such extraordinary breaches of the embargo, which were by no means infrequent, prompted many to question whether NATO's monitoring procedures were adequate, or whether its members thought it mattered.[38]

In dwelling on these instances of inconsistency, however, historians are simply playing a game at which contemporary critics excelled throughout the 1960s. For to demonstrate that NATO's policy was not always what it claimed to be is not to describe what it was. If NATO policy fell short of a clear cut decision between Portugal and the nationalists, if it wavered between adherence to its democratic principles and obligations to a long-established member, this was not always to Portugal's advantage. Salazar's successor, Marcellino Caetano, was often bitterly critical of NATO's lukewarm support for its colonial mission. As he reminded the National Popular Action Movement in September 1970:

> ... the fact is that by definition NATO is only concerned with the North Atlantic area and forbids the use of its weapons outside that area. Several of our allies in the organisation do not hide their hostility to our position in the southern hemisphere

and act as our adversaries. We receive no support from NATO or from any other source, organisation or alliance.³⁹

Such denials, however frequently expressed, need not be taken at face value, but it would be equally unwise to disregard them altogether. Most arms sales were *ad hoc* in nature. That the embargo could only have been effective had arms transfers to Portugal as well as the colonies been stopped altogether is irrefutable, but hardly to the point. Comprehensive sanctions would have been tantamount to expulsion; those who advocated such draconian measures deluded themselves if they ever thought that the matter was a serious subject of discussion. There were some members of NATO who discussed whether Portugal should be expelled, but they were too few and carried insufficient weight to command attention. Their counsels went unheard or unheeded. Although condemnation of Portugal came from many quarters, in the main it came from Africa, and for the most part it was directed at the Western Alliance as much as Portugal. 'Portugal is only able to wage a colonial war', Nkrumah observed in May 1961, 'because fundamentally she has the backing of the North Atlantic Treaty Organisation. If this backing were withdrawn tomorrow and Portugal was excluded from NATO, Portugal's colonial rule would collapse the day after'.⁴⁰

Since the ensuing controversy persisted until the decision was taken out of NATO's hands in 1974, we might well ask why the Alliance baulked at the idea of expulsion, why it continued to hope right up to the end that a solution could be found without a fundamental change of regime. The Americans were hamstrung from the beginning by the importance they attached to the Lajes base on the Azores which they had leased from Portugal since 1951 and which Dean Acheson once described as 'the single most important we have anywhere'.⁴¹ From its facilities on the island chain it was possible to track submarines within a radius of 1000 miles – the midpoint that linked the US Sixth Fleet in the Mediterranean to its major supply depots on the eastern seaboard of the United States. No less important were its two airbases at Terceira and Santa Maria which handled 14 000 departures in 1961, or more than 40 flights a day and which would have been crucial in a general airlift of American forces. Although the number of aircraft by volume fell by 60 per cent between 1962–68, 560 flights a month were not uncommon.⁴²

When the lease expired in December 1962, protracted negotiations for renewal enabled the Portuguese government to blackmail the United States with the threat of cancellation. The dilemma in which the Americans found themselves was summed up succinctly in the guidelines which the State Department drew up in 1963:

> The US faces a dilemma in its policy and operations towards Portugal. On the one hand, we want to continue to have use of base facilities in the Azores and to keep Portugal in NATO. On the other hand, we are convinced that Portugal must face reality concerning the future of its overseas territories; accept the principle of self-determination for these territories and prepare them for the exercise ... Our problem is one of a delicate balance – making certain that in working to achieve one set of objectives we do not sacrifice the other.[43]

In a memorandum prepared for the Secretary of Defence, the Joint Chiefs of Staff seized upon the dichotomy for their own ends:

> The importance of Portugal lies primarily in the importance of US base rights in the Azores and *secondarily in the membership of Portugal in NATO*. Loss of the Azores would seriously degrade the responsiveness, reliability and control of major US forces.[44]

Throughout the 1960s, Portugal successfully forced America to balance these two options by refusing to extend the lease on Lajes on other than a temporary basis. It was only during the visit of the Portuguese Foreign Minister to Washington in 1970 that the government expressed an interest in formal renewal in the expectation of winning a generous aid package in return. In December 1971, the two governments exchanged notes in Brussels giving the United States the right to remain in Lajes and the naval base at Praia de Vitoria until February 1974. Two days later the final seal was placed on the agreement during a summit meeting between Presidents Nixon and Pompidou, hosted appropriately enough in the Azores by Caetano.

The Azores Agreement of 1971 omitted any reference to Southern Africa even though in his defence of it the Undersecretary of State reiterated America's continued support for the principle of self-determination.⁴⁵ Caetano himself spoke with more frankness when, in a speech in December, he welcomed the treaty as a 'political act' between two friends and allies.⁴⁶ It was left to Senator Fulbright to ask why Portugal as a member of the Western Alliance could not itself assume responsibility for the 'very minor activity' conducted from the Azores, and why the Administration had not taken up Caetano's offer in March to change Lajes into 'a NATO base whose use will be restricted to the objectives of the Alliance and to nothing else'.⁴⁷

In fact, the original agreement of 1951 had allowed the United States access to the base in the event of a war in which the Atlantic Alliance was involved. Successive administrations, whenever challenged, had always adopted the defence that the base fell within the North Atlantic area.⁴⁸ One cannot help suspecting, however, that Portugal would never have negotiated a separate NATO Treaty if the Americans had made this a condition of the lease. For that matter, would its NATO partners have considered the Azores strategically important enough to have paid the price demanded by Caetano's government?⁴⁹

What of America's allies? Why did they remain silent during most of the 1960s instead of speaking out? NATO was very conscious that it had to defend its good name against its critics whether they were humanitarian and anti-colonial organisations, or the BENELUX and Scandinavian members who became increasingly vociferous in their opposition. In the early 1960s, the consensus among most pundits had been that Portugal would probably leave the Alliance within a few years. Alastair Buchan urged the NATO Council to debate the matter and not to feel inhibited from exercising its ultimate sanction: expulsion. At the time he wrote, Portugal's military contribution was negligible, its strategic importance much diminished.⁵⁰

His concern was echoed by the American Political Commentator, Arnold Rivkin, who cautioned against presenting the argument in terms of an intractable dilemma: winning the friendship of the newly independent African states, or preserving the friendship of an ally. The question of Portuguese colonialism was one of the few issues on which every African state agreed. Because consensus among them was rare the issue took on an added importance. If, in keeping with the Alliance's support for the principles of its charter, it thought it right to support self-determination, then expulsion seemed the sensible option. To equivocate on the issue would be to run the risk of alienating both sides while winning the respect of neither.[51]

Such views were frequently expressed before 1965, hardly at all thereafter. Instead, there was general concern that Portugal might withdraw from NATO without waiting to be expelled. In 1966, France had set a precedent by pulling out of the Alliance's integrated operations, forcing its naval command post to be transferred from Brest to Lisbon. Dr Grainha do Valle, the chief of the Atlantic Pact section of the Portuguese Ministry of Foreign Affairs, had already expressed his own disillusionment with NATO, noting that countries who were not members often had much less difficulty obtaining arms. Obviously Lisbon began to weigh very carefully the advantages and disadvantages of following France's example and went so far as to refuse to install long range aid to navigation facilities (LORAN-C) on its territory as its allies had asked.[52]

Whether the time would have been opportune to have pressed for political reforms in the colonies, the Alliance had to take account of reality as it was and not what it would have liked it to have been. Many efforts to discuss the matter with the Portuguese in the NATO Council foundered on the profound concern of several governments, not only the United States, that Portugal's voluntary withdrawal or forceable expulsion would present a challenge to the very future of NATO. This fear was cogently expressed by two contemporary writers:

> Although her departure might not materially weaken the military position of NATO it would nevertheless represent a distinct political and psychological loss in terms of the dynamic image of the Alliance much as a single national defection from the Soviet bloc would mar the dynamism of the communist camp, or the expulsion or resignation of a member of the United Nations would be taken as a bad omen, as though the organisation had passed its historic peak.[53]

These concerns were manifested in the reluctance of Portugal's allies to press matters to a conclusion. They explain also why the limited actions which were taken fell short of African expectations.

Canada was one of the NATO members most outspoken in its criticism of Portugal. Like the United States, it had suspended arms shipments that could be used in its overseas territories even before the Security Council embargo of 1963. Canada had always pursued a more radical programme in Africa than most NATO members including the United States. Volunteer workers from the Canadian University Service Overseas (CUSO) operated in countries in which US Peace Corps operations had either been phased out (Tanzania, Malawi), or the Corps itself had never been active (Zambia). For a time Ottowa even had a military mission in Tanzania which drew criticism at the time from conservative circles for training the Tanzanian army as a potential foe of Portugal, as a 'front line' force deterrent against Portuguese raids on FRELIMO bases from which guerrilla attacks were launched into Mozambique. The mission finally closed in December 1969 after five years work and $14m expenditure.

It is interesting, however, that the Conservative Party in Canada was actually critical of the Trudeau government for not condemning Portugal more robustly. In a speech in Ottowa in February 1970, its Foreign Affairs spokesman went several steps beyond the Liberal government's official position. Urging that funds be channelled through the OAU to the liberation movements in the field, he urged Canada to re-examine 'the paradoxical implications of its membership of NATO when one of our partners, Portugal, with material assistance from NATO members, conducts a ruthless war against freedom fighters in Angola and Mozambique'.[54] The implication of these remarks was that Canada should not withdraw from NATO itself, but that Portugal should be expelled.

It is possible of course to read too much into Canadian opposition. Its radical posture was often more rhetorical than real, and at times not even particularly vocal. It was not until the Commonwealth Conference of 1973 that it publicly recognised 'the legitimacy' of the national liberation struggle, although this somewhat belated recognition did not constitute full recognition of their claim to be the sole representatives of African opinion. Unlike Britain, however, Canada did not reserve its position on the wording of the final communiqué which committed it to providing material assistance to the guerrillas.[55] The question of whether it was right to provide such assistance sparked off a heated public debate which actually postponed its implementation but which nevertheless, won international respect for Canada's wish to disassociate itself from Lisbon's policies.

But although relations remained outwardly close, criticism of Portugal grew more vociferous every year. The Norwegian Foreign Minister raised the question of humanitarian assistance for the liberation movements during the NATO Council meeting in Lisbon in 1971 against the advice of most present. Although the meeting left hardly any mark, Norway continued to denounce Portuguese colonialism as contrary to the principles enshrined in the UN Charter. Two years later the Norwegian government played host to a conference organised by the United Nations and the Organisation of African Unity (OAU) which two months before the NATO defence ministers met in Copenhagen, articulated the theme of race conflict and the challenge to white supremacy. Among the members who sent representatives were Turkey, Denmark and Iceland.

At his opening press conference, the new Dutch Foreign Minister, van der Stoel, promised to bring the subject up at Copenhagen, which he did without appreciable result.[56] Nevertheless, the Netherlands granted nearly $5m in financial aid to the liberation movements. Moreover, it made the aid unconditional. Although it would have preferred the money to have been used for non-military purposes and distributed through the UN Development Programme, the Dutch Minister for Development Aid stated that had the government requested such guarantees it would have incurred the justifiable charge of paternalism.[57]

There were already signs by the time of the *coup* which overthrew Caetano's government in April 1974 that criticism was beginning to gather momentum. During the election campaign of 1972, the Dutch Labour Party asked its own government to condemn Portugal and, against the wishes of its leadership, voted to leave NATO altogether if in four years' time Portugal was still a member or still engaged in suppressing the peoples of Angola and Mozambique. Even more surprising was the increasing and visible disenchantment of the West Germans when the Wiriyamu massacre in Mozambique came to the attention of the general public through the pages of *The Times* of London. The German government responded with a strongly worded denunciation not only of the event, but also the circumstances in which it could have happened. When the incident was reported in the German press, the Minister for Development Aid remarked that NATO could no longer tolerate two Vietnams – one in Southern Africa, the other in South-East Asia. It was not only a question of morality or even the right of self-determination, important though both were; it was also a question of German interests.[58] Willie Brandt's response was notably more critical of Portugal than that of his predecessor. Shortly afterwards, his party received a FRELIMO delegation headed by its deputy leader, Marcellino dos Santos.

Perhaps, criticism from these governments would not have been forthcoming at all but for the mounting success of many different pressure groups in bringing Portuguese colonialism to public attention. The critics were all the more successful for articulating their claims in a popular idiom. The late 1960s saw a proliferation of pressure groups in NATO countries including the *Angola comité* in the Netherlands, the Committee for Freedom in Mozambique, Angola and Guinea in Britain, the *Afrika Komite* in the Federal Republic, the *Comite National de Soutien aux luttes de liberation dans les colonies Portugaises* in France and the *Movimento Liberazione e Svilupo* in Italy. Growing disillusionment with Portugal was compounded by growing impatience of many rank and file party members with their own political leadership, a fact which was true not only of the Labour Party in the Netherlands but also Britain. The swing of public opinion under the influence of such pressure groups served notice to governments that NATO's own behaviour would not long escape public scrutiny.

NATO, of course, was not the only organisation of which Portugal was a member: it also belonged to the Organisation for European Economic Cooperation (OEEC) and the European Free Trade Association (EFTA), but the pressure groups and public lobbies concentrated their energies and attention almost entirely on the Western Alliance, embracing as it did the United States, a veritable symbol of the external support upon which Portugal continued to count. Like the nationalists with whom they worked closely, they objected to Portugal's membership on the grounds that NATO's constitution pledged its signatories to respect the principles of democracy, liberty and the rule of law. Portugal, even more than the Greece of the Colonels (1967–74), appeared to be governed under a political system which could not be squared with the democratic and constitutional values to which its allies paid lip-service both at home and abroad.[59]

Both the pressure groups and public lobbies drew strength from one another. Political initiatives, electoral and agitational alike, were increasingly moulded into organisations with broader constituencies. By 1973, they began to insist that individual members take their side against Portugal, and did so in a manner which NATO must have found ominous: by presenting clear policy options which had to be taken seriously. The *Angola Comité* wanted the General Assembly to defer West Germany's membership of the United Nations until it had agreed to comply with its own resolutions suspending arms shipments to Portugal.[60] The London-based Committee of Freedom proposed several courses of action against the NATO members upon whom Portugal relied most heavily for support, particularly Britain who had already come under attack in the Commonwealth for its arms policy towards South Africa. The General Assembly, it advised, should press for international control and supervision of the arms embargo similar to that exercised by the Sanctions Committee on Rhodesia, of which Britain was chairman.

As the *Angola Comité* noted in 1969, the year it was founded, it was precisely in the political arena that the issue would eventually be determined:

> The question remains whether NATO as an organisation has anything to do with the criminal Portuguese policy in Africa. NATO as an organisation has never protested against the fact that advantage is taken of Portugal's membership to carry out criminal arms sales. NATO as an organisation has never protested against the fact that NATO troops and armaments are withdrawn from the NATO area to be used elsewhere . . . One would be mistaken if one supposed NATO were solely a military organisation: the political aspect of NATO is equally important.[61]

Nevertheless, despite the fact that governments were beginning to become more responsive to popular protests, and despite the fact that many more of their own party members were beginning to voice them, the pressure groups never really presented a serious challenge. Their criticism had much less impact than condemnation on the inter-state level; it was only when NATO found itself in opposition to the OAU that it began to take stock of its own position.

THE ANGLO–SOUTH AFRICAN CONNECTION

Apart from the criticism which Portugal's membership of the Alliance raised, South Africa's links with the West, and with the United Kingdom in particular, aroused equal controversy. Indeed, in many quarters South Africa's alleged 'associate status' in the Western Alliance was treated with ever-increasing emphasis by the United Nations and the OAU. Not only was the myth of collaboration common to Soviet propaganda; it was also shared by the majority of African states, Marxist or non-Marxist alike. The Anglo-South African connection honed the prism through which South Africa's critics looked at the Atlantic Alliance even though that connection was less a portent for the future than the remnant of passing British imperial responsibilities which survived into the 1970s to everyone's surprise but the British.

Anglo-South African cooperation was a legacy of the 1930s. When South Africa had debated whether or not to enter World War II on Britain's side, it had had to ask itself whether the security of both countries was indivisible, or whether South Africa could survive in a world in which the Commonwealth, with Britain at its head, no longer guaranteed the freedom of the seas. The debate bitterly divided South African opinion. In the end, the vote to enter the war was carried in the face of bitter opposition from the National Party. South Africa's cooperation in the war, with the vital contribution it made to the security of the shipping lanes in the South Atlantic, was bought at the expense of domestic unity in South Africa itself.

Was Britain's security indivisible with South Africa's? It was an important question, the answer to which influenced, and to some extent determined, South Africa's decision to seek continued cooperation with the West after the war had come to an end. The threat of Soviet expansionism in Europe seemed to be at one with Communist subversion in Africa. But this time the issue of military cooperation with Britain produced a domestic consensus which had eluded Smuts in 1939. In this respect, if no other, Smuts and the National Party leader, Dr Malan, were in total agreement. In his last year in office Smuts had talks with the Chief of the Imperial General Staff about the problems of Western security. When the North Atlantic Treaty was signed two years later Malan, now Prime Minister, expressed the hope that it would eventually be extended to include all Africa, not merely the French dependencies north of the Tropic of Cancer.

In 1948, the South African ambassador at large spoke to Robert Lovett, the American Under-secretary of State about the possibility of South Africa becoming a party to the North Atlantic Pact. This was the first intimation of the seriousness of the South African request to be included in Western defence planning, and the first recognition that the Western powers might themselves be interested in securing South Africa as a transit base in military operations east of Suez.[62]

Before leaving for London to attend the Commonwealth Conference of 1950, Malan added that South Africa would be prepared to join NATO if invited to do so. '... In view of the dangers . . . here within our borders', he reminded the Senate on his return, 'we too may need those powers or any other powers that have interests here in Africa.'[63] At the conference itself he urged the United Kingdom to admit Italy and Germany without delay. His reasons were not entirely disinterested. Although Britain remained South Africa's only dependable ally until the early 1960s, the South Africans, from the beginning, saw cooperation with the British in the wider context of Western security. Increasingly aware of Britain's declining power, increasingly disenchanted with its colonial policy, South Africa resolved to play a role less and less in the context of the Commonwealth, and more and more in that of NATO.

As time went by, government ministers spoke increasingly of South Africa as an auxiliary of the Alliance.[64] In an interview with a French newspaper in 1952, Malan predicted that a future war would not be confined to Europe and that many of the Treaty powers had territories in Africa which they might find difficult to defend without South African assistance.[65]

The last time South Africa's membership was seriously under discussion was immediately after the admission of Greece and Turkey. In the interim the South Africans had sent air crews to help in the Berlin airlift and the 2nd Squadron of the South African Air Force (SAAF) to Korea. In September 1950, the British government raised the question of associate status. At this stage it still envisaged the possibility that NATO would ultimately be extended to include a Commonwealth country other than Canada. But its opinion was rapidly revised once it was realised that if South Africa were included, British policy in the

Middle East would have to come under the influence, if not the control, of Brussels. Neither London nor Pretoria welcomed such a prospect. Britain's immediate needs in the Middle East were met by further guarantees by the Americans and more important, the admission of Greece and Turkey.[66]

Moreover, neither Britain nor its allies, least of all the United States, were prepared to acknowledge that a threat to Africa actualy existed. This emerged most clearly in 1951 at a conference in Nairobi sponsored jointly by South Africa and Britain to which five NATO members – Belgium, France, Italy, Portugal and the United States – were also invited. It also emerged at the Dakar conference of 1954 at which the same powers were in attendance and which once again failed to reach agreement on the form cooperation might take. The South Africans, in fact, asked for too much – South African leadership of a regional defence organisation modelled on NATO in a continent which its putative partners did not consider was under threat, and which they themselves could do little to defend since they resolutely refused to allow black troops to be used, or to abandon their own policy of white enlistment.

What finally emerged was a purely Anglo-South African agreement centred on the decision to abandon the whole idea of a regional pact in favour of a bilateral understanding on naval cooperation. The United Kingdom's principal interest was to ensure itself continued access to Simonstown in time of war. South Africa agreed to expand the base so that it might be used, not only by the RN, but by all 'ships serving with the RN and by navies of allies of the UK in any war in which the UK is involved'.[67] The agreement also allowed some scope for cooperation in the defence of Southern Africa since the South Atlantic wartime command was extended to include a designated 'South African area' which extended as far north as the Mozambique Channel.

Quite apart from the close cooperation between Britain and South Africa which followed the conclusion of the agreement, the decisions reached in 1955 were also important in a NATO context. As well as making provision for combined training with the RN, the decision to purchase British equipment introduced the fledgling South African Navy (SAN) to NATO contingency planning, NATO signals and NATO naval doctrine. South African pilots of the fleet air arm received their training for many years afterwards at the RN air station at Lossiemouth. Far from lessening South Africa's primary reliance on the Alliance, the clause in the agreement which gave Britain's allies automatic access to Simonstown even in a war in which South Africa itself was not engaged gave it an implicit stake in Western security. This remained the case even after South Africa left the Commonwealth. Indeed, in February 1962 its Foreign Minister, Eric Louw, insisted that cooperation with Britain had never stemmed from purely Commonwealth interests, but from the interests of the Atlantic community. Despite its withdrawal from the Commonwealth, those interests had in no way diminished and Britain could rest assured that there would be no significant departure from the existing pattern of defence relations.[68]

But if the Simonstown agreement for South Africa was an expression of closer relations with the Western Alliance, quite a different gloss was put on it by the British. In the years that followed, it became clear that the two countries had an entirely different conception of what it meant. Neither party had given a guarantee to the other that it would come to its defence if attacked, a point the British themselves made clear when they registered the exchange of correspondence at the United Nations. The South Africans probably imagined the agreement would be followed by a multilateral defence pact between the republic and Britain's allies, resolving once and for all the question of reciprocal guarantees within a much broader security framework.[69] Indeed, there was no reason to think that a specific guarantee from the old enemy Britain would have been acceptable to the rank and file membership of the National Party, many of whom no doubt looked to NATO to sweeten the bitter pill of alignment. Isolationism, after all, had only recently been one of the main planks of the party's platform.

Why then were the South Africans deceived? In part, because they were still living in the past. While it is true that both countries acted upon strategic assumptions which were, in all essential respects, similar in 1955 — that a future conflict at sea would involve a protracted conventional war and that shipping would be most at risk in the South Atlantic[70] — the British continued to distinguish between the defence of the southern oceans and the defence of South Africa. Indeed, the distinction was specifically made so that Britain, and by implication NATO, would not be faced with the stark alternative of writing the area off as strategically unimportant, or admitting South Africa formally into the Western Alliance.[71]

A year after signing the Simonstown agreement South Africa's new Prime Minister, J. G. Strijdom, expressed the hope that eventually France, Portugal and the United States might become parties to the treaty. Together with Belgium, all three countries attended a conference in Cape Town in 1958 at which maritime security was widely discussed, while the United States sat in on the defence meetings between British and South African planners which took place once a year between 1956–59. But despite growing military involvement, the West was sensitive to international apprehension over its relationship with South Africa – the idea of a formal alliance was as unpopular among the colonial powers as among their non-colonial partners.

Simonstown Revisited 1961–67

The Sharpeville massacre of 1960 and the outcry it arose around the world, in Europe no less than Africa, soured relations between the Western powers and South Africa and complicated relations between South Africa and Britain. South Africa had not been prone to conflict in the middle decades of the 1950s, belying the stereotypes which had been thrown up by decolonisation in the rest of the continent. And in the immediate aftermath of Sharpeville, when the opposition was driven underground and its nationalist movements savagely proscribed, South Africa was left with a government that was even more committed to maintaining internal order than it had been before trouble had broken out. Nevertheless, its very success in crushing the civil disobedience movement of the 1950s provoked the United Nations into punitive actions, then quite unique in its history.

Britain remained especially sensitive to these international developments as a member of the Commonwealth. To escape embarrassment, naval visits to Simonstown were drastically curtailed. Between 1961–65, only five frigates and four submarines, together with a few Royal Fleet auxiliaries, visited the base, the frigates spending only 16 weeks each undergoing maintenance and repairs. The UN arms embargo of 1963 to which the British subscribed together with all their NATO partners made it particularly difficult to honour the terms of the 1955 agreement.

While South Africa was no stranger to repression, the British believed that not all weapons could be used for repressive purposes and that arms could, indeed, must be sold if the South African Navy was ever to undertake its obligations off the Cape. In 1964, Britain's Foreign Secretary reminded the House of Commons:

> ... if the Simonstown agreement is regarded as important ... and if our view is that the strategic needs of it remain strong, we must obviously continue to be prepared to provide arms which are necessary for the support of Simonstown and for the self-defence of the country. It is still unreasonable to think that we can have a total embargo of arms to South Africa and still expect that country to continue with the Simonstown agreement.[72]

Unfortunately, the problem of selling arms for self-defence and insuring that they were not used for domestic repression raised a series of sensitive questions to which the United Kingdom and its NATO allies had no answer. With the South African defence forces still heavily dependent on British technological and logistic support, including spare parts and replacement systems, the questions became increasingly pressing.

In 1967 the British themselves asked to revise the agreement. Faced with the need to retrench, they insisted on withdrawing their Commander-in-Chief South Atlantic and the frigate which had been permanently based in Simonstown since the 1950s. By then the base was a mere ghost of its former self, no longer the main base of the South Atlantic squadron, although still the headquarters of the South Atlantic command. By the mid-1960s, all that was left was the headquarters itself, and the Youngsfield airfield with its radio station and a solitary frigate. Under the terms of the renegotiated agreement Britain agreed to station a single liaison officer at Simonstown with the right to assume complete command of the South African Navy in time of war, an automatic carry-over from 1955 which no-one took very seriously ten years later. For the rest, the base itself, the dockyards, the communications facilities, even the ships in the area were now manned by South Africans.

By 1967, both parties were forced to recognise that strategic and political considerations for the United Kingdom, as well as South

Africa, had altered fundamentally. The decision to renegotiate the agreement intimated that Anglo-South African cooperation, which had been the link in South Africa's informal contribution to the Western Alliance, had become less important for both parties. Indeed, it had raised the question which had been posed in opposition by Sir Alec Douglas-Home that if the Simonstown agreement was to survive at all it would have to become 'an informal extension of NATO'.[73]

The decision had not been taken lightly. The arguments employed on Simonstown's behalf by Britain's Foreign Secretary would have been familiar to the Conservative government of 1964. In the light of the vast increase in shipping round the Cape which had followed the closure of the Suez Canal in 1967 and which had given Simonstown itself a new lease of life, the base should surely be kept at a high state of readiness. Between June–December, 46 British warships called *en route*, as well as four French, and one Belgian. Was not Britain even more dependent on it than ever?[74] But dependent was an elusive word and among naval men and politicians its meaning varied. The waters off the Cape no longer dominated naval thinking as they once had; the absence of Soviet ships in the area meant they no longer had to.

To a Labour government anxious to deny South Africa what President Nyerere of Tanzania called a 'bridge of respectability', none of these arguments appeared convincing enough to justify the sale of arms. Britain's reassessment was a severe blow to South Africa's self-esteem. It was not so much the actual denial of arms which rankled, but the inference that many of the assumptions about the strategic significance of the Cape route which had been taken for granted in 1955 and the provisions which had been accordingly made for Anglo-South African cooperation in its defence were no longer as persuasive as they had once been.[75] After all, if South Africa was not to be given the arms necessary to fulfil its allotted role and if the RN no longer was prepared to undertake the role itself, or even to maintain a frigate on the South Atlantic station, did the United Kingdom consider the Cape strategically important at all? In exasperation, South Africa's Defence Minister was moved to ask in January 1970 whether the time had not come for the British themselves to declare whether the Simonstown agreement, in letter or spirit, had any meaning for the British themselves.[76]

Simonstown's changing role derived both from Britain's diminished capabilities and from its altered objectives. The appearance of the Soviet Navy in the Indian Ocean not only prompted the British to reconsider their decision to pull out of the area, but also re-opened the question whether cooperation with South Africa might be useful after all. The Conservative government's response to that question took two forms: first to build up the SAN's strength in home waters; secondly, to increase the frequency of exercises and manoeuvres with the RN. In African eyes these moves were highly suspect. They had objected for years to the close professional relations between the British and South African navies, which they interpreted as the expression of the high regard in which South Africa was held. The decision to renew the sale of arms seemed to offer further proof that Britain intended providing South Africa with the means to defend itself against forces which were likely to be less predictable and more dangerous.

It was in order to defuse criticism of its arms policy that the British shifted their ground. Instead of contending that the sale of arms was essential to British security, they argued they were logically obliged to sell arms under the terms of the Simonstown agreement. Since the latter were known only to a few interested parties, the British government hoped it would be easier to stand its ground. As Edward Heath discovered at the Commonwealth Conference in Singapore (1971), many African leaders were unfamiliar with the terms of the agreement either in its original version, or the revised version of 1967, the text of which had never been made public,

> ... One African leader wanted to know if the Simonstown agreement had been published. Another thought that the Simonstown agreement involved an undertaking by Britain to defend South Africa against its neighbours. President Kaunda of Zambia admitted towards the end of the discussion that the issue was much more complex 'than he had originally thought'.[77]

Where strategic arguments in the past had conspicuously failed to convince its Commonwealth partners, Britain hoped that legal obligations would prevail. After returning from Singapore, Sir Alec Douglas Home reminded the Royal Commonwealth Society:

No-one openly suggested that if a legal obligation was established Britain should break it ... It was noticeable that no-one asked us to scrap the Simonstown agreement. On the contrary, it was admitted we should keep it. We had to explain that in order to keep it ... it would be necessary to sell some naval arms and that no-one else could decide for us what was required to preserve our service in being. There could be no substitute, therefore, for our own judgment.[73]

Eventually, in February 1971, the government published a white paper on the legal obligations arising from the Simonstown agreement. Much of the opinion was concerned with technical questions, such as the type and quantity of vessels, aircraft, and equipment to be supplied. In addition, however, the law offices considered that, although

1. 'HMG undertook no obligation itself to supply arms or equipment' the express undertaking of South Africa to place firm orders for certain vessels, including anti-submarine frigates, implied an obligation on the part of the UK 'to permit the export of any material purchased under the agreement' and thus necessary to the achievement of its purposes;
2. the government was obliged 'if so requested by the South African government to permit the supply of replacements of the initial equipment and stores and base reserves for the vessels supplied from the UK and of any other equipment which is necessary to keep these vessels efficient for the purpose of carrying out the objects of the agreement;'
3. but the agreement did not impose 'a general and continuing obligation, upon HMG to permit the supply of any further arms that might in the future be requested by the South African government.

In fact, the law officers determined that all Britain was required to do under the terms of the agreement was to supply a limited number of WASP helicopters and several frigates. All but one of the helicopters were duly sold; the frigates were not.[79]

The really important feature of the debate in 1970–71 was the extent to which the dissatisfaction of the African states voiced both at the OAU heads of state meeting and the Commonwealth Conference in Singapore forced the British to reassess their own position in law. From the legal point of view its position was considerably weakened by the fact that the treaty had been so radically modified by subsequent practise that it was unclear whether the circumstances which had weighed so heavily in the minds of the signatories in 1955 any longer obtained, whether – to take the most obvious example – the agreement to supply frigates created an obligation 15 years later to supply naval reconnaissance aircraft. If the practise of warfare at sea had changed, had the terms of the treaty passed into history as well? In the event, the legal obligations, of which so much was made in 1971, were pared down to a minimum.

In November 1973, the news that Great Britain was in the process of delivering seven Westland helicopters in fulfilment of an agreement signed in February 1971 did not rouse anything like the opposition which its decision to renew arms sales had provoked a few years earlier. The muted response was due, in large part, to private assurances that Britain had no intention of making any further arms deals with South Africa, or flying in the face of African opinion.[80]

The fact is that Britain's enthusiasm for selling arms to South Africa in 1970 was yet another example of its unwillingness to undertake the defence of the sealanes itself. The sale of arms, of course, was only one element in British policy; expanding Britain's naval contribution another. But as budgetary constraints bit even deeper, as the government battled to come to terms with the country's economic decline, so it came to rely increasingly on South Africa's contribution. As Douglas-Home despairingly admitted, the defence of the sealanes should have been of equal concern to its allies:

> but it is not now, and for the present unless NATO changes its policy there is only one way in which the sea routes in this area can be adequately policed – that is by the British and South African navies together . . .[81]

A report prepared for the Conservative Party's Commonwealth and Overseas Council a few months earlier recommended the appointment of a British Commander-in-Chief for the area in the absence of a NATO commander, with command of an aircraft carrier task force and one or more nuclear-powered submarines.[82] As the South Africans themselves argued so avidly at the time, the only way to counter the Soviet Union was to maintain a naval and air presence in the Indian Ocean so formidable that it would have required a direct challenge to displace it.[83]

But with the services battling against defence cuts the most the RN could do was to exercise with the SAN on a periodic basis. In July 1970, the two navies undertook combined naval exercises in the South Atlantic. The following year the naval exercises were commanded for the first time by a South African officer. Later manoeuvres included a combined operation in July 1973 in which the nuclear submarine *Dreadnought* took part. In a press conference on his flagship HMS *Tiger*, Admiral Clayton looked forward to further cooperation by the two navies in the future.[84] Since the late 1960s, every naval exercise had been more extensive than the preceding one with the largest of all in October 1974 involving a flotilla of 11 British warships including a helicopter cruiser, four frigates and a submarine. Yet this 14 day operational visit provoked such controversy that it forced the incoming Labour government to cancel the Simonstown agreement.

Its cancellation was quite logical in the circumstances. It had never really been clear how increased Anglo-South African naval cooperation could prevent the Soviet Union from increasing its naval presence in the Indian Ocean, much less deter it from attacking allied shipping. The British correctly judged that the South African Navy could not deter the Russians itself since the embargo on arms denied it the capability to project power out to sea; and that *in lieu* of a NATO task force (which was only discussed in 1976)[85] the increasingly ageing navy would need British support. But the Conservative government which came to power in 1970 was too sanguine about its own contribution; too muddled in its thinking to recognise that only a NATO Task Force could have made a decisive contribution. As Professor J. E. Spence noted at the time, neither a British contribution to an essentially South African force, nor a South African contribution to a British standing force in the area could have deterred the threat to Western shipping if it was as grave as the Conservatives claimed.[86] If the Soviet threat really was serious then the most appropriate response would have been to persuade the NATO allies to take action on a multilateral basis. But from the evidence of SACLANT planning, Britain's allies were simply not impressed by the need to divert resources to what was still in 1974 only a secondary theatre.

The most convincing argument of all, as it happened, was

volunteered by the British themselves in the briefing note which formed a substantial part of the Prime Minister's speech in Singapore. The United Kingdom, he argued, was not attempting to maintain a maritime presence in the Indian Ocean on a war footing; it was not thinking of military confrontation at all. Britain wanted to be in a position to monitor developments in the area, to detect hostile moves in good time, to make clear that it was prepared, if necessary, to defend its interests. For this purpose, he concluded, there was no substitute for a visible presence, notably ships patrolling the sealanes and demonstrating their commitment to the freedom of the seas.[87]

If that was indeed the case, the British should either have acted on their own account, or if they were incapable of doing so, with their NATO allies. For there was no justification at all in asking South Africa to undertake the task itself as long as it was denied the status of a recognised ally. NATO, not surprisingly, was suspicious of British intentions; suspicious of general statements about the Soviet threat which did less than justice to the complexity of the situation, and that gave South Africa, within the terms of reference she herself had mapped out, an opportunity to secure associate membership of the Alliance.

SOUTH AFRICA AND SACLANT, 1972–74

From 1968, NATO began to show increasing interest in the Cape route. Delegates at a NATO Conference in October 1969 were told that the Soviet Navy could inflict severe, and possibly fatal damage, to allied shipping in the area within a matter of hours of the outbreak of hostilities.[88] Every day half a million tons of oil was carried round the Cape, 3300 fully laden tankers plied the Cape sea passage; the density of shipping to and from the NATO countries of north-west Europe was of the order of 22 ships per 100 miles of water; the Cape route accounted for approximately 25 per cent of all trade to and from its shores, while the volume of overseas trade had been increasing at a rate of $8\frac{1}{2}$ per cent by value for Europe as a whole, and $5\frac{1}{2}$ per cent for the United Kingdom.

Confronted with statistics which by themselves were impressive, and in the context of Soviet naval power much more so, NATO planners hoped that cooperation with South Africa might extend, if not to the NATO area, at least, to the area round the Cape. At a conference organised in 1972 by the Royal United Services Institute in London, most of the speakers agreed that the Alliance should extend its responsibilities, either as an organisation, or through the efforts of its individual members, or through a defence group in which the United Kingdom would play a leading role. All agreed that the British might more usefully make a contribution south of the Tropic of Cancer rather than adding another division to their forces in Western Europe; all hoped that Britain would be able to impress upon its allies the importance of the Cape and prevail upon the NATO Council to extend its maritime responsibilities.[89]

Almost from the time of his appointment the Secretary-General of NATO, Joseph Luns, thought that the Cape ought to be included in the Alliance's defence perimeter, although he had recognised the difficulty of establishing close working relations with the South African Navy in the political climate then prevailing.[90] The first firm intimation that the question had been discussed within NATO came in a communiqué issued by the NATO ministers in June 1973 which confirmed that the Supreme Allied Commander Atlantic (SACLANT) had been instructed by the Defence Planning Committee (DPC) – on which all members sat, except Denmark and France – to draw up contingency plans for the defence of shipping south of the Tropic of Cancer.

When SACLANT was later asked whether the Alliance intended to extend its operations into what its own report had termed 'an area of concern' it refused to comment. Inevitably, this gave rise to speculation that South Africa had been consulted directly, or sounded out informally on the matter. The United Nations produced a report of its own which, by quoting an anonymous NATO official who had been involved in drawing up the SACLANT study, claimed that cooperation with South Africa had been discussed; even more, that the SACLANT study had been intended as a smokescreen to obscure the contacts that already existed.[91]

The report left the reader in no doubt as to where, in the authors' opinion, the Alliance's priorities lay. It went on to claim that the main instigator of the study, the United States, had asked its own National Security Council to produce a policy brief (National Security Study Memorandum 39) which, in all essential respects, had anticipated the SACLANT plans. The Nixon

Administration vigorously denied this. In reply to the allegations, a government spokesman informed the chairman of the House subcommittee on Africa that NATO had never discussed South African participation, nor issued any public statement which could be construed as indicating tacit, or open, support for the use of Simonstown. If some of its members wished to use the base on an *ad hoc* basis, that was entirely a matter for themselves and South Africa. At most, the DPC had looked into the logistic, communications and support facilities in the area that the NATO members might make available to one another. In a crisis, obviously the Simonstown agreement was by far the most important. The South Africans themselves, however, had not been consulted.[92]

Indeed, when the full text of NSSM 39 was leaked to the press later in the year it became clear that the Pentagon had not been at all impressed by South Africa's putative contribution to the common defence. From the beginning, it had been clear why the South Africans were so anxious to cooperate with the West: 'South Africa is eager to be included in Western defence arrangements as a sign that it is accepted as part of the Western community'.[93] The Administration, contrary to popular belief, never accepted that South Africa could play a useful role in its own defence, let alone the defence of the Cape. It even upheld President Johnson's ban on the sale of naval reconnaissance aircraft despite persistent requests for the planes to replace its aged and frequently grounded Shackleton Mark IIIs. As the Secretary of State informed the press in the very early days of the Administration, the United States and Britain had 'agreed to disagree' on renewing arms sales to South Africa.[94] The cost of replacing many of South Africa's ageing vessels, most of which already faced obsolescence, threatened to be prohibitively high. The Pentagon was being quite honest when in May 1974, in response to a telegram from the chairman of the House subcommittee on Africa, it denied that any decision had been taken in 1969 to 'preserve a balance in Southern Africa'.[95]

Although America's attitude to the situation in the Indian Ocean was thrown into increasing confusion by the growth of the Soviet Navy, South Africa figured hardly at all in its calculations. When the NSC drafted two separate memoranda on the Indian Ocean between 1970–71, South Africa was not discussed at all, much to the astonishment of one of the NSC consultants, Dr

Chester Crocker.[96] Although the Director of the State Department's Bureau of Politico-Military Affairs and the Deputy Assistant Secretary of Defence both volunteered the opinion that South Africa had a role to play in securing the Indian Ocean from the Russians, it was clear from their testimony to the House subcommittee on National Security that they had not given the matter much thought.[97]

Subsequent reports suggested that four NATO governments – Denmark, Norway, the Netherlands and Canada – had objected to the SACLANT plans and that the row had come to light during an investigation into NATO policies by a Dutch parliamentary committee.[98] Yet only the previous year, a NATO spokesman had confirmed that the members were free to adopt the recommendations or not as they wished.[99] When questioned in Parliament, the British Foreign Secretary admitted that studies had been made, but added that they involved no commitment on the part of any of the members to engage in operations or exercises outside the NATO area, much less to cooperate with South Africa.[100]

Out of this complex story it is not easy to unravel the threads of what actually happened from the many rumours surrounding the SACLANT study. Britain and the United States, it appears, took the lead in asking the Military Committee of the North Atlantic Assembly to set up a subcommittee to review the Soviet maritime threat. The draft working paper which had been completed in June 1972 only explored the possibility of cooperating with South Africa in time of crisis. Later on the paper was extensively revised to take note of African opinion. When discussion continued in the North Atlantic Assembly, it was decided that SACLANT itself should look into the problem more thoroughly. At a ministerial meeting in Brussels, the suggestion was accepted subject to three conditions: that the final plans were to be approved by the Military Committee before they were discussed at a ministerial level; that they were not to be implemented without the prior approval of the Defence Planning Committee; and that SACLANT was to make clear in its final report that NATO's sphere of operations was still limited to the North Atlantic area.

It is still not clear whether SACLANT ever saw the report prepared by the Military Committee or, for that matter, whether such a report ever existed. SACLANT was unable to identify the draft working paper on the Soviet maritime threat despite the fact that as a rule all work undertaken by the staff of the Committees was normally drafted with the full participation of the SACLANT staff. As the subject of Soviet maritime operations had been under discussion within NATO before a decision was taken to authorise contingency planning in 1972, such a staff study would almost certainly have incorporated SACLANT staff views from an earlier period.[101] What the SACLANT story illustrates, however, is how little South Africa itself figured in NATO planning; indeed, how little Africa figured at all. It was evident that the Western powers were not prepared to flout African opinion, that the risks of cooperating with South Africa could not be so easily dismissed which, in turn, suggested that South African hopes were grounded in illusions. The options were not clear-cut. The priorities of diplomacy, no less than those of defence, strongly exerted themselves to circumscribe NATO's freedom of choice and action.

4 NATO and Warsaw Pact Intervention, 1970–78

Until 1970, the West had never had to deal with a very credible Soviet threat. The Soviet Union's disastrous attempts to influence the outcome of the Congo crisis reinforced its own weakness. NATO largely forgot that the Soviet bloc had interests in Africa which were in no way served by the predominant position of the Western powers. The days of direct military intervention might have passed, but the West had other weapons at its disposal by which to defend its entrenched privileges.

It was, of course, particularly unwise of the West to have based its policy on the understanding that it could deter the Soviet Union from intervening with the threat to retaliate and yet avoid retaliation; particularly so when it was in Africa's interest to redress the balance of the old world by calling in the new. In two of the case studies we shall consider, the Soviet Union was requested to intervene by African governments, only one of which was avowedly Marxist–Leninist in its sympathies. Yet only in the last of these cases did the West recognise, from the outset, that its own freedom of manoeuvre was largely negated by the remarkable coincidence of Soviet and African interests.

NATO's attempts to counter Soviet influence, although seriously pursued, were ineffective in practice because the most vigorous policies were blocked by the passivity or active obstruction of the OAU. Without some African support, the West simply could not impose its will. The implementation of its own policies depended on the good will of African governments (notably the Front Line States in Southern Africa); and they concurred with those policies only when they accorded with their own interests. They might cooperate to limit all forms of foreign intervention, but not to oppose the intervention of the Warsaw Pact if it meant that they would depend even more on the West in the process. Western policy in the 1970s, in short, was a record of pious hopes and lost opportunities, rather than real achievement.

THE SOVIET UNION AND THE DEFENCE OF GUINEA, 1970–74

There were several reasons why the Soviet Union took up Guinea's invitation to defend it against Portuguese aggression in 1970 – all of them consistent with its past actions and attitudes, and all dictated by a view of its own security interests.

The PAIGC was arguably Africa's most successful liberation movement in the early 1970s; witness the foolhardy and reckless Portuguese operation against the Conakry government which was bound to 'internationalise' an already divisive conflict. By 1970, the PAIGC had liberated over half the countryside. For once the provision of aid to an African country (Guinea) could be seen as a logical extension of aid to a liberation movement, mandated by the United Nations itself. In 1965, the General Assembly had appealed to all states to render moral and material assistance to the nationalist movements in revolt against Portuguese rule. The extent of its assistance to the PAIGC (the most generous to any liberation group) had prompted Lisbon to intervene directly against the country from which the guerrillas directed their operations. The next logical step in support of the movement was to protect Guinea itself.

In November 1970 a *Pravda* commentator wrote:

> The Lisbon rulers have been confronted with major successes by the patriots of Guinea-Bissau . . . despite NATO assistance and the colonial authorities' use of every neo-colonialist strategem and effort.[1]

In 1969, the Portuguese army had captured 50 tons of Soviet equipment; in 1970 it captured another 50 tons but barely interrupted PAIGC operations. By deploying a naval squadron in Guinea's defence, the Soviet Union was able at one and the same time to supply the nationalists and strengthen its own influence in Conakry.

Another reason for its willingness to intervene directly in 1970 was that West Africa was still its main focus of attention. The Soviet Union had met with a number of severe setbacks in the late 1960s including the overthrow of two respected allies, Nkrumah and Keita in Ghana (1966) and Mali (1968). Guinea's invitation came at a critical moment in its own relations with the African continent, and provided an unexpected but much welcome opportunity to rescue something from the collapse of its own efforts.

Strategic calculations were also important. Access to base facilities in Guinea could provide the Soviet Union with the means to protect its growing merchant fleet, as well as to monitor NATO fleet movements in mid-Atlantic. At the same time, Portugal's membership of NATO provided a rare conjunction of African and Soviet interests. For both countries NATO posed a common threat. For once African rhetoric justifying a very close Soviet connection went far beyond the inflated aspirations and invented values of radical African states. For once the rhetoric reflected the very real pre-occupations of an independent African country.

The decision to despatch a naval task force to Guinean waters was also the first occasion on which an African issue was debated within the Warsaw Pact. At the heads of state meeting on 2 December 1970, its members issued a joint communiqué which insisted that the Portuguese attack proved the importance of redoubling the efforts towards the ultimate objective:

> The imperialist aggression against Guinea demonstrates once again the insistent necessity of the speediest possible and complete liquidation of the colonial and racist regimes.[2]

In the Security Council debate which followed on the return of the UN investigative commission, the Soviet ambassador referred to this Warsaw Pact statement; its promise of assistance; and its conclusion that:

> until there is no longer a single colonial regime or colonial bridgehead on the African continent and until all troops have been withdrawn and all colonial military bases dismantled, the peaceful and independent existence and development of the African states will be in danger.

The ambassador concluded his address by calling for 'demonstrations, blockade and other operations by air, sea or land forces' if sanctions failed to deter Portugal in the future. Since the resolution calling for economic sanctions was rejected by the United States, the Soviet Union, with the backing of its Warsaw Pact allies, provided unilateral military assistance instead.

The naval patrol by three Soviet ships began in December and continued in one form or another until 1978, four years after the liberation of Portuguese Guiné. It was upgraded briefly in February–July 1971. Its main area of operations was adjacent to Portuguese territory – the area through which any seaborne invasion force would have to travel. It is likely that similar assistance would have been offered to the other target of the Portuguese army, Senegal, had not the French agreed to stand by their pledge to defend it against civil disorder. The presence of a substantial French force in Dakar provided a credible deterrent to Portuguese attack.

In time, the West Africa squadron was gradually transformed into a permanent naval presence. Submarine tenders were deployed in the Gulf of Guinea from 1972; the squadron, much augmented in size, was employed off the coast of Angola during the Angolan civil war. Long range reconnaissance flights began from the extended Conakry runway in July 1973 and continued until 1978 when the government ordered the base to be closed to prevent it from being used in the airlift of Cuban troops to Ethiopia which Seke Touré as the President of Guinea opposed.

In the light of these other uses to which naval operations were put, it is well to bear in mind that the West Africa squadron did, in fact, perform the role for which it was originally intended. Portugal did not attack Guinea again. Moreover, when the PAIGC leadership was kidnapped in January 1973 after the assassination of its leader-in-chief, Amilcar Cabral, the Soviet Navy managed to intercept the vessel before it reached Guinea-Bissau. Indeed, the most detailed account of the Guinean story concludes that the Soviet action in 1970 was a highly responsible use of a measured deterrent. It is really impossible to substantiate the claim of Admiral Zumwalt (Chief of Naval Operations at the time) that:

the Soviets did not hesitate in a part of the seas quite remote from their sources of supply to challenge a member of an alliance accustomed to maritime supremacy.[3]

In fact, the Soviet Union did not commit naval forces until it was clear from the private and public requests by Guinea, the international condemnation of Portugal at the UN, and the private assurances sent to Conakry by Portugal's own NATO allies, that its acceptance of Guinea's request would meet with very little, if any, opposition. Even then it refused to provide a permanent squadron until 1971 when it was clear that Lisbon would not repeat its mistake and when its public complaints at being let down by its allies showed that their patience was near exhausted. Finally, when the presence was made permanent, the re-allocation of naval units at Conakry quite substantially reduced the risk of an inadvertant clash with the Portuguese navy.

NATO thought so little of the Soviet squadron that it did not make its presence public until naval reconnaissance missions began in summer 1973; and it did not bring any pressure to bear on Conakry to restrict Soviet operations until the Conakry base was used for the Angolan intervention two years later.

Perhaps, the main reason why the West Africa squadron aroused so little concern was that its deployment at no time persuaded the government to accede to Soviet requests for a permanent naval base on Tamara, despite repeated Soviet representations. Later Mozambique, Angola and Ethiopia all refused to comply with similar requests, although they allowed *ad hoc* use of their own airfields. The one exception was Somalia which permitted the Soviet Navy use of a base at Berbera. But Berbera also became an exception in 1981 when the Somali government allowed the United States to turn the port into a major base for its own Rapid Deployment Force (RDF). It is also worth adding that consistent and generous military support for the PAIGC did not lead to close military collaboration between the Soviet Union and Guinea-Bissau when the latter attained independence. Guinea-Bissau became the first of the ex-Portuguese colonies to turn to the West for financial assistance; with Luis Cabral's assassination in 1978 it also became the first Marxist–Leninist state to lose its government in a military *coup*.

SOVIET INTERVENTION IN ANGOLA, 1974–76

The collapse of Portuguese rule in Angola by comparison triggered off a series of events which profoundly altered the attitude of the Western Alliance to Soviet intentions. Many Western observers, foremost among them the American Secretary of State, Henry Kissinger, were profoundly shocked that the Soviet Union had chosen to intervene in 'a peripheral area of the globe removed from traditional Western interests'.[4] But the intervention of Cuban troops, financed, transported and sustained by the Soviet Union found the Alliance divided and uncertain in its response. Although Africa had begun to figure in the debates of the NATO Council and the reports of the Political and Military committees of the North Atlantic Assembly, the dangers in these early days were unclear, its responsibilities blurred and definitions of vital interest easily obscured. It was only after the debacle of Western policy in Angola that the Alliance fully woke up to the threat to its own security.

A month after the mutiny of the fifth infantry regiment at Caldas da Rainha, the Portuguese government was overthrown in a bloodless military *coup*. The officers who led the conspiracy and who subsequently formed a ruling *junta* under the leadership of Antonio de Spinola, the hero of the campaign in Guinea-Bissau, had no intention of transferring power in the colonies immediately; some had no intention of transferring it at all. General Spinola himself assured NATO at a ministerial meeting in May that the army would remain in Angola until 1976. But whether the officers were militant or conservative, eager to rid Portugal of its colonial burden or to fulfil its colonial responsibilities to the end, most of them had taken to heart a document circulated by the junior officers on the eve of the *coup* which had called upon the government to recognise 'the irreversible and undeniable reality' of African nationalism and its aspirations to self-rule.[5]

Spinola, ever mindful of the fact that the Caetano regime had faced an *impasse* from which it could only have been rescued by military defeat, accepted the need to open talks with the nationalists, but chose to work with the FNLA rather than the avowedly Marxist–Leninist MPLA. His removal from power in September brought these clandestine negotiations to an end and encouraged the *junta* to work for a tripartite transitional government which would act as midwife for the new nation. The Alvor agreement concluded in January 1975 after eight months of discussion created a national defence council for the commanders of the respective guerrilla forces and a council of ministers in which cabinet portfolios were allocated to one of the three parties, with the under-secretaryships in each ministry devolving on the remaining two. In the event, the new government barely survived the first outbreak of fighting. The Portuguese peacekeeping forces, undermanned and overstretched, were placed in an impossible position. As the independence date approached, they were concerned not with transferring power to the legal administration but ensuring that the white settlers escaped in time. As the liberation movements recklessly used their forces to stake out their own claims to power, all semblance of order collapsed and with it the Portuguese army's already suspect morale.

The civil war in Angola multiplied the uncertainties of a confused situation. Portugal's precipitate decolonisation in Mozambique, more orderly to be sure, but no less swift, opened up a 300 mile front on Rhodesia's eastern frontier, while depriving Salisbury of a valuable ally. The crisis in Angola exposed Namibia's northern frontier at a point where South Africa's control was at its weakest. Under pressure from South Africa, Salisbury had already embarked on the first of a series of negotiations with the nationalist leaders which ended finally, and perhaps unexpectedly, at Lancaster House five years later. But as one American official noted at the time, the collapse of Portuguese rule made the prospect of military struggle more attractive than a negotiated settlement and the management of change in the area much more difficult.[6]

It is clear why the West wanted an orderly transition of power in Southern Africa. With so much at stake in terms of access to raw materials it could not afford to see its interests threatened directly or indirectly by Soviet actions. But the Russians themselves appear to have intervened for reasons which were not dissimilar: it seemed improbable that the Soviet Union, following the recent success of the nationalist struggle in Angola, would readily accept the exclusion from power of its own protegé, the MPLA.

When fighting broke out between the rival movements in March, the Soviet Union began to airlift arms to the movement on a massive scale, enabling it to take control of the capital in July and to extend its authority over most of the country. But by August, US covert aid had assumed such major proportions that the MPLA faced the very real possibility of defeat.

The Russians also seem to have been concerned about NATO's interest in naval bases in the south Atlantic, of which they had made so much in their propaganda in the 1960s.[7] Concern that Angola might become a centre of NATO operations on the route along which their own shipping passed on its way to the Indian Ocean provided them with another reason to stand by the movement they had supported since 1965.

During the Angolan civil war, the Soviet case against the West provided a faithful refrain of African sentiments. On 8 November, *Pravda* declared 'that it is no secret that under the guise of a 'civil war' intervention by imperialist and neo-colonialist forces has begun in Angola'. The sources of 'external aggression' were frequently cited in the Soviet journal *New Times*: 'A conspiracy is being planned against Angola on which there focus today the interests of NATO strategists, international cartels and South African racists'.[8] What evidence, if any, did the Soviet Union have for these claims?

The most alarming evidence of a conspiracy to deny the MPLA political power was the collusion between the United States and Zaire – an American client state of long standing; a NATO surrogate in all but name. The Russians could not ignore Zaire's support of the FNLA even if they had been disposed to do so. In terms of its immediate impact, it was far more important than the covert assistance provided by the United States. A Zairean armoured column entered Angola in July, a month before Castro offered the Russians the use of Cuban forces. By the time the first Cuban detachment disembarked in Angola, five Zairean battalions were already in the field.

Kissinger later accused the Cubans of taking 'unilateral advantage of a turbulent local situaiton', conveniently ignoring the fact that Zaire could well have incurred a similar charge. The United States had initially only provided aid to the FNLA to retain Mobutu's confidence.[9] Zaire was seen in some circles in Washington as a showcase of African capitalism, a future that worked without the socialism to which most of its neighbours subscribed. The Americans had always hoped that Zaire would save Africa by its example, if not by its exertions. Briefly in the summer of 1975, its exertions became very important.

The first question that needs to be asked about American objectives in 1975 – understood as the exclusion of the MPLA from government – was whether it was plausible. From the outset the Americans harboured no illusions about the FNLA's competence; their one hope was that the FNLA and UNITA between them might produce a military stand-off. If they hoped that, they remained oblivious to the internecine conflict between the parties and to the MPLA's military strength; if they hoped the Soviet Union would accept a stand-off which would nullify its 15 year investment in the MPLA, their hope suspended belief. But as we have seen, the question was somewhat narrowly put – Western intervention in Angola had two dimensions to which the Russians were acutely sensitive. They were aware that, but for Zaire's lobbying, the United States might not have intervened at all; and that, but for its intervention, they might never have been called upon to intervene themselves.

The Cubans probably took the decision to intervene to secure the MPLA from defeat before 11 November – the date the Portuguese intended to transfer power to whichever of the liberation movements was in control of the capital. Initially undertaken in merchant ships and civil airliners, to disguise Soviet involvement, by October Soviet An-12s and An-22s were airlifting 400 Cuban soldiers a day.

Quite fortuitously, the Cubans arrived in the front line in time to meet a South African invasion from the south. Worried by the initial drift of the civil war, the South Africans decided to intervene to bolster the claims of UNITA. Their intervention in the event had a political impact out of all proportion to the scale of the operation.

Once the Cubans intervened in force in November, they were able to reverse the tide of war which up to that point had been running strongly in the FNLA's favour. South Africa's invasion, by contrast, came too late to affect the outcome. In February, its forces withdrew, frustrated in their attempts to dislodge the MPLA by fear that the West was about to sell them short.[10]

South Africa's intervention inevitably fuelled suspicion that NATO had been involved. At the height of the operation, *Pravda* claimed that 'secret cooperation between South Africa and the militant organisation of NATO is so advanced that a real if not legal military union now exists'.[11] These claims did not go unheard or unheeded. They were widely believed. They were given credence from an unlikely source when President Ford admitted that the United States would not have intervened at all but for concern that South Africa's position in the area might be made untenable.[12] Later Vorster complained that South Africa would never have intervened had it not been assured that its forces would be resupplied if they encountered major oppositon;[13] that it had only intervened at all on the express understanding that the United States would continue to arm the SADF if it suffered heavy losses.[14]

The reasons why South Africa intervened were many and varied; the extent of American collusion is still unclear. What can be said is that the Western powers could only have offered very marginal support, certainly much less than the South Africans later claimed. Why, if the United States had agreed to make up their losses, did they refuse to commit their Mirage IIIs at a time when their forces could not proceed without substantial air cover? If South Africa's understanding was that the West would intervene rather than stand by while the FNLA collapsed it was soon disabused. As a government official told Congress, no American government could undertake to resupply South African forces during a conflict in which its own forces were not directly engaged. He even underlined the fact by reminding it that the United States had scrupulously adhered to the arms embargo throughout the conflict.[15]

America's ambassador at the UN may have been speaking for the Administration when he accepted that American and South African objectives in Angola were one and the same,[16] but the United States did not attach quite the same importance to the objectives in question. Since the South Africans knew by December that they would be outnumbered and outgunned by the spring, their decision to remain on can only be explained if they anticipated Western intervention. There was no likelihood of this after the NATO meeting in December when the Americans were advised in the clearest terms that the Western Alliance could not afford to be seen fighting on South Africa's side. When an American team from the State Department visited London in the first week of January the British advised them against making South Africa's withdrawal conditional on Cuba's. The Africans, they advised, would never condemn Cuba's presence in Angola while South African soldiers remained on Angolan soil.[17]

In their preoccupation with Africa's reaction, the Europeans responded to America's association with South Africa with suspicion and procrastination. When Kissinger warned his colleagues of the dangers, he foresaw if the FNLA and UNITA suffered total defeat,[18] he found them unwilling to express their political purpose in military language. When Joseph Luns later criticised Congress for cutting off funds to the two liberation movements,[19] he spoke only for the Secretariat, not for the member nations. The Europeans, like the United States, wished to rescue Angola from communism but, as one South African politician aptly put it, they were not prepared to pay the price if it meant South African assistance.[20]

In the wake of these disquieting developments, it was entirely expected that a number of African states should suspect NATO of involvement. Collusion with South Africa, as we have seen, was never, in fact, part of the Alliance's policy. The understanding between South Africa and the United States was little more than a tacit agreement which was not discussed before South Africa intervened and which won little or no support when it was eventually debated at the foreign ministers' meeting in December.

But what of the Soviet Union's other charge: that the Alliance was intent on establishing itself in the South Atlantic? Certainly the question of NATO policy south of the Tropic of Cancer became even more pressing after 1975 when Portugal's withdrawal left a vacuum which the Soviet Union would swiftly fill. If NATO's response to events was not entirely determined by its appreciation of the future naval balance in the South Atlantic, there is no doubt that the security of allied shipping weighed heavily on its mind. A report prepared for the allied Chiefs of Staff at a meeting of the Defence Planning Committee in December 1975 pointed with alarm to the increase of the Soviet West African squadron, the use of Nigerian ports by Soviet warships, and naval facilities in Guinea, all of which posed directly, or indirectly, a threat to the lifeline between North America and Europe, and between Europe and the Middle East.[21]

The lure of base facilities on the Angolan coast seemed very great. Luanda, the country's capital, and second largest port provided a natural sheltered tidal harbour with depths of up to 100 feet. Deep water berthing facilities were available at the main pier. Although there were no major shipyards or repair installations, its foundry could perform minor, above water repairs. The country's largest port, Lobito, was a natural coastal harbour protected by a peninsular. It had two deep water wharves and re-fuelling facilities, but again no major facilities for repairing major damage to ships. Mocamedes, the third port of any size, was located on Angola's arid southern coast. It could provide safe anchorages at depths of up to 56 feet, as well as a good berthing space at its main pier.

Most American naval planners were convinced that unless the MPLA was defeated, a victory would assure the Soviet Union domination of the South Atlantic. A year after that victory had been secured, the Joint Chiefs of Staff produced a highly pessimistic Theatre Appraisal report that paid extensive attention to South Atlantic developments. It concluded that 'increased Soviet naval capabilities to operate along the littoral of Africa have put increasing pressure on our ability to protect important South Atlantic trade routes', and suggested that the only way out of the predicament would be to secure bases for Air Force Atlantic (AFLANT) 'in the South Atlantic region'.[22]

The main conclusion that the Chiefs of Staff had arrived at in the light of the Angolan affair was that some form of cooperation with South Africa might well be desirable. Failing that, the West would have to rely more and more 'on underway replenishment and (to) accept greater risks to forces deployed to protect South Atlantic lines of communication'. William Lewis, who worked in the Defence Department during this period, has suggested that the military planners who urged the United States to oppose the MPLA argued that unless it was defeated a victory would 'virtually assure the Soviet Union's domination of the South Atlantic'.[23] Despite these assessments, however, the Soviet Union's main interest in 1975 appears to have been the wish to underwrite a new political order in Southern Africa, rather than to secure base rights or to reduce fleet maintenance costs by securing right of access to Angola's ports.[24] Neto was actually opposed to the establishment of foreign bases, although he was not quite as categorical as Article 16 of the Angolan constitution which explicitly forbade foreign bases on Angolan soil. Neto left the door partially open when he claimed that base rights might be provided if they were essential to Angola's national defence.[25]

It is not clear why the Soviet Union would have needed access to the country's ports, or why it should have been willing to pay so high a price. Prior to its intervention, it had concluded 13 agreements for port access along the African coast. Several years later, Luanda did replace Conakry as the centre of its reconnaissance flights in the South Atlantic, but relations with Guinea during the Angolan crisis were very good. Conakry, after all was actually used as a staging post for the airlift of Cuban troops.

A clue to Soviet intentions may well lie in the deployment of Soviet naval units at the height of the crisis. During the civil war, the Russians despatched a number of warships to the South Atlantic – at one time or another a cruiser and a destroyer, both armed with guided missiles; an amphibious landing ship with naval infantry aboard; as well as several auxiliaries. At least three other missile armed ships may have been kept in reserve near the Straits of Gibraltar. Their initial deployment appears to have been defensive: to meet the threat of Zairean patrol boats intercepting sea transports off or near Pointe Noire; to prepare for the possibility of withdrawing Soviet advisers had the MPLA front collapsed as seemed, for a brief moment, possible after its defeat at Quibala (9–12 December); and later to deter the United States from intervening. One of the most interesting features of these operations was their keen sensitivity to the African reaction. During the OAU summit in January, the *Kresta* II SSM cruiser and a *Kotlin* class guided missile destroyer – the two most powerful ships in the Soviet Task Force – were withdrawn. Both vessels remained in port long after the summit had ended in deadlock. The Soviet Union appears to have been acutely aware of the charge of 'gunboat diplomacy' which it had levelled against the United States so often and so successfully in the past.[26]

These developments showed how flexible and mobile Soviet naval operations had become; how naval facilities in West Africa gave it the advantage because of their proximity to Angola. But in a real sense the operations themselves were even more significant. Soviet forces provided an effective deterrent against Western intervention in an area of the world which, as Dr Kissinger made plain, had traditionally been a Western sphere of interest. Moreover, naval units were deployed in a way that suggested an effort to anticipate US naval movements, something completely without precedent before Angola. In February 1976, the USN almost deployed a task force in the South Atlantic grouped around the carrier USS *Enterprise* but the government thought better of it and the force never left home waters,[27] an episode which showed that the Soviet Navy was now better organised and trained for operations in a variety of circumstances and locations.

Nevertheless, there is no evidence that NATO defence chiefs ever seriously thought that the denial of bases was, in itself, sufficient argument to intervene against the MPLA, or to defy African opinion, still less to underwrite, by word or deed, South African intervention.

After Britain cancelled the Simonstown agreement in November 1974, South Africa had announced its intention of expanding the facilities at the base to enable warships to dock outside as well as inside the quays, so that the dockyard could handle up to 50 ships at a time and all but the largest nuclear aircraft carriers.[28] After 1969, the South Africans tried with consistent lack of success to translate their bilateral agreement with the United Kingdom into a multilateral treaty with its NATO partners. Since the closure of British and American bases in Libya (1970), they had been inclined to see themselves as NATO's southern flank. General Hiemstra, when head of the SADF, had postulated that since the Russians had successfully encircled the Alliance's flank in North Africa, the logical countermove would be to outflank the encircling movement in turn by coopting South Africa in Europe's defence.[29] The South Africans never considered co-ownership of the base as entirely remote: political implications apart, the Defence White Paper of April 1969 had rightly pointed out that the Simonstown base was too large to justify exclusive use by the RN, but large enough to play a useful role in the naval strategy of the Alliance [30]

South Africa doubtless expected that the argument would win far greater support after 1975. In January, six Republican Congressmen, headed by a member of the House Armed Services Committee, visited the base on the invitation of the South African government, briefing the Secretary of the Navy on their return.[31] A visit organised by three Democratic Congressmen, two of them members of the Armed Services Committee, also returned from South Africa favourably impressed. The South African Minister of Information visited Washington in September when he conferred briefly with the head of the Office of International Security Affairs. Speaking at a National Press Club luncheon, Connie Mulder reminded the United States that South Africa was prepared to play its part in defending the South Atlantic and Indian Ocean, if the United States was prepared to do the same.[32]

Nevertheless, Simonstown seemed likely to prove a troublesome liability for the Western Alliance, jeopardising relations between Africa and the Western powers at the very time that they relied on the MPLA to deny base facilities to the Soviet Union even after coming to power with Soviet support. The political implications of using Simonstown could hardly be overlooked. Kissinger was probably speaking for the Administration as a whole when he warned the House Armed Services Committee in closed session that it would be politically disastrous if the USN found itself based in Simonstown at a time when South Africa itself came under attack or was involved in a confrontation with one of its neighbours.[33]

These doubts were clearly reflected in the Alliance's cautious and divided response to the Soviet airlift in Angola. The Europeans, conscious of Africa's suspicions of NATO, were unwilling to intervene against any of the nationalist parties, even the MPLA. The United States, anxious not to put *détente* entirely at risk, did not believe that it could deter the airlift of Cuban forces even within an area that had long been regarded as a Western sphere of interest.

There was no support among America's allies for the measures which at one time were threatened against Cuba and the countries which allowed their airfields to be used as staging posts in the Cuban airlift. The United States did what it could to terminate the airlift. In Guyana, it first pressed Texaco to desist from refuelling the transports in Georgetown and then bullied the government by threatening to bomb the airfield.[34] An MPLA commission headed by Major Carvalho visited five Latin American countries to persuade them to resist American pressure on the somewhat questionable grounds that the aircraft were ferrying supplies to Cuban instructors and not Cuban troops.[35] They were not successful, but the delay proved fatal to the United States. By the time the Americans had persuaded Barbados to close the José Martin airport, the Cubans had been using it for an average of 15 flights a week. In the end, the Cubans were forced to fly direct from Holguin (Cuba) to Maya Maya (Brazzaville) using smaller transports, and airlifting fewer troops by which time the Russians were already providing them with long range transports.

None of these operations had the support of America's allies. The NATO response was so uncoordinated, in fact, that in January 1976 Washington had to lodge an official protest with the Canadian government about elicit return flights by Cuban transports from Brazzaville to Gander (Newfoundland) two days after President Trudeau had reminded Havanna of the International Civil Aviation agreement to which both countries were signatories (and which forbade flights of this nature).³⁶

The Europeans appear to have been equally unhappy about America's attempts to prevent a repetition of events in Namibia and Rhodesia. In Dallas, Kissinger had warned Havanna that the United States would resort to 'forthright and decisive action' if it attempted to carry its operations over into Namibia. The following day during a news conference in Atlanta, he refused to dismiss the possibility of military action against Cuba itself if its warnings went unheeded. Shortly afterwards the National Security council and the Joint Chiefs of Staff were asked to review the military options which might be taken, although Kissinger went out of his way to reassure the Senate that neither review meant that the United States and Cuba were already locked into 'a crisis situation'.³⁷ By that stage, the Administration may well have overplayed its hand. While Kissinger was in Southern Africa the Defence Secretary, Donald Rumsfield, advised the press not to exaggerate reports of preparations for military intervention against Cuba; no such decision in fact had been made.³⁸

After the initial shock and consternation had receded, the West was a little less inclined to view the whole affair as the first in a series of intemperate adventures by the Soviet Union to undermine the regional order in Southern Africa. In the course of time, it saw it as an *ad hoc* attempt to exploit an opportunity for which Western policy in the last 15 years had been, in large measure, responsible.

All in all, the Western Alliance emerged from the Angolan affair bloodied and bowed. Historians will long debate the extent to which the Western powers accurately perceived the mainsprings of African nationalism, or the nature of the civil war; whether the FNLA or UNITA deserved their support; whether prompt recognition might have made the MPLA less dependent on the Soviet Union after the fighting had ended. In retrospect, a study of NATO deliberations, and particularly America's role, leaves one with the impression that the Alliance felt itself buffeted by forces beyond its control; perhaps even beyond its understanding.

SOVIET INTERVENTION IN THE HORN, 1977–78

Because of its geographical location astride the route to the Mediterranean through Suez, the Gulf of Aden and the Persian Gulf, the Horn of Africa has always occupied a position of great strategic importance. Superpower competition in the area has a long history in the region dating back to the independence of Somalia in 1960. As with so many African countries, the pattern of boundaries Somalia inherited at independence conformed only nominally to the actual distribution of peoples in the area, fuelling pan-Somali irredentist claims which extended not only to Ethiopia and Djibouti, but also large stretches of northern Kenya, at this time still under British rule.

The political stability of the Horn proved too fragile for the West to steer a neutral course through the cross currents of competing nationalisms and ethnic rivalries. Reluctant to allow the Russians to exploit Somali grievances, it was even more unwilling to encourage Ethiopia's dismemberment. Border clashes between Ethiopian and Somali forces in August 1960 and April 1961 convinced the West it could no longer distance itself from the controversy without forfeiting the sympathy of both protagonists and winning the friendship of none.

America's refusal to help Somalia meet its national deficit was interpreted by Mogadishu as final confirmation that she had taken sides. As a result, Somalia moved rapidly from a pro-Western position to one of 'positive neutralism', winning as a consequence the largest *per capita* credit that any country had ever received from the Soviet Union.[39] Their alignment with the Soviet bloc was largely an act of faith forced upon the Somalis by the unwillingness of the West to underwrite their nationalist ambitions. It did not, however, dispose of the problem of translating the rhetoric of pan-Somalism into the realisation of a greater Somali state.

Pressure on the Soviet Union to honour its pledge to modernise the armed forces came at the time of its own build-up in the Indian Ocean. The way in which events in the Horn intermeshed with great power politics was evidenced in the Senate hearings of 1970 which identified Somali irredentism as the most immediate challenge to Ethiopian security, and the most serious threat to the US defence satellite communications system in Kagnew.[40] It was evidenced even more by the increasing interest which the Russian

Navy began to show in the use of Berbera, a natural deep water harbour in the Gulf of Aden.

Even before the Friendship Treaty was signed in 1974, the Soviet Navy had been given exclusive use of one section of the pier and the right to put one of its own officers in the port as harbour master. Having dredged the harbour in the late 1960s, Soviet construction crews started expanding the facilities in October 1972, assembling a three-section floating pier, adding 50 000 barrels of oil storage capacity and laying down an oil pipeline to a military airfield outside the town to make up for the loss of Mersa Matruh, from which they had been recently expelled by Egypt.

The Russian presence in Somalia was not confined to the naval dockyard at Berbera. Naval reconnaissance aircraft flew missions over the Red Sea from airfields at Uanle Uen and Hargeissa. They also maintained smaller depots at the southern port of Kismayu and a network of communications and observation posts along the Somali coast.[41] In every case, the Soviet Union's overriding consideraton was to increase its own strategic advantage in the area without necessarily meeting Somali demands for equipment, or allowing them to dispute the control of large stretches of the Ogaden with America's principal ally in the Horn.

The revolution in Ethiopia which overthrew the imperial dynasty in 1974 did not alter the balance of power immediately. The United States tried hard to come to terms with the military government, despite the latter's Marxist sympathies. Indeed, Ethiopia received its largest sales credit from the United States after the revolution, not before. True, the regime negotiated an arms agreement with the Russians in December 1976, but at this stage it was concerned merely to diversify its arms suppliers, not to make itself entirely independent of the United States. The Ethiopians were in the middle of buying $40m of arms and spare equipment at the time diplomatic relations were finally suspended. Far from precipitating a breach, their belief that Ethiopia would continue to remain dependent on spare parts for at least another ten years made the Americans confident, in the event quite foolishly, that they could come to terms with the revolution, and that the revolutionary regime would eventually come to terms with the United States.

As relations began to sour, the Carter Administration issued several warnings that the old arms agreement would not escape unscathed. In February 1977, it announced that the fiscal budget for 1978 would not allocate any funds for military aid; in April, that the staff of the Military Assistance Advisory Group would be reduced by half and that Kagnew would be closed before the lease expired. Not to be outdone, the Ethiopians expelled the entire MAAG mission and ordered the base to be closed within three days. Thus began a series of moves and counter moves in a diplomatic game of harassment by both sides which ended as it had always threatened to, with the signing of a Treaty of Friendship and Cooperation with the Soviet Union in November 1978.

But between the expulsion of the MAAG mission and the time the treaty was signed, Ethiopia itself came near to disillusion. As secessionist struggles flared up in the Ogaden and Eritrea and the government in Addis Ababa struggled to maintain power, if not its authority, in the country at large, the Somalis took the decision to intervene. That they should have done so is hardly surprising considering that at the time the United States had suspended arms shipments entirely and the Soviet Union had not yet offered to make good its losses. Although Ethiopia had received limited supplies since December 1976, these were soon revealed to be elderly T-34 tanks which could in no way match the M-68s which the United States had been prepared to sell, nor for that matter the tanks which the Russians had already supplied Somalia.

The battle for the Horn which followed saw a bizarre line-up of political forces with the Russians centre stage walking a political tight-rope as the principal military suppliers to both protagonists, alternately suspending and resuming arms supplies in an impossible attempt to maintain good relations with their Somali allies without forfeiting Ethiopia's friendship. Even at the time, the competition between the superpowers seemed extraordinary. The conflict in the Horn, after all, was entirely one of conflicting nationalisms, not competing ideologies. From this dilemma the Soviet Union was eventually rescued by the decision, first by the United States, then by its main European allies, to supply Somalia with military equipment to meet its 'legitimate defence needs' – the strongest reason that Ethiopia could have been given for going over to the Russian side.

Throughout this period, the geopolitical game played by the superpowers resembled the feints and counterfeints of two players, neither of whom could rely on their own forces in the front line. Possibly, the Russians in their attempt to be all things to all men simply miscalculated. They had agreed to modernise the Somali army in the expectation that it would become even more dependent on Soviet spare parts and military supplies, both of which they were careful to keep in short supply. Even the petrol they provided for Somalia's tanks and aircraft never exceeded two months' supply.[42] They deceived themselves, however, if they expected that modernisation would render the Somalis entirely dependent on outside support. Although large by African standards, the Somali army was small enough to operate independently of the Russians for the three months that Mogadishu calculated it would take to occupy the Ogaden and dig in to await the inevitable Ethiopian counter-attack.[43]

The war itself followed the course the Somalis had predicted. In order to secure the Ogaden, the Somali army had to capture three towns – Dire Dawa, Harar and Jijinga. Dire Dawa was the main Ethiopian airbase in the region and a rear supply base for the army; Harar the headquarters of the Third Division; Jijinga its main tank base.[44] Dire Dawa eventually proved the most important of the three since it was Ethiopian air superiority, coupled with its greater fire power, which eventually helped to win the Ogaden war.

At first, the Somalis carried all before them. The high point of the campaign came in November with the thrust to Harar, in which Ethiopian defences in Jijinga were out-flanked and out-manoeuvred, and ultimately outgunned. The defeat of the Ethiopian forces that summer must largely be attributed to dissatisfaction within all ranks and the collapse of morale. Nevertheless, by the end of the first phase of the war, neither side could reasonably claim to possess an advantage. It should be noted that, contrary to what many Western analysts claimed, the failure of the Somali forces to reach all their objectives owed nothing in the initial stages to the airlift of Cuban troops who had agreed to intervene after a personal request from Mengistu. The Somali drive had already peaked by the time the first Cuban divisions arrived on the battlefield in December.[45]

The front line had also stabilised outside Harar before the arrival of the first shipment of Soviet arms. There is no reason to believe that Soviet intervention, of which so much was made by NATO, either, in the form of arms shipments, or the airlift of Cuban troops, decisively altered the military balance in the first and decisive stage of the war when the Somalis tried, but failed to reach their objectives, or that the eventual outcome would have been very different if the Soviet Union had not intervened. What Soviet intervention did also, of course, was to expose the unwillingness, or inability of the Western powers, to supply Somalia with the arms it needed to defend the little ground it had gained.

Between November and early January, the Russian airlift which involved some 225 aircraft (about 12 per cent of the entire Soviet transport fleet) strengthened the Ethiopian forces by up to 1500 Soviet advisers and 10 000 Cubans. Such an unprecedented demonstration of Soviet power was no doubt intended as a reminder to the Western powers that the Soviet Union could come swiftly to the aid of its friends. Compared with the massive airlift of Soviet arms in the three months in which it took both sides to build up their forces, the Western response to Somali requests was muted. The only positive support came from Iran which originally promised to transfer American Phantom jets until prevented from doing so by the United States during Carter's visit to Tehran in February 1978. Apparently the sale of equipment was not one of the 'constructive steps' which the two countries had agreed upon to defend Somalia from invasion.[46] Although Carter accused the Soviet Union of sending 'excessive quantities of weapons' to Ethiopia and of 'unwarranted interference in the area',[47] the United States was anxious to dispel any notion that it countenanced the Somali invasion.

In January, the Ethiopians moved out of their defensive positions at Harar, using heavy artillery bombardments which forced the Somalis to abandon their prepared positions in front of Jijinga. Parachute drops enabled their forces to establish a bridgehead for their armoured units. The main attack was launched in a costly but successful operation through the Garda Marda pass. Victory at Jijinga brought the conventional phase of the war to an end. It was a victory made possible by overwhelming fire power and the brilliant use of armour which had been arriving by the shipload from the Soviet Union since September. It was a victory which might have proved elusive if the Somali air force had had the use of Iranian Phantoms with their air-to-air missiles which outclassed the MiG-21s the Ethiopians had recently acquired. Only a massive infusion of arms from the West would have prevented the problems the Somalis had begun to experience as early as September from exceeding the limits of what they could cope with and thus threatening the gains they had already made.

Much as the Western Alliance was opposed to Soviet intervention, it had to admit that Somalia had been the aggressor. There was never any likelihood it would have gone to Somalia's help; none at all that it would have challenged Ethiopia's right to defend itself. In Angola, South African intervention had disarmed the West completely; in the Horn of Africa, Ethiopia could rely on the sympathy of the majority of African states. Obtaining absolute unity of views in the OAU on almost any issue was virtually impossible. In Angola the organisation, working at cross purposes for much of the time, had been unable to respond quickly enough to a rapidly changing and increasingly dangerous situation. But the crisis in the Horn brought forth no such confused response. From the outset the OAU gave grudging, but almost unanimous support to the Soviet Union who trumpeted its respect for one of the most important principles of the OAU Charter: the recognition of post-colonial frontiers. Brezhnev made great play of the fact at a luncheon given for the MPLA leader Angostinho Neto on 28 September 1977:

> Many of the dangerous armed conflicts including some very recent ones, have stemmed from attempts to revise and forcibly change existing borders between states. A regrettable example is the fighting between Somalia and Ethiopia. Of course, the frontiers of the present African states have in most cases not been established by them but by foreign colonists . . . But today the most important thing, as we see it, is that the principle of the inviolability of borders be universally observed in the interests of peace, security and the progress of peoples.[48]

Even the West's friends in Africa had expressed concern at Somalia's cancellation of the Treaty of Friendship with the Soviet Union in November 1977 which they had continued to see, right up to the end, as the only guarantee of stability in the Horn, one of the few elements of restraint in an uncertain situation. In March 1978 when it was already clear that the invasion of the Ogaden had failed, Kenya sent a 12 man delegation to London and Washington to obtain a firm pledge that neither power would re-arm the Somalis to the extent that they would ever again be able to mount a similar operation. These fears had never been wholly absent in earlier times, but they were undoubtedly more openly expressed than ever before.

It is not altogether surprising, therefore, that the Western powers were embarrassed by the charge levelled by the Somalis in September that they would not have entered the Ogaden at all but for an unspecified 'understanding' that they would be re-armed during the operation. The charge reminded Africa of South Africa's complaints after its withdrawal from Angola, but like Angola very few aspects of the question have lent themselves to open examination. The United States, Britain and France had announced in July that they would assist Somalia defend its 'present territory'; by early August, less than a month later, American officials were already insisting that the promise could not be made good until Somali national forces had withdrawn to the border. Britain and France were equally insistent on the matter, equally aware that they were susceptible to charges of collusion. Later, the United States insisted that the assurances that Somalia's leader, Said Barre, had been given had not been of a nature that 'a prudent man would have mounted an offensive on the basis of them', a remark that was as oblique as it was pointed.[49]

What actually was said in July 1977 is open to interpretation, but the Western powers were determined that there should be no misunderstanding in future. At a meeting in Washington in January 1978 which convened after the ambassadors of five NATO powers – the United States, Britain, West Germany, Italy and France – had been called in by the Somali President and warned of an imminent invasion by Warsaw Pact forces, NATO agreed to ask the Soviet Union to restrain Ethiopia from crossing the frontier into Somalia. For it was quite abundantly clear that the Western powers themselves could do nothing to deter the Soviet Union from intervening. A few months later, the United States decided against moving an aircraft carrier task force into the area because no one knew what it would accomplish when it arrived. Its presence off Ethiopia would have contributed very little to the resolution of the crisis.[50] A five nation NATO task force steamed off the Horn in May in the hope of reassuring the Somalis, yet it deliberately denied itself air cover so as not to provoke the Russians. At the height of the crisis, the United States deployed seven destroyers offshore, all to little or no avail. Only the deployment of a Kittyhawk class carrier could have materially affected the military balance. Given the number and calibre of its aircraft, the Ethiopian air force could have offered no defence even with its MiG-17s and 21s.[51]

The projection of Soviet power overseas – exemplified most of all by the 225 transport planes which at the height of the crisis took off from airfields in the Transcaucasus every 20 minutes – shocked and discomfited NATO planners. 'We used to console ourselves with the thought that the Soviets were not very good at this kind of thing', one NATO official commented, 'now, they have shown first in the Middle East, then in Angola and now in Ethiopia that they can organise things very effectively when they want to. They are getting better all the time'[52] Echoing this sentiment, the West German Defence Minister, Georg Leber, observed that Soviet transport planes had become a 'new strategic element' in the East–West balance to which NATO, as yet, had no answer.[53]

The success of the Soviet airlift led many to conclude that diplomacy was the only answer. The NATO Military committee, while acknowledging that the Russians were pursuing a long term goal of out-pointing the Alliance in the Red Sea and the headwaters of the Gulf, advised against military intervention.[54] A response which was firmly grounded on a political approach to the crisis might, at least, elicit a political response from the Soviet Union.

At the risk of oversimplifying, it seems clear that the West's response, such as it was, was the very simple one of getting back to the *status quo antebellum*. The history of the conflict had been extensively discussed in January and it seemed clear at the NATO summit, that a better understanding of the past could only improve the chances of acting wisely in the future.

First, therefore, it refused to treat the problem as an East–West issue, much to Somalia's annoyance. At its summit meeting in May, NATO agreed to coordinate the national policies of its members so that the Africans might at least defend themselves: while stopping short of providing arms which would allow them to embark upon irresponsible adventures. When Barre began a tour of NATO capitals beginning with London and Bonn in June, and ending in Paris and Rome in September, he found that the Europeans were reluctant to supply any equipment until he had agreed to withdraw his support from the guerrillas who were still fighting in the Ogaden. Although the bulk of the Ethiopian forces had been transferred to the Eritrean front, casualties in the Ogaden were still high and the Ethiopian air force continued to fly sorties across the border. The British informed Barre that they could not consider selling arms until Somalia had renounced its territorial claims against Kenya. The Germans, obviously reluctant to get involved at all, reminded him that *détente* was indivisible and that to be valid it must apply in Africa as well as Europe. Most discouraging of all, the United States indefinitely postponed the departure of the team it had originally agreed to send out to Mogadishu to ascertain the arms the Somalis might need. The Americans were clearly unsure whether to believe Barre's assurances that he would only use the weapons he was given for self-defence. At the end he had nothing to show for his two European tours and the intense lobbying that had preceded them except a few anti-tank weapons and surface-to-air missiles supplied by an ever unpredictable France.

The Somalis subsequently complained that the Western Alliance had been deeply divided over matters of principle and interpretation, that it had allowed itself to be bullied by the United States into passive disregard for its own interests. The fact that a senior member of the Carter Administration had believed that the presence of Cuban troops in Africa represented 'a stabilising factor' on the continent (a reference to a remark made by the US ambassador to the United Nations, Andrew Young) seemed to Barre to indicate that NATO was prepared to allow the Russians to threaten the oil producers in the Gulf rather than defy African opinion.[55] But, as we have seen, even more fundamental to the politics of the crisis was its apprehension that, without African support, the Soviet Union might be given a free hand in Southern Africa. The nature of the crisis in 1978 and the opposing African and European reactions to it raised the question whether the Alliance could any longer afford to dismiss African opinion. It also transformed the recent crisis of confidence in Angola into a profound crisis of uncertainty.

Somalia had set out, after all, confident that it could persuade the West that the Soviet airlift in Ethiopia represented a far greater threat to Western interests in the Middle East than any immediate or collateral damage to the West's relations with the OAU. In this it gravely miscalculated. While it is true NATO needed and, for the most part, wished to deter the Soviet Union from intervening in an area so close to the Gulf, at the same time it did not wish to forfeit OAU support for the Zimbabwe and Namibia negotiations. That the OAU would have condemned any Western intervention in the Horn on Somalia's behalf was confirmed in January when it warned Iran not to transfer Phantom jets to Somalia to meet what the communiqué called 'hypothetical strategic situations' in the Red Sea.[56]

At the NATO summit in May, one of the issues most widely discussed was Brezhnev's letter to Neto in April pledging 'further assistance and support' for the liberation movements in Southern Africa. The crisis in North-East Africa so focused international attention on the area that it temporarily obscured the underlying reality of the power struggle in the southern half of the continent which for the West, if not for the Soviet Union, was more important. Such were the fears about Soviet intentions in Southern Africa that Said Barre complained that the Western powers had reached a compromise with the Russians at Somalia's expense – allowing the latter freedom of manoeuvre in the Horn in return for a free hand in the south.[57]

At the time of the NATO summit, the United States called for a concerted Western response to Soviet adventurism in Africa. But what emerged at the end of the conference was a clear appreciation that the response would need to take a diplomatic as well as a military form if it was not to lead to a clash between the Western Alliance and Africa and foreclose the dialogue with the OAU which offered promise of a settlement to the potentially dangerous conflicts in Zimbabwe and Namibia.

The Somalis had based their territorial claim on the argument that the border between the two countries had been determined not by a European colonial power, but by Amharic imperialism in the 19th century. It was a claim which, whatever its historical plausibility, failed to win a single vote. Its subsequent claim that its forces had only entered the Ogaden to support an indigenous revolt was disbelieved as well. As a result, the Somali case went by default, and with it Western intervention. In the Horn, as in Angola, the OAU was unable or unwilling to take a stand against the Soviet airlift. In different ways and for different reasons its members felt they had good grounds for giving the Russians what support and encouragement they could. The crisis in the Horn followed much the same pattern as that in Angola. It left the Cubans in occupation and the Western Alliance in considerable disarray.

5 France and Western Security, 1974–83

From what we have said so far, it is clear that the security of the Atlantic Alliance was profoundly affected by events outside Europe. This was to be expected in a coalition of powers dependent for its very survival on international trade and raw materials. Yet as we have also pointed out, the planning and execution of Alliance policy concentrated hardly at all on Africa even though the planners were fully alive to the fact that political instability on its southern flank might have broad ranging repercussions.

This was particularly noticeable in the discussions of the Atlantic Policy Advisory Group, whose members were drawn from the foreign ministries of the NATO powers. Most agreed that developments outside the Treaty area should not become the subject of multilateral action by the NATO command, though the smaller powers raised no intrinsic objection to cooperating, as and when the occasion required. On the whole, most were opposed to military postures in sensitive areas such as Southern Africa. Commenting on these meetings many years later, Robert Elsworth concluded that the members seemed to believe that external security problems would never detract from European security; and that the broad-based interest which was already beginning to be expressed in Southern Africa's mineral wealth and the protection of shipping at the Cape was self-executing as well as self-evident.[1]

Although their relationship with African countries and the sensitivity to African opinion significantly differed, the United States, Britain and France were by 1974 quite confident about the future. Since 1970, the French had given increased importance to the metropolitan *force d'intervention* in place of their permanent garrisons in Africa. Air mobility was less embarrassing than maintaining bases in the face of local opposition. The French denied that they had any bases in sub-Saharan Africa, arguing that metropolitan France was the only true base for the defence of French interests. Armed garrisons seemed to be consistent neither with the independent status of African states nor with modern military doctrine.

The British showed even less inclination to press defence agreements on reluctant Commonwealth members. The United States directed two-thirds of its military aid and four-fifths of its military deliveries to one country, Ethiopia. Events gave the Americans a wide latitude in deciding how to respond to challenges to internal security, and whether to rely on their European allies to intervene on their behalf. Even French forces in Africa were substantially cut back in favour of small highly mobile units that could be airlifted from Europe to the scene of conflict.

Yet, Soviet intervention in Angola produced a complete change in the fundamental assumptions and orientation of NATO's policy. The retrenchment of French power and America's slow turn away from global responsibilities were both reversed. The Europeans were now aware of the need to act, but realised that they could no longer act on their own against Soviet-inspired subversion and the actual presence of Soviet proxies. In a speech in 1976, Giscard d'Estaing denied that France alone could meet the threat to global security; in contrast to de Gaulle who had attempted to stake out a separate claim in Africa, President Giscard d'Estaing expressed the opinion that the West must act where the vital interests of all were threatened:

> Our world is an over-armed world in the case of the East–West conflict and a world which is looking for a North–South balance. On the other hand, it is a very unstable world for a series of reasons ranging from ideology to under-development which explains that everywhere we witness a general destabilisation of security.[2]

His suggestion that the Western powers should act together raised some uncomfortable issues at home where his policy was denounced by a former Gaullist Defence Minister, Michel Jobert, as 'a return to NATO'.[3] It was not only the Gaullists who suspected that it would not be long before France would begin to act in NATO's name. Many African leaders, finding themselves successively unable to prevent the great powers from intervening in Southern Africa or the Horn, or from building up their naval forces in the Indian Ocean, began to suspect the French of defining their own interests in terms of allied cooperation. How far this was true, how far the allies acted separately, how far, for that matter, the Africans believed what they themselves claimed is the subject of the chapters that follow.

The arrival of Giscard d'Estaing brought to an end the ten year old policy of military disengagement from Africa. The language employed during the Pompidou presidency had indicated that many still thought France had a role to play in Africa in defence of Western interests. For Giscard, the display of French military power was an even more important indicator of the West's determination to defend its own interests than it had been for his predecessors. His decision to increase the effectiveness of the *force d'intervention* was made in the knowledge that French military power would be used rather than simply displayed.

In the new analysis made of French defence policy, Army Chief of Staff General Méry argued cogently for a more interventionist role in Africa to subsume the nuclear stalemate in Europe. 'The possession of a nuclear arsenal and the response capabilities it provides may inhibit action at home, but it also provides the necessary stability which makes possible overseas operations',[4] Giscard's own arguments were more modest. In proposing that France's special mobile force be expanded, he merely suggested that it should possess an interventionist capability which 'would correspond to her stature as a world power'.[5]

It was in pursuit of such a goal that France intervened twice in the Western Sahara. In October 1977, Polisario attacks on the Zouerte mines in Mauritania and the capture of two French technicians prompted Paris to act on Mauritania's behalf. During the next two months, French troops were flown into the country and in December, the government authorised a number of air strikes against guerrilla forces. All of these actions seemed far in excess of what was necessary to secure the release of the French prisoners. A further intervention in May 1979 after a new outburst of Polisario attacks, indicated that Giscard was still, as he had said before, opposed to the creation of mini-states.

Nevertheless, when the Polisario guerrillas unilaterally declared a cease fire with Mauritania, while continuing the struggle against its former ally Morocco, who now laid claim to the entire Western Sahara region, the French declared their willingness to act as mediators in discussions concerning the possible creation of an independent West Saharan state. None of these discussions led anywhere. It could well be asked whether after alienating Algeria (over intervention) and then Morocco (over mediation), Giscard knew exactly what policy in the Western Sahara best served French national interests.

Those interests were defended in the late 1970s by the *force d'intervention* which had formerly been drawn from the 11th Parachute Division in the south-west of France and the 9th Marine Infantry Division in Brittany. Soon after Giscard came to power, it was decided to develop the 31st Demi-Brigade (eventually to comprise 3000 troops by 1982) in Provence as an adjunct to the other forces, having lighter and more mobile weaponry.[6]

The understanding that in the past fire power had given way to the need for speed and mobility, and that in the future the first might be more important than the second, made certain additional *materiel* seem desirable. The 11th Parachute Division received new combat helicopters in 1977 and Milan anti-tank missiles in 1978. Matters went rather too far when the government refused to rule out committing tactical nuclear weapons to the interventionist forces.[7] As it happened they were never deployed in military operations during Giscard's presidency. But what did become evident was that French military solutions could not, in themselves, resolve disputes that were endemic to particular regions, and that the nature of French military power was such that even for quite limited operations assistance from its NATO partners might in future be required. Both these factors were evident in its two recent operations; in Chad and Zaire.

CHAD AND FRENCH UNILATERALISM, 1969–83

French policy in Chad suffered from almost as much confusion as it did in the Western Sahara. In both countries the government intervened almost out of force of habit; as well as from an often unexpressed wish that a state that France had created might be ruled by an administration, at least to some extent, sympathetic to French interests. The hopes of Pierre Messner, de Gaulle's

Minister of the Armed Forces, that France should stay out, were dashed by the persistence with which the experts on African affairs thought some form of military intervention inescapable.

The conflict in Chad between the Muslim north and the mostly pagan, partly Christian and considerably more Europeanised south, had persisted in one form or another since the country became an administrative entity in 1920. Because units of the French army remained in the north for some years after independence (1960–65), the situation appeared rather more stable than it was. So stable in fact, that one observer was able to describe the civil strife that began in 1965 as merely the continuation of Chadian politics by other means.[8]

While the economic importance of the territory had always been considered minimal, its strategic location had for long been considered vital. In the first instance, France's aim in conquering the territory was to unite its northern and central African empires. Later, the military base at Fort Lamy became a central mainspring of its own security. De Gaulle was quite happy in 1960 to offer the Chadian government the possibility of logistical assistance in the event of internal unrest.

When in 1968 a group of tribesmen (having only tenuous connection with the revolutionary movement, the Chad National Liberation Front (FROLINAT)), staged a revolt in the northern provinces of Boukou, Ennedi and Tibesti the French became concerned that President Tombalbaye's government might fall. The fear that the rebellion in Chad might deprive them of the power to defend the continent if Fort Lamy were also to fall, was central to their eventual decision to provide military assistance to the government, and then in 1969 to undertake military operations themselves.

Three reasons were advanced at various times for the French decision. The first argument was that a cooperation agreement had been signed between the two countries, and a decision not to intervene would affect France's relations with other Francophone states. A second argument was that French interests in other areas might not long survive if Chad fell. Uranium deposits had been discovered at Arlit in Niger and at Bakouma in the Central African Republic (CAR) and both might later become important. Libya might well become interested in the Arlit mines. If a power vacuum were to be created in central Africa as a result of Chad's fall, other states might gain access to areas of French interest.

The government's third contention which took the form of an African 'domino theory'[9] was that the collapse of the Tombalbaye regime would undermine the support of other governments in the region. The Central African Republic and Congo-Brazzaville were both potentially explosive countries in which political authority was weak.

Led initially by General Arnaud, the French military had little initial success, and it was only when the command of French forces passed to the more aggressive General Cortadellas that intervention in Chad began to bring the desired results. A number of FROLINAT bases were destroyed, and soon after the rebels were forced to disperse their forces. By December 1970, many of the rebellious areas were under control. But the political problems that had given rise to the insurrection were not resolved so easily, and Tombalbaye's refusal to introduce the administrative reforms which de Gaulle had demanded as the price of French support only compounded the political problems that the government continued to confront.

The new government of General Malloum originally felt confident enough to order the evacuation of French bases in 1975. Within a year, however, it chose to negotiate two new military assistance pacts which served as the basis of French logistical support to the Chadian air force during FROLINAT's new summer offensive in 1977.[10] A year later, more French *legionnaires* were sent in at the government's 'specific and urgent' request. Although Giscard claimed that these reinforcements had been sent only to ensure the security of French nationals, and that none of the troops (which by 1979 numbered 3000) would take part in counter-insurgency operations, only French intervention enabled General Malloum's government to survive FROLINAT's southern offensive in April–May 1978.[11]

When, after extensive negotiations, FROLINAT's President, Hissène Habré, was appointed Prime Minister by Malloum, there were many who hoped that a political solution might, at last, be in sight. The new government established in 1979 preferred the French to leave. The French for their part were only too happy to oblige; at a $1m a day the anti-FROLINAT operation had incurred a great deal of criticism.

Giscard, who had all troops withdrawn from Chad by May 1980, placed all his hopes on the negotiated settlements which had been hammered out in Nigeria, and on the possibility that an inter-African force, supported by the OAU, could keep the peace. The emptiness of these hopes was shown after the new President Goukouni Ouaddai signed a mutual defence pact with Libya in June, and announced a merger between the two countries the following January, shortly after Libyan military forces had moved in to the north. Knowing that French intervention would have met with little, if any, support Giscard chose to stay out. Military units were increased in the CAR, Gabon, the Ivory Coast and Senegal; new military cooperation agreements were signed with neighbouring Niger and Cameroon, but the knowledge that any attempt to dislodge the 10 000 Libyans from Chad would have resulted in a great deal of bloodshed, and have done little to advance Giscard's aim of advancing African solutions to African problems, ensured that the French kept out.[12]

The inter-African force, however, did not prevent Hissène Habré from retaking the capital in June 1982. Goukouni Ouaddai was forced to take refuge in Cameroon. Yet, just when the OAU at its 19th summit meeting in Addis Ababa recognised the Habré government, a revolt broke out in the north in the name of the transitional national union government of Ouaddai, backed by land and air forces supplied by Libya. On 24 June 1983, the insurgents took the principal oasis in the north, Faya-Largeau, lost it in July and then took it back on 10 August. It was at this point that Hissène Habré, with the support of the OAU, appealed to France.

President Mitterrand could not ignore these developments, even if he had little respect for Habré's government. The intervention of Libya was of serious concern to many African states. In the first place, Libya was militarily one of the most powerful African countries. Much of its oil income had been spent in building up well-equipped armed forces with 3000 tanks of Soviet design and 550 combat aircraft of French and Soviet origin. In the second place, the *de facto* annexation of the Aozou strip, then the occupation of N'djamena in 1981 followed by half the territory of Chad in 1983 seemed incontrovertible proof that Libya was pursuing an expansionist policy aimed at modifying colonial frontiers to its own advantage.

Within three weeks of Mitterrand's decision to intervene, 1500 men had been moved to Chad, together with armoured cars, anti-tank missiles and detection equipment reportedly so sophisticated that it had yet to be used by the French army. Yet it remained a phantom presence, almost unreported. In spite of their military hardware, French military aid to the government was purposefully kept to a minimum. They did not sell Hissène Habré anti-tank and anti-aircraft systems; and there was no suggestion that this was ever discussed.

The arrival of the French brigade stabilised the situation, but at the cost of a *de facto* partition of the country roughly along the line between the arid Muslim north and the non-Muslim south which the French used to call *Tchad utile* in the days of empire. The security line to the south of which French forces were deployed could be crossed only with difficulty by Ouaddai's forces because this would have taken them beyond the range of action of the combat aircraft deployed on Libyan territory. It was clear that Mitterrand's preference was for negotiations between the warring Chadian factions followed by yet another OAU peace-keeping force which would be jointly financed by France and Libya.

What is interesting about the whole episode is the extent to which it revealed the limits of allied consensus. In August 1983 the United States had despatched AWACS electronic surveillance aircraft, some F-15 fighter escorts and several other reconnaissance planes to support Habré's government. France was not consulted about these shipments. Indeed, it soon expressed growing resentment at the way the Americans had forced the pace of intervention in a conflict which Paris saw in less dramatic terms than Washington. The Elyseé showed distinct signs of impatience at being upstaged by the Americans. The Reagan Administration, in its almost obsessive urge to defeat Colonel Quaddafi, had intervened on the basis of at least three seriously flawed assumptions. The Administration overestimated Libyan capabilities – as opposed to ambitions – in central Africa; underestimated French reluctance to assume yet another military burden; and presumed to take sides in a war about which astonishingly little was apparently known in Washington.

This chapter of Franco–American misunderstanding also struck a chord in Europe. France's European allies were not parties to its African alliances. They had never tried to be. No one had asked them, but in 1983 they did express concern at French intervention in an interminable conflict to which there was no end in sight. In the summer of 1983, there were just under 15 000 French troops deployed overseas. In view of the need to rotate troops deployed outside France, it could be deduced that all these commitments corresponded to the limits of French capabilities (about 20 000 men). This level could hardly be raised since conscripts could not be used for overseas operations without a vote in the National Assembly.

These considerations may have played a part in the government's decision to set up a special force of 45 000 men, partly drawn from French forces in Germany for deployment either in Europe or overseas. This decision was clearly of concern to its NATO allies, as was the brief rift with Washington when the AWACS were sent home, and its failure to consult its allies through the normal NATO channels.

NATO was, in addition, concerned about the intensity of the conflict, and the fact that France believed it necessary to deploy some of its more sophisticated equipment, most of which should have been stockpiled in Europe. The logistical operation was so complex and extensive that it was described by the local French commanders themselves as the most important French military operation since the Algerian war 20 years earlier.[13] The all-purpose Transall troop carriers were able to use a new base at Bouar in the Central African Republic which had been developed both as a supply post and an electronic listening post linked to the Breguet Atlantic airborne listening system. These planes were in constant touch with a number of African bases accommodating 20 Jaguar fighter-bombers, some of which were moved to N'djamena.

The French themselves were not entirely happy with their extensive commitment in Chad. They were always haunted by the fear that one day they might be forced to confront Libyan or East German troops, some of whom were seconded to Ouaddai's forces. Testimony to this is Mitterrand's evident embarrassment at the Franco–African summit the year before, when Mobutu, President of Zaire, had thanked him for guaranteeing Africa's security. The government had responded by warning him that expectations raised so high might well be disappointed.[14]

In 1983, the French clearly recognised that the contending political leaders in Chad had few, if any, perceptible ideological differences. Both were warlords from the north of the country with a long experience of extracting arms and money from a wide variety of foreign backers. The danger was that their parochial disputes might widen into a crisis of disproportionate dimensions as outside powers were drawn in. The muted French response was

more realistic than the militant stance adopted by Washington.
But some of France's allies would also have preferred no
intervention at all; for them the conflict in Chad was a civil war in
which Libyan involvement was peripheral.

For many Europeans, the conflict was almost surreal. What
was the strategic prize at issue? In the 1890s, Lord Salisbury,
seeking to explain one of those innumerable agreements which led
to the drawing up of frontiers in West Africa, had noted:

> Anyone who merely looks at a map and measures distances
> may think that France has gained a great deal of land. But land
> must be measured not only by its extent, but its value. What
> France has gained is what agriculturalists call 'very high land'.
> That is to say, the Saharan desert.

It may never have crossed Lord Salisbury's mind that one day
there would be another dispute for this desert region from which
the state of Chad originally emerged. But he would certainly have
recognised the considerations which led Paris and Washington to
concern themselves with the fate of the second poorest country in
the world. Great powers suffer from a horror of power vacuums;
they dare not concede territory to a rival even when that space is
worthless in itself.

FRANCO–BELGIAN INTERVENTION IN ZAIRE, 1977–78

In April 1977, the government of Angola, exasperated by Zaire's
continuing support for the National Front for the Liberation of
Angola (FNLA), lent its support to an invasion of the mineral-
rich province of Shaba by 7000 Katanganese *gendarmes*. The
gendarmes, who by this time called themselves the Congo National
Liberation Front (FNLC), were the remnants of the force
originally formed in July 1960 from the nucleus of Congolese
troops in Katanga who had initially fought for Tshombe against
the UN and then briefly reappeared when he became Prime
Minister shortly before his career was brought to an end by a
military *coup*.

When they struck in 1977, Zaire was in the throes of the worst
economic crisis in its history, produced largely by a decline in the

world price of copper three years earlier which had left the country with a critical deficit in its current account. Revenues from exports of copper had fallen to three-fifths of their former value. As a result, the country was unable to meet its commercial debt obligations or service its medium and long term loans. Debt servicing, nevertheless, continued to swallow up 20 per cent of its export earnings. Despite standby loans from the International Monetary Fund and a package of austerity measures which promised more than the government of Zaire could actually deliver, the picture remained bleak. In addition to a deteriorating economic situation, the threat to President Mobutu's control appeared to arise largely from deteriorating relations with Angola, one of the legacies of the recent civil war.

The invasion of Shaba threatened to undermine Western efforts to rescue Zaire from its own economic mismanagement, the result of squandered resources and endemic corruption. If Shaba, which provided 70 per cent of the country's export revenues, were to secede the economy might collapse, and with it Mobutu's pro-Western regime. Many of the long term loans from international banks whose servicing was long overdue had also been invested in exploiting the province's non-renewable resources. The IMF had only just concluded that if copper exports could be maintained at projected levels, Zaire's general state of indebtedness might ease by 1980. Thus in April 1977, all factors combined and all to the West's disadvantage.

The crisis translated concern into public policy. The Western powers had no alternative but to intervene themselves. The Zairean army was in a low state of morale, apathetic because of low pay, paralysed by a recent purge of the armed forces in which ten generals had been arrested or dismissed. President Mobutu could only count on support from his Western friends. The United States, describing the situation as 'serious', sent $1m worth of military supplies and equipment. Belgium flew in two C-130 transports, France spare parts for Zaire's six Mirage fighter-bombers.

The Mobutu regime represented everything that more radical countries, Tanzania included, despised – yet the OAU was not happy with reports of Cuban involvement, following so swiftly upon the civil war in Angola; but for the apparent evidence of Cuban links, the West might not have gone to Mobutu's assistance. The American embassy in Kinshasha reported that

2000 Cuban soldiers were waiting to enter Zaire at the first opportunity, a claim which seemed to be substantiated by the alleged discovery that the FNLC was 'officered by men specialised in guerrilla warfare who had come from across the Atlantic'. The Defence Ministry in Luanda vigorously denied the charge, claiming that the invasion had met with widespread internal support.

With the FNLC poised to take Kolwezi, and with Zaire in such disarray that at one point the rebel leader was able to conduct an interview from Europe through the telephone exchange at Kinshasha, the Europeans acted swiftly. France used its influence in Morocco to persuade the government to send a rescue force transported by the French air force. The Moroccans needed little persuading. They saw similarities between the situation in Shaba and the Western Sahara where they were engaged in a protracted struggle against the Polisario guerrillas.

In both cases vital raw materials were at stake; in one the copper deposits of Shaba, in the other the phosphate rock deposits at Bo Craa; in both cases the guerrilla movements appeared to be funded and supported by the Soviet Union. Although many Western observers believed that the Moroccans could have mounted the airlift with their own Hercules aircraft, they turned to France for logistical support to reinforce their claims to Western assistance in the Sahara, to identify themselves with a rescue mission largely underwritten and directed by the Western Alliance.[15]

The intervention of 1500 Moroccan soldiers, transported over the course of a week by 11 French air force planes, decisively turned the tide in Zaire's favour. Once in Shaba, they were joined by 65 'non-combatant' French soldiers and 85 Belgian military personnel. The speed of the airlift and the success of combined operations on the ground enabled the Zairean army to recapture the town of Mutshatsha, 60 miles west of Kolwezi, 11 weeks after the emergency had been declared. The Moroccans headed a two-pronged attack against the town of Kapanga in the north, and the strategically important railway town of Dilolo on the Angola/Zaire border. Within three months operations were brought to an end by the capture of the strategic crossroads towns of Kasaji, Kisenge and Luashi.

The first invasion of Shaba merely underlined the weakness of the Zairean body politic. It did not emasculate the FLNC, nor did it convince everyone in the West that the regime was worth saving. The United States, for once, refused to make too much of the episode's East–West implications.[16] Thus it came as no surprise that Shaba was invaded the following year, nor that the invaders were more formidable and better organised. This time, however, the West's response was more prompt, its intervention more decisive. Fearful that the invasion would precipitate the collapse of Zaire's economy, the Western powers acted with rare unanimity, prompting SACEUR (Alexander Haig) to congratulate NATO on its first concerted response to the Soviet–Cuban presence in Africa.[17] The United States put the 82nd Airborne Division on full alert and despatched C-141 aircraft to lift 1200 Frenchmen and 1700 Belgians into Zaire. In the first instance, they were charged with creating an air corridor which would allow their respective nationals to flee the country; but once on the ground the French were ordered to stay on for a new mission – that of policing the area after the invaders had retired to Angola.

The French gambled in 1978 on getting the support of the United States and their NATO allies. Perhaps, the most significant aspect of the Shaba I and Shaba II crises, was the extent to which France believed it could act only with the connivance and cooperation of its Atlantic partners. 'I came to the conclusion', Giscard d'Estaing told an American magazine in July 1977, 'that the United States and Western Europe were absent in Africa at a very critical moment and that it was necessary to act on our own to preserve the security and territorial integrity of a Western orientated state which, by definition, means the protection of Western interests.'[18] No wonder that many Africans looked at the actions of individual European countries through a NATO lens when countries such as France claimed to be acting in Europe's name. After Shaba II, the army Chief of Staff, General Méry, proposed that the cooperation between Europe and Africa, symbolised in the economic sphere by the Lomé Convention, could be extended to a defence pact with France representing the Western powers.[19] No wonder that Giscard's domestic critics attacked France as the *'gendarme Otanien de l'Afrique'* and the 'spearhead of the Atlantic Alliance' and condemned what they saw as a return to *'la politique des blocs'*.[20]

The Gaullists were especially scandalised that France had had to rely on very extensive American assistance so that the costs of the operation would not be great and the gains of marginal value.

The scale of the Shaba II exercise raised the question whether the French and Belgians could have acted at all without American logistical support, and whether they would have acted anyway if they had not been convinced that the Americans would have been forced to intervene had the Cubans moved into Shaba in support of the FNLC.

At the NATO ministerial meeting in Washington on 30 May 1978 President Carter reminded the delegates that:

> the activities of the Soviet Union and Cuba in Africa are preventing individual nations from determining their own future. As members of the world's greatest Alliance we cannot be indifferent to those events because of what they mean for Africa and because of their effect on the long term interests of the Alliance itself.[21]

Indeed, US Readiness Command was involved from the outset, though the extent of its involvement was not widely reported. As well as sending a joint communications support element to Kinshasha, which was responsible for coordinating the airlift, the 82nd Airborne Division was placed on full alert. The airlift itself was an object lesson in cooperation with the French who were the first to recongise that even modest forces could not be projected into central Africa without American support.

Nevertheless, the operation was not a NATO exercise whatever President Carter might have intimated at the Washington summit. Although US European Command (EURCOM) was nominally in charge of the airlift, its primary role was to keep the NATO allies informed. EURCOM had no operational role. The airlift was mounted from the United States not Europe; and it was in the United States that the troops, who were alerted for possible employment in Zaire, were based.[22] NATO as an organisation was consulted only after the episode was largely over, even though its channels of control and communication were extensively used throughout.

In fact, most Europeans were highly sceptical of the Franco–American role in the whole affair. The swiftness with which the Western Alliance acted conveyed to friends and enemies alike, the importance it attached to Zaire. But did the character of the action fit the character of the objective? The rescue mission could easily have proved a failure if circumstances had been different. The lessons of Shaba II merely reinforced those of Shaba I. Both missions had been made necessary, not by the strength of the FNLC, but by the vulnerability of the Mobutu regime. Actual military operations had been limited because the FNLC had offered no real opposition. Its performance in the field, when it came to the test, had proved as lack-lustre as that of the Zairean army. That is why the Francophone states, who had few enough forces of their own, were prepared to provide a peacekeeping force after the initial airlift and why the Belgians could think of pulling out only 72 hours after their arrival.

Secondly, although France was determined to reassert Mobutu's authority the forces of change, had they been stronger, might well have defied the control and direction of any external power. Although the French insisted that they had only intervened to save the state from collapse and to give the government another opportunity to put its own house in order, neither they nor the Belgians found it very easy to disengage once it became clear that nothing had really changed. In February 1979, only nine months afterwards, Belgium despatched 250 troops to Kitana, a town 300 miles from Kinshasha, to deal with a further outbreak of instability. Clearly, the Europeans would have been forced to underwrite the regime to a much greater extent had violence been more widespread, or support for the FNLC more broadly based. In the event, President Mobutu very sensibly made peace with Angola, recognising that a third incursion into Shaba might not have had the same happy outcome.

The most serious difference of opinion arose between the two powers who actually mounted the rescue mission, Belgium and France, and latterly between the United States and Britain. The first was a re-run of 1977 when the Belgian Prime Minister, Renat van Elslande, had accused the French of poaching on a Belgian sphere of influence. This time it was the turn of the French to hurl accusations, accusing the Belgians of dragging their feet and raising unhelpful obstacles while the mission was in progress. Together with Denmark and the Netherlands, Belgium had opposed open-ended support for Mobutu in the aftermath of Shaba I. Now they questioned whether Shaba II should be seen in an East–West context at all. Writing several years later, the Belgian Foreign Minister, Henri Simonet, argued that it would be folly to expect African countries to join in the struggle between the blocs

> ... to force them to join the kind of alliance that is close to our own would tempt the West to impose its own ideologies on Africa and therefore to view the African continent as being divided into two camps: its own and that of its rivals. Trying to draw them into our camp would invite the other camp to step in ...[23]

Such reservations were decisive in dissuading other NATO members from giving the French and Americans their uncritical support. In Washington, President Carter supported France in its view that Soviet power had penetrated beyond the North Atlantic area and that the Alliance could no longer afford to be indifferent to what happened in the continent. The British, however, were sceptical of America's new-found interest in Africa. James Callaghan complained of new Christopher Columbuses setting out from the United States to discover Africa for the first time and, on his return to London, came out in support of the OAU's right to defend itself without interference from NATO.

At the last minute, the final *communiqué* was altered to take account of these reservations, to stress that not all crises should 'be viewed exclusively in an East–West context and (to reaffirm) the importance they attached to encouraging peaceful settlements through negotiation by the countries and regional organisations themselves'.[24] Of the ten hours of talks at the Washington meeting, over half were devoted to the discussion of African security. Yet, while the Americans found that most NATO leaders agreed that the Soviet–Cuban presence in Africa should be closely monitored in the future, most were unwilling to divert resources to Africa itself. These reservations were given expression in Section 5 of the *communiqué*, which called upon its members to use force only as a last resort.

French efforts to organise a pan-African force also met with considerable opposition even though the use of NATO troops was not discussed. At the fourth Franco–African summit in the aftermath of Shaba I, Giscard had proposed a security pact between Africa and Europe though not, as widely reported at the time, between Africa and the North Atlantic Alliance (certainly nothing like the *Alliance Atlantique Africaine* which his critics in France accused him of promoting). In proposing a Eurafrica pact, he had acted without consulting his European allies – indeed he had no brief to offer any such agreement. France was clearly embarrassed when Leopold Senghor of Senegal asked for European backing for a West African defence pact. It knew full well such a scheme would be totally unacceptable to its allies.[25] At his final press conference, Joseph Luns reiterated that the situation in Zaire was not something which NATO could concern itself with as an Alliance, but which its members acting either individually or collectively could deal with as they saw fit.[26] But Dr Luns' statement concealed more than it revealed. If some members agreed to help the Africans help themselves by building up a pan-African force, would the decision require formal NATO endorsement? For the controversy which ensued raised a more far-reaching question. African solutions to African problems may have been a deceptively simple formula but the latter was symptomatic of a general disposition within the Alliance to limit the West's role in solving security problems in a region where the risks were high but where, in the judgment of most, no vital Western interests were at stake.[27]

It was such considerations which prompted Nyerere and Obasanjo, the President of Nigeria to question the sincerity behind the whole pan-African scheme. Would NATO ever be prepared to supply standardised defence equipment to a peacekeeping force unless it was in control of the force itself? And once the interests at risk were classified as vital, would such an arrangement be considered adequate, or would NATO intervene? To many Africans Shaba II reflected a flexible and pragmatic response to security problems: pragmatic, because it had not ruled out a NATO interest in an area outside its defence perimeter; flexible, because it had allowed the three countries who could intervene most quickly to interpret whether Western interests were threatened or not. Yet it was precisely in order to keep their response both flexible and pragmatic that most NATO members eschewed formal defence commitments and wanted nothing to do with training and equipping a pan-African force.

FRENCH OPERATIONS SINCE 1978

Since the Zaire operation, France has continued to cite its role in the context of Western policies. Speaking in 1981 at the *Institut des Hautes Etudes de Defense Nationale* the Minister of Defence, Charles Hernu, stated the views of President Mitterrand: who during the

Zaire operation only three years earlier had been one of Giscard's most vocal critics:

> The geographic and political situation of France places it at the centre point of the two great axes around which modern international relations revolve – North/South relations on the one hand, East/West on the other. That is the reason why the policy of the President takes note of these axes.[28]

France, he went on to say, 'was inevitably concerned with the conflicts and contests that are played out in the Third World'. The following year, Charles Hernu returned to the theme in an article written for the *Revue des Deux Mondes*. Citing the many conflicts which had broken out in Africa as a result of great power competition, he remarked that:

> the privileged relations between France and numerous African countries, and the great vulnerability of the continent as a whole, are the two essential realities on the basis of which any French role in Western security must be considered.[29]

The fact that French presidents have succeeded in preserving the African dimension of French power no less than the European one, has ensured that France will continue to play a unique role. The system of Franco–African relations which de Gaulle nurtured, though it has changed over time, has continued to guide French foreign policy. It is not surprising that this role is increasingly defined in terms of Western security, though no reference to NATO as such is ever made. The extension of that role to Portuguese speaking (Lusophone) Africa, and Zaire which began under Giscard, has become the most important element in the Mitterrand government's stance towards Africa. The desire to consider Africa as a whole rather than a collection of traditional spheres of influence, has animated much of what the new socialist administration has done.

Two conclusions which have been reached by France are bound to have some influence on the relationship between the West and Africa. The first is that the role of military power in French policy has changed. There is a growing recognition that it may not be sufficient, given the ever increasing resolve of local African forces to deal with every crisis. The costs of intervention have risen as the conflicts have multiplied. Drawing from America's experience of Vietnam, the Minister for Cooperation, Jean-Pierre Cot argued recently that:

> Policy based on military power alone is not an adequate answer to a changing world. France believes that a more sophisticated and long term concept of national interest is called for. . . . Today in the Third World established disorder goes under the name of oppression and underdevelopment. To fight against such disorder without subsuming this struggle in the conflict between East and West is one way to escape from the Yalta legacy . . .[30]

For most French socialists, the world has become a place in which geopolitical success is best measured by a country's responsiveness to the call for changes in the international system rather than by its ability to maintain its privileged position by force. Giscard used to emphasise the theses of interdependence and cooperation which governed relations between France and Africa, yet his military policy seemed to imply that France had very specific interests in very specific countries, and that his grand designs were only a mask for rather less grand concerns. To some extent this has now changed.

The second explanation for France's increasing propensity to see its role in Africa in terms of its Alliance obligations, is the increasing visibility and cost of such operations. The importance of ensuring that France can intervene in Africa has remained undiminished and no major changes in the *force d'intervention* (the *force d'assistance*) have taken place since the socialists came to power. The Franco–Senegalese exercises in November 1983, which combined men from all the services, but particularly from the 21st Marine Infantry Regiment, revealed the much improved mobility of French forces over a long distance with military equipment which previously the parachute units had been able neither to transport nor use.

In the Indian Ocean as well, French units have been highly visible. Until the massive build-up of the Rapid Deployment Force (RDF) the four infantry companies based at Djibouti with two anti-tank squadrons, Mirage fighters and a 12-20 complement of ships including the guided missile frigate *Dusquesne* and five dual purpose frigates, constituted by far the largest foreign military presence in the Gulf. Just before the RDF's Bright Star manoeuvres in the region, the French Southern Zone Armed Forces conducted their own 'Orchids 1981' exercise using 1800 men in a simulated two front invasion of Réunion.

France continues to maintain control of four small islands in the Mozambique Channel (Glorieuses, Juan de Nova, Bassas da India and Europa) on which it had a number of airfields central to the surveillance of shipping. Until the appearance of the American Rapid Deployment Force in the early 1980s, its forces in Djibouti (together with the aircrew of a Mirage squadron) were the largest military presence close to the Gulf.

It is worth remembering that while Britain deploys a surface task force in the Indian Ocean every year and the Netherlands deploys a frigate or destroyer group every second year, the French maintain a permanent Indian Ocean Fleet which at one time (1976) eclipsed both the Soviet and American navies in the number of shipdays in the area. At present, their fleet consists of 15 ships, including four corvettes, a command ship, several patrol vessels in the Gulf and the Mozambique Channel and occasionally an aircraft carrier which can be converted into a helicopter assault ship if required.

Precisely because of its visibility, the French have been anxious to reduce cooperation between their navy and the RDF to a minimum. Even when France joined Britain and the United States in patrolling the Arabian Sea during the Iraqi–Iranian war, France refused to cooperate or even consult its NATO allies so as not to appear to be planning the defence of vital interests common to all in a specifically NATO context. Nevertheless, the defence community in France has increasingly recognised the need to cooperate more extensively with its NATO allies to ensure that future French operations meet with continued success. It is well aware that France has too few ships and too many commitments in home waters to permit the deployment of more than a token force overseas. Evidence of consultation between France and the United States is not easy to come by, but it does exist. In August 1978, to cite only one example, the commander of the American Middle East Task Force (MIDEASTFOR), the forerunner of the RDF, paid a visit to the commander of the FAZSOL (French Indian Ocean Fleet) to discuss joint operational planning. Shortly afterwards the French commander paid a return visit to Diego Garcia.[31]

There has been some support in France for a joint NATO task force in the Indian Ocean flexible enough in its operational design to allow individual countries, notably France which is not a member of NATO's integrated military command, to patrol stretches of the Indian Ocean in which they are already active. An obvious area for the French would be the Mozambique Channel through which their oil tankers pass *en route* to the Cape. If the French could be sure that their allies would be responsible for a part of the area which they now patrol on their own, their navy would be able to benefit from shorter deployment times as well as higher employment cycles. This would allow much greater rationalisation of units which are, at present, deployed as part of their Indian Ocean fleet.

In Africa itself, the French are finding the burden of intervention increasingly costly. Here too they could benefit from greater cooperation with their allies on a scale considerably larger than that shown in 1978. At present, France can sealift a motorised division of its marine infantry or airlift a two brigade parachute division. It has also re-opened the C-160 Transall production line and has provided some of its new aircraft with inflight refuelling. But even when added to its existing airlift fleet they will still not be able to carry heavy artillery or tanks. Recent military operations in Africa have served to highlight its costs. The war in the Western Sahara and the conflict in Chad have seen the deployment of Jaguar fighter-bombers, Breguet Atlantic reconnaissance aircraft and Transall transport planes; in the case of the Jaguars and Transalls 10 per cent and 25 per cent respectively of the entire fleet. These percentages are so large that they must prompt the question: whether sustained military operations are any longer possible without some form of allied support.

Nor is the political picture very promising. Both the extent and scope of any future operations will almost certainly be determined by the current availability of enlisted men. Conscript forces as a rule are not sent overseas. The Foreign Legion, not the regular army, saw service in Chad (1970) and Zaire (1978). And with 10 000 men already stationed in Africa defending commitments which are fast becoming open-ended, the manpower situation must be considered somewhat doubtful. Here again there is every reason to consider the wisdom of cooperating with other European forces, or even, for that matter, the United States.

6 NATO and South Africa, 1974–83

Critics of the Western Alliance have accused NATO of collusion with South Africa ever since the Alliance came into existence. No doubt the option has been discussed, if it has not been acted upon. But what the critics offer as evidence does not in itself explain anything that we do not already know. And if the lesson we draw is that the Alliance has only been prevented from working closely with South Africa for fear of being discovered, we do less than justice to the facts. Despite all accounts of NATO's 'collusion' with South Africa, accounts indeed that are beginning to constitute quite a large corpus, it cannot be established with any accuracy that collusion on any significant scale has ever taken place. Instead, NATO's political leaders, representing a wide spectrum of political opinion, have seen South Africa as a country suffering from internal pressures too intense for it to serve any useful role, or indeed for it to want to.

An entire school of analysts, of course, has postulated quite the opposite hypothesis, a school that owes much to the writings of superannuated generals and admirals. Yet, there is little evidence that bears the hypothesis out. What the evidence does show and why it is worth discussing is that NATO has never had much reason to admit South Africa through the back door. It is also a reason why we must reject much of the criticism that is available. Matters of fact, of speculation and of political fancy have not been clearly distinguished.

Much of the evidence has centred on the sophisticated electronic equipment furnished for project Advokaat – a comprehensive surveillance, monitoring and communications programme which was installed at Silvermine, not far from Simonstown, in 1973. Since then South Africa has been able to maintain surveillance across the South Atlantic to Brazil and across the Indian Ocean to New Zealand. Silvermine itself is a computerised three-storey maritime communications centre, fully equipped with teleprinters, radarscopes, crypto machines and other communications equipment necessary to acquire, collate and maintain a continuous picture of the 20 000 ships which pass in sight of the Cape every year. The centre also has space for officers of NATO navies which could be made available in time of war.[1]

The critics of the link argue that it drags the Alliance into the Southern Africa conflict, even though, as of 1976, 11 non-NATO members had utilised the codification system in one form or another. The British anti-apartheid movement which discovered the link in the early 1970s submitted a memorandum to the United Nations Special Committee against apartheid showing that orders for parts had been placed with companies in the United Kingdom, the United States and the Federal Republic of Germany using NATO forms and NATO stock codes. It concluded that South Africa had been admitted into the NATO code area and that all future military equipment and spare parts would be codified and recorded as for all other NATO members.[2]

Most of the evidence, in fact, relates to West Germany which originally built the codification system and trained a team from South Africa in its use in May 1974. Evidence acquired from the South African embassy in Bonn reveals that the Federal Republic receives information on shipping movements through the RAF communications centre at Rheindahlen free of charge.[3] Together with the United States and Britain, Germany continues to supply spare parts even though Norway, the Netherlands, Denmark and Canada refused to do so after the Oslo ministerial meeting in 1976. By then the Central Intelligence Agency (CIA) had already concluded that Silvermine made America's own communications facility on Diego Garcia unnecessarily expensive.[4] In 1976, America finally pulled out its last electronic intelligence gathering ship from the South Atlantic, in the expectation that South Africa would continue to gather the same information at much lower cost.[5]

Nevertheless, the facts of the case are somewhat more complex than often made out. The special number code had been given to South Africa at the request of France. South Africa had used the codification system since the early 1960s, long before the construction of the Silvermine station – indeed, the supply of equipment to the base in 1973 had been, in all essentials, a commercial exchange between South Africa and West Germany. It could hardly have been otherwise since the system was never officially classified, even though the subject came up for discussion at the ministerial meetings in Oslo (1976) and London (1977).

At both meetings, the NATO ministers were lobbied by the British anti-apartheid movement, the second time successfully, in so far that Britain itself bowed under the pressure and agreed not to supply spare parts in the future. In the circumstances, however, it is hardly surprising that the major maritime powers in the Alliance should have wished to monitor shipping in the sea lanes off the Cape, the most congested in the world.

The South Africans obtained first the hardware and later the computer software for cataloguing ship movements in the categories employed by NATO, and then provided it with the information. Later it was alleged that the Silvermine complex was used to handle weapons inventories in South Africa on the basis of NATO codification forms. Since the forms were usually unclassified the allegation is probably true, but hardly of the significance credited by NATO's critics.[6] Although the exchange of data between Silvermine and the NATO centre for satellite monitoring of the sea lanes may be fairly extensive, there are no direct links between the two intelligence gathering authorities as the commander of Silvermine recently admitted.[7] The information is exchanged only after it has been processed, a fact which is periodically drummed home whenever Pretoria releases public data on the movement of Soviet shipping.

Collusion of a rather different sort was alleged in 1976 in a report by Sean Macbride describing a secret agreement between Henry Kissinger and South Africa's Prime Minister, John Vorster, with the then SACEUR, Alexander Haig. As a former United Nations Commissioner for Namibia who was briefed by Dr Kissinger during his initiative on Southern Africa, Macbride's allegations enjoyed wide currency both within the United Nations and outside it. Macbride claimed that two agreements were reached at a meeting in Zurich, the second of two conferences in Europe which Dr Kissinger held with John Vorster before he set off on the first leg of his ill-fated Southern Africa shuttle; the first, to extend collaboration between the SADF and NATO's military commanders, knowing that any attempt to extend the Alliance's territorial limits would meet with opposition from the Netherlands and the Nordic members; and to supply military equipment contrary to the arms embargo of 1963.[8]

Do either of these claims ring true? Macbride himself admitted that he had no positive information that any NATO member, apart from Britain and France, had ever been informed of the agreement, or that Dr Kissinger had ever relayed it to the State Department. He did claim, however, that the text was communicated to the military command in Brussels and it is interesting in this connection that while Joseph Luns assured the British anti-apartheid movement at Oslo that the international staff did not maintain contact with South African officials, he refused to provide such an assurance for the national staff at SHAPE.[9]

Sean Macbride's allegations do not stand alone. There have been many charges of collusion between South Africa and NATO which differ only in the emphasis they place on where the responsibility lies and the motives which underlie their interests in working together. But there is no disagreement on the conspiratorial nature of the partnership, or the inevitable consequence that each conducts its foreign policy so as to avoid collision with the other.

Suspicions about informal liaison have been fuelled by ambiguous comments emanating from South Africa itself. In 1975, the South African Defence Minister remarked that his country's military relationship with NATO was 'not official, but friendly'.[10] Such charges have always been emphatically denied. When the chairman of the UN Special Committee on apartheid visited Brussels in February 1975 he was assured by Dr Luns that the Alliance had well defined geographical perimeters which did not include South Africa; that SACLANT's study of sea lane protection in time of war had at no time involved any contact with the South Africans at a political, diplomatic or technical level; and that the NATO Council had never discussed the use of Simonstown.[11] The evidence in support of such denials is, of course, open to interpretation, but the case for the prosecution has yet to be proved. Perhaps it is significant that when the Secretary of the Federal Ministry of Economics returned from a visit to South Africa in 1978 convinced that Silvermine had a crucial role to play in the defence of the oil supply from the Gulf, he was surprised to learn how little contact there had been, even on an informal basis, between the SADF and senior officers at SHAPE.[12]

The evidence that the arms embargo has been breached is also very questionable. In 1978, NATO was asked to provide the Security Council with details of all transfers of patents and licenses for items such as the Mirage F-1 fighter-bomber and Airbus transport plane.[13] Occasionally, individual members have been singled out for criticism. The sale of Mirage F-1s and licenses for the FN–762 gun figured prominently in the condemnation of Belgium at a meeting in Brussels in April 1978.[14]

There is no doubt that individual NATO governments have been lax in chasing up loopholes in the arms embargo and have not always acted sensibly. There were noticeable discrepancies, for example, between the official German denial of arms sales published in January 1977, and the evidence produced by independent West German defence journals which confirmed the delivery of several items on the government's list.[15] The German anti-apartheid movement submitted new evidence to the OAU during a summit meeting in Nairobi in June 1981. The report alleged that since the UN mandatory embargo of 1977 West Germany had sold to South Africa:

> ... equipment for its nuclear enrichment plant which is outside the international safeguard control; 3000 military trucks; an assembly plant for engines ... used in military vehicles (and) ... two mine sweepers in October 1980 ...[16]

These claims are difficult to substantiate; like a great many others, their accuracy may be in question. Even if this is not the case the examples cited conflict with the general pattern of the last ten years.

TABLE 1 *Ships and aircraft sold to South Africa 1975–78 in FFr and as a percentage of total French exports of those categories*

	1975		1976		1977		1978	
	FFr	%	FFr	%	FFr	%	FFr	%
Ships	2.6	0.1	33.0	1.4	365	15.0	815.0	26.6
Aircraft	166.9	9.2	648.1	27.5	465	19.1	36.6*	1.0

*Almost entirely spare parts

SOURCE: Christopher Hill 'French and West German relations with South Africa' in James Barber (ed) *The Uneasy Relationship: Britain and South Africa* (London: Heinemann, 1983) p. 125.

The question of military cooperation with South Africa was raised during Chancellor Schmidt's visit to Zambia in June 1978. West Germany had previously exempted France from 'the final destination clause' which had prohibited the re-sale of German arms to countries 'in areas of high tension'. France, as South Africa's leading arms supplier in the 1970s brought this exemption into question. The following month the Pietschke amendment came into force which introduced a new licensing system which effectively closed this loophole. In all other respects, there was no doubt where Germany's sympathies lay. In the late 1970s, it was in the forefront of attempts to promote a peaceful transfer of power, or a transfer with the minimum of violence. Its membership of the Contact Group in Namibia, the economic consultants it seconded to the Zimbabwe Peoples Union (ZAPU), its decision to step up development aid to Zaire after Shaba II to find 'a political and economic solution' to the crisis, may have reflected a wish to underwrite the more conservative forces of change in the region. They did not illustrate any intention to oppose the more militant forces by tacit support of the existing *status quo*.

The result of claims, to the contrary, has been, first and foremost, an enormous expenditure of time, attention and energy by African governments on the one hand, and anti-apartheid movements on the other – on a myth that has been long in the making. It has also blinded many pundits who have urged closer cooperation between NATO and South Africa to the fact that South Africa has never had much to offer the Alliance; that by nature and history it is an African country not a Western one, probably more averse to entangling alliances than ever.

In the early 1950s, Malan, Prime Minister of South Africa, had no doubt that South Africa could only defend itself in partnership with the NATO powers. 'South Africa's aim', he claimed:

is to take responsibility *in so far as agreement can be reached with other countries* for territories to the north of South Africa. We want to help in the protection of our neighbours.[17]

By 1961 the perception had changed radically. Commenting on NATO's tendency to treat the SADF as a complementary force, the government declared that the country would have to build up a completely autonomous unit, adding that if the SADF had to fight on NATO's side, it would do so more effectively if its men were fully integrated.[18]

The reassertion of South African nationalism was not surprising. In all other respects except defence, it has always been a fiercely nationalistic country, the first African state to launch a nationalist revolt against European imperialism, the first to achieve self-government within the Commonwealth. Except for Simonstown there has never been a foreign base on its soil. After 1961 and its withdrawal from the Commonwealth, the South Africans tried to carve out an independent political role for themselves, to treat it as a vocation and in all respects play it as an African power. The fact that Africa would not allow it to play the part, or to play any role at all in the context of pan-African politics, forced South Africa by default to think itself part of the Atlantic community. This, in turn, re-emphasised for a time the deep personal and moral commitment which many whites already felt for the West, especially Britain, and which made it all the more difficult, of course, to develop an African identity.

Disillusionment with the Western powers, and with Britain in particular, led the National Party in the late 1970s to return to its isolationist tradition. The old nationalist rallying call was taken up once again in a speech made by the Foreign Minister at Zurich in March 1979 in which he threatened to give serious consideration to a neutralist position in the struggle between the blocs.[19] The speech echoed the warning of its first Foreign Minister Eric Louw, 20 years earlier, that South Africa's very strategic significance, of which the government made so much, was likely to make the NATO powers even more interested in the future political dispensation, more alert to whether the whites could maintain control, more prone to intervene if they could not. Even in the 1950s, the era of greatest Afrikaner self-confidence, Louw believed that South Africa's association with NATO might undermine apartheid, not underpin it, if the Western powers should ever make their defence guarantee conditional on the reform of the political system.[20]

The event which undermined South Africa's confidence in the West was its failure to stand by it in Angola. Whether or not the SADF had intervened with or without America's tacit approval, the episode confirmed once and for all that South Africa would not be resupplied with arms in a crisis in which Western forces were not themselves engaged. It was this realisation which undermined the central plank of alignment with the West, for in defending the Simonstown agreement in 1955 Strijdom's only argument for abandoning neutrality had been Britain's agreement to sell arms in the spirit of the Simonstown accord.[21]

The Angolan debâcle confirmed its suspicions that the Western Alliance could live, not only with a Marxist Angola, but also a non-white South Africa. Dr Kissinger's shuttle in 1976 and the Contact Group initiative on Namibia which followed shortly afterwards seemed to confirm Louw's prediction that the West would intervene once it was convinced that the whites were on the way out, or had demonstrably lost the will to maintain themselves in power.

Calls for neutrality have been voiced quite often since P W Botha asked whether South Africa could put any faith in 'the timorous Western world which is so captivated by the soft music of *détente*', a doubt which has not abated, despite the fact that *détente* has worn rather badly. The Western Alliance has been charged with everything from seeking South Africa's destruction to remaining impassive in the face of Soviet penetration, and even undermining South Africa's efforts to reach an understanding with black Africa, in its eyes the most culpable charge of all.[22]

With the appearance of the Rapid Deployment Force in 1980, South Africa briefly stepped up its offer of Simonstown as a base. As the Prime Minister commented on opening an expanded section of the harbour:

> These facilities are at the disposal of anyone who wished to be on good terms with us to their own great advantage.[23]

Torn between the 'neutralist' and 'integrationist' options, even as late as 1980, it is not all that surprising to find that the Defence Minister Magnus Malan was still an integrationist at heart. Malan was, after all, the last South African officer to be trained at the US Army's Command and General Staff Course at Fort Leavenworth in the early 1960s:

> It is time that the United States and its allies included Southern Africa in their global strategic design instead of drawing the line at the Tropic of Cancer and trying to believe that what lies to the south of this line cannot possibly affect the security of the West.[24]

Perhaps, however, it was indicative of the future that South Africa remained strictly 'neutral' during the war between Britain and Argentina in 1982. Pretoria may even have sold arms to the Buenos Aires government while the conflict was at its height. It did offer the Royal Navy the use of Simonstown, but only on conditions that the British government could not meet: a guarantee of weapons supplies that could not be obtained on the open market.[25] From South Africa's point of view, the conflict gave it an opportunity to demonstrate its declared intention of 'no longer being taken for granted' in any future war involving one or more of the Western powers.

Recent events have also raised the question of a more aggressive posture which would have been inconceivable before 1975. Although the South African Navy is, on its own admission, no longer capable of patrolling the sea lanes despite the extension of its territorial waters to 200 miles, it has shown itself quite able and willing to threaten Western shipping in time of tension. In January 1980, South African air force and naval units 'harassed' a US naval battle group as it sailed round the Cape.[26] This may have been an isolated incident, but it showed just how far the South Africans may be prepared to go to express their avowed 'neutrality'.

The question of non-alignment has prompted South Africa to ask whether in terms of its strategic priorities it is already an African power; whether its navy should be changed from an ocean going force into a coastal inshore mine-sweeping unit; whether the airforce should give up its role of maritime support in favour of that of an inland strike force.

The force structure of the SAN suggests that in time of crisis, South Africa will show great caution both in evaluating and responding to the Soviet presence in the Indian Ocean. Possibly the Navy, many of whose officers have no experience of joint exercises with allied navies, would strike out to sea, but the West can hardly rely on it to do so. In the long run only its own naval forces can meet such a threat, or prevent the situation from ever arising.

The bulk of the present fleet was acquired during the period of close collaboration with the RN, including two destroyers transferred in the early 1950s, seven frigates (four of which were launched during the last war, the rest, including the flagship *President Steyn*, in the early 1960s), ten mine-sweepers sold prior to

1960 and five light Fori class vessels purchased at the same time. The West had also consistently refused to supply naval maritime reconnaissance aircraft to replace seven recently modernised, but ageing Shackleton Mark III and 18 Piaggio P1665 aircraft. That is one reason why most reconnaissance missions, routinely conducted within 100 miles of the coastline, detect only 60 per cent of commercial traffic. It is also one reason why Pretoria has been forced to shift emphasis from frigates to smaller but faster corvettes and strike craft. South Africa does relatively little routine patrolling along its coastline in part because it acknowledges, quite openly, that the Soviet Union poses no real naval threat to its security. Because a large part of the SAN will face obsolescence by the end of the decade, it has no alternative but to abandon ocean going anti-submarine operations for the less demanding role of inshore patrol.[27]

Early in 1972, the Defence Minister warned that South Africa had long ago defined the Navy's task as anti-submarine warfare and mine sweeping – it could not defy a greater power, nor had this ever been its policy.[28] Six years later the SAN chief, Admiral Walters, finally admitted that the Navy could no longer look to its 'voluntary duty to care for the security of the Cape route', but would in future have to 'concentrate on its primary task' of defending its own coast and harbours and patrolling its traditional fishing waters.[29]

For its part, NATO has long had doubts about the capacity of the SAN to perform the mission Britain expected in the 1970s, and so too the French who have not carried out joint manoeuvres with SAN since March 1974. The new priorities outlined in 1978 expressed regional anxieties rather than global concerns; the concern of a state that had finally come to terms with its own history and recognised that it could never be more than an African power. This recognition may well make the eventual emergence of a non-aligned black South Africa much less traumatic for the Western Alliance than many commentators have predicted. It also explains why, despite traditional African fears, NATO has never had much interest in forestalling majority rule.

SOUTH AFRICAN INTERVENTION IN SOUTHERN AFRICA

Far from acting as a surrogate of the West, South Africa has now become an independent military power. It is striking that the conflict which saw the triumph of the MPLA and prompted some Western observers to dismiss South Africa as a significant military power was followed by a notable increase in military operations. Since 1976, the SADF has repeatedly crossed the frontier into Angola to attack road and rail installations and the bases of the South West Africa People's Organisation (SWAPO) against which it had been fighting for the past ten years. Although these operations have been described as raids, the term is somewhat misleading. On occasions they have amounted to full-scale invasions, involving armoured cars, fighter bombers and large detachments of troops – considerably larger, in fact, than those involved in 1975. Clearly, Pretoria's failure to contain the forces of change at home has prompted it to compensate by putting even more emphasis on the use of force beyond the *laager*.

For a number of years these raids tended to be seen almost exclusively against the backdrop of the Namibia negotiations. It seemed clear that after 1976, South Africa needed to show that armed struggle would not always triumph as it had in Angola and Mozambique. The government apparently made a profound connection between the chances of peaceful change at home – on its own terms and at its own pace – and military victory or defeat, actual or perceived, in Namibia.

Nevertheless, the raids after 1980 were clearly very different, particularly in scale, from anti-SWAPO operations. It is interesting, for example, to compare Operation Protea in August 1981 with the invasion of Angola five years earlier. The number of men involved in Operation Protea, 11 000 in all, was considerably greater than the force committed six years earlier. But then the somewhat smaller raid – Operation Smokeshell in 1980 – had represented the largest mobilisation of South African military strength since 1945.

Operation Protea not only called upon a greater number of aircraft, but also the use of high speed bombing strikes against the civilian population. No attempt was made to win civilians over to UNITA's side. Indeed, South Africa deliberately injected new uncertainty into the Angolan scene which became more tense and potentially more dangerous than ever. Operation Smokeshell had also involved three squadrons of Mirage III and Buccaneer bombers which might well have turned the tide of battle had they been committed four years earlier.

In addition to relying on air support, the forces used in 1981 were also equipped with 90 Centurion tanks as well as 250 armoured cars. At the same time, 120mm and 155mm guns were used in combination with the air force to bombard several towns in the province of Cunene before ground troops moved into the area.³⁰ The main reason for the increase in force and equipment numbers is that South Africa has no longer been fighting guerrilla units, but a highly trained, well-equipped modern army with sustained experience of modern combat. It is the Angolan army, not SWAPO, whom they have engaged. The Cubans are so unreliable and their morale so suspect that they have been used almost exclusively for garrison duty in the main towns.³¹

Operation Protea yielded 3000 tons of equipment, including 300 vehicles, more than 100 SAM-7 missile launchers, many still in their crates, and ammunition stacked ten feet high. The capture of such extensive supplies confirmed that the Angolan army to whom most of the vehicles and heavier weapons belonged, lost even more in the assault than SWAPO. At a press conference in Luanda, President Eduardo dos Santos reported that, contrary to South African claims, the operation had been directed against regular army units which had suffered 60 per cent of the total casualties.³²

A subsequent raid on two Angolan missile sites under construction at Cahana and Chibemba, two towns north-west of Xangogo, provoked the Angolans for the first time to put up real resistance, bringing to an end a tacit understanding that the two countries would not engage each other's forces along a narrow corridor running 200 miles north of the border. The South African commander later claimed that, despite alerting the Angolans of the assault, they had 'awaited' the advancing column and attacked it 'with premeditation', an episode, which if true, marked the first time the army of a neighbouring state had tried to stand its ground against South African forces.

Since the beginning of 1981, South African incursions into Angola, the great majority of which have gone unreported,³³ have taken one of several forms: reconnaissance flights over the provinces of Moçâmedes, Huila and Cuando-Cubango; bomber raids in the eastern province of Moxico; and long range sabotage missions by special units, of which by far the most dramatic was an attack on the Petrangol state oil refinery in Luanda in November 1981.

By supporting the UNITA guerrillas, South Africa has been able to harry the Angolan government at the point where its control of the country is at its weakest. Although the conflict in the south has produced many conflicting, exaggerated and unverifiable claims, the movement has undoubtedly disrupted the life of the country. From a demoralised band of 3000 men who fled into the bush at the end of the Angolan civil war, UNITA's leader, Jonas Savimbi, claims to have built up a force of 30 000 men who are active in every province up to the 10th parallel.

The true extent of South African support for UNITA is unknown. Many of its trucks and most of its petrol is supplied by Pretoria, as are some, although not all, of its weapons. Savimbi's reason for fighting on is to force the MPLA to re-open negotiations with him on equal terms. It is doubtful whether his allies are really interested in such an outcome. With UNITA in the government, rather than out, the South Africans would have no excuse for destabilising Angola, or for focusing attention on what is happening elsewhere in the region in order to distract attention from what is happening in South Africa itself.

It is much more likely that their main interest is not the support of Savimbi, but the indefinite economic dislocation of Angola. Although the country is one of the world's least developed states, it has been forced to spend more than 50 per cent of its budget on defence.[34] A report prepared by the Angolan government estimated that in the 18 months between June 1979 and December 1980, the raids had produced damage to the tune of $230m, nearly as much as the preceding three years.[35]

Undoubtedly, the worst dislocation has been the refugee problem, which, after Somalia's, is the second worst in Africa. Since 1975, half a million Angolans have been made homeless by the fighting. Operation Protea added 80 000 refugees in less than three weeks. One of the worst hit targets, Lubango, is the distribution centre for relief supplied by the UN Emergency Programme. Having abandoned their fields and lost their herds of cattle, many thousands of peasants have been reduced to a state of permanent dependancy. Many have become refugees in their own country. Many more have not survived at all. Intermittent warfare has turned southern Angola into Africa's southern Lebanon and, like the Lebanon, the government's pleas for international assistance have gone largely unheeded.

Since 1980, the scope of South African intervention has

extended well beyond Angola. ANC bases have been attacked in Mozambique to prevent the movement from attacking power plants, rail links and government installations in the Transvaal. Pretoria has also tried to prevent the nine members of the Southern African Development Coordination Conference (SADDC) from escaping from South Africa's economic orbit.

South Africa's concept of security is no longer confined to the protection of communications centres and other installations within its own borders. By a 1976 amendment of the Defence Act 'service in defence of the republic' was redefined to include the suppression of ANC units beyond its frontiers. Since the Soweto summer of 1976, the ANC has been deluged with young recruits crossing the frontier into Botswana, Lesotho and Swaziland from where they have gone on to training camps in Zambia and Angola. One of the most important developments of recent years has been the re-emergence of the ANC as the most popular nationalist movement.

The SADF has launched several raids against ANC offices in the suburbs of Maputo, notably in the summer of 1983 and January 1980 when its assault destroyed three of its planning and control centres. In December 1982, it also carried out an operation into the heart of Lesotho's capital, Maseru. Ever since the head of the South African security police warned that Lesotho was becoming an ANC staging post, the country has been at risk.[36] It is doubtful whether the South Africans would want to bring down the existing government, but clearly they wish to demonstrate that they are quite prepared to reciprocate if the ANC is allowed to operate without restriction. In one way or another, this is a message which South Africa appears intent on sending to its neighbours.

The NATO powers have every reason to be concerned by these developments. No country in Southern Africa is likely to acquiesce voluntarily in what amounts to a *pax Afrikaanse* enforced by the application of military intervention. If South Africa continues to threaten its neighbours it will have to face the consequences. It is doubtful whether it has thought the consequences through. Quite apart from the West which it appears to hold in no particular esteem, it might have to contend with the Soviet Union. As long as Pretoria insists on intervening to pre-empt attacks by the ANC, the Front Line States will see no recourse but to ask for outside assistance. There appears to be every likelihood that the more implaccable and unyielding South Africa remains, the more they will feel impelled to look to Moscow or East Berlin.

Indeed, in a telegram to the UN Secretary-General after Operation Protea, Angola warned that it might be forced to invoke Article 51 of the UN Charter and to invite outside assistance in what was fast becoming 'a war with unforseeable consequences'.[37] Such commitments of assistance can be found in the defence treaties which both Angola and Mozambique have signed with the USSR and the GDR. The treaty with Mozambique was activated for the first time in January 1980 following the raid against the ANC offices in Maputo. Within days of the attack, the 16 000 ton carrier *Alexander Suvorov* arrived in Beira. The treaty with Angola came into play the following year when a small contingent of Soviet ships stood off the Cunene river while a South African raid was actually in progress.[38]

The likely consequences of these actions cannot be predicted with any certainty. But the possible danger is provided by an episode in June 1979. Anxious to forestall recognition of the internal settlement government by Britain and America and the attendant repeal of sanctions against Rhodesia, the Warsaw Pact tried to persuade the Front Line States to underwrite a plan to recognise a Zimbabwean government-in-exile in a guerrilla controlled area of Rhodesia adjoining the frontier with Mozambique. To forestall a Rhodesian attack, the plan called for the mobilisation of the Mozambiquan army and the occupation of the area by a Mozambiquan mechanised battalion complete with artillery and anti-aircraft weapons.[38] What is so interesting about the plan is that its authors were completely oblivious to the consequences of such action – a dangerous internationalisation of the conflict at a critical moment in relations between the Front Line States and the West.

It was largely for this reason that it was vetoed by the Patriotic Front leaders, who had no wish to escalate the conflict into a conventional confrontation that would ultimately have threatened their own independence, and provoked a major Rhodesian invasion of Mozambique, perhaps, even an attempt to destroy the government of Samora Machel, with or without South African assistance. In all probability, too, it would have involved Warsaw Pact intervention on Mozambique's behalf, including most dangerous of all, the commitment of ground troops, East German rather than Cuban.

So far the Front Line States have acted with remarkable restraint. They have been fully alive to the consequences of close military ties with the Soviet Union. But this restraint is predicated on the willingness of the Western powers to use their economic and political power to produce a diplomatic solution to the problem of minority rule in South Africa itself. As long as the two can work together there can be no convincing case for ignoring the opportunities which a non-violent solution might offer.

If the Western powers fail to act in time, and more immediately, if they prove incapable of deterring South Africa from threatening the political viability of the Front Line States themselves, the situation may well get out of hand. Far from postulating an informal understanding between South Africa and NATO, South Africa's complete failure to take note of the new situation and the possibility of Warsaw Pact intervention, raises the question whether it has any real interest in defending Western interests, as opposed to its own which are somewhat more narrowly defined.

In fact, Southern Africa has become a battlefield in which the Soviet Union and South Africa appear to have developed surprisingly similar objectives. Both countries seem to expect political gains from a continuation and increase in hostilities; both are lukewarm, if not openly hostile, to the West's attempts to find a permanent solution to regional problems which, in one form or another, have preoccupied the West and the Front Line nations for the better part of ten years.

But the West is involved more directly. For South Africa's not unsuccessful attempts to disrupt the plans for the SADCC have brought into question NATO's relations with Pretoria in a way that has not been seen since 1949. SADCC was born in May 1978 when the FLS meeting in Botswana decided with Zimbabwe's imminent independence that the time was right to increase regional cooperation. Although its nine members were among the world's poorest countries, they found themselves in a strategically significant area of the world.[40] It was largely because of this that the West felt the necessity of underwriting the venture designed to loosen ties with South Africa and to strengthen ties with each other. At the Maseru conference in January 1983, Canada and the United States pledged an unspecified amount; six other NATO countries pledged $107.6m. The Western input is already important; together, the nine member states have only survived with Western assistance – a fifth of all Western aid to the continent of Africa.

The extent of the SADCC should not be exaggerated. Before the Maseru conference, few of the 106 projects which had already been identified had taken shape. Only three had been implemented; 35 were in 'the design, construction, or delivery phase'; 20 were under 'submission to financiers', and 35 had not even been discussed.[41] But this slow progress had in no way alleviated South African fears. By the end of 1982, Mozambique's harbours and railways were already handling about half of all the rail traffic from Malawi and Zimbabwe, as well as the daily trains from the copper mines of Zambia and Zaire; two countries which a few years earlier, had moved most of their goods through South Africa.

As soon as Mozambique became pivotal in the SADCC's attempts to divert transport and communications routes away from South Africa, its ports and other strategic installations became vulnerable to sabotage. The *Resistencia Nacional Mocambicina* (MNR) has successfully blown up the railroads linking Zimbabwe with the Indian Ocean ports of Maputo and Beira. Beira's oil storage tanks were destroyed in December 1982 causing landlocked Zimbabwe serious fuel shortages. The MNR, originally set up by Rhodesian intelligence in 1977, passed under South African control after the Lancaster House Conference. The South Africans after training its forces in camps in the Transvaal, have continued to supply it by air and sea at points north and south of Beira.

It is notable that since South Africa took over the movement, little interest, if any, has been shown in its earlier objective of creating 'liberated' zones and winning popular support. Instead, the MNR has set about producing the maximum disruption to local life in the seven provinces in which its forces are active. Because of Mozambique's size and geography, it is almost impossible for the country's army to patrol every line of communication. Yet its rail and road links are absolutely central to the success of the SADCC – in particular the rail link from Zimbabwe to Maputo, the road and rail links near Beira and the oil pipeline from Beira to Mutare (Umtali) which opened six months behind schedule because of guerrilla attacks.[42]

Two other members of the SADCC, and two of the signatories of the Lomé Convention, have also suffered from South African attacks in recent years, which have also been intended to defer the day when they escape South Africa's orbit. In Zambia evidence of economic destabilisation was brought to light when an EEC Commission of enquiry found that many Zambian villages had come under attack since 1980. The most sustained form of aggression had been the laying of land mines, which in addition to causing loss of life and a decline in agricultural production, had also deterred several mining companies from investing in the region.[43] The strategy of destroying Zambia's economic infrastructure became apparent in July 1982 when, in the wake of an attack by two battalions of South African troops, the government was forced to declare the whole of the Western Province a disaster zone.[44] The EEC Commission's condemnation of these attacks recalled Britain's complaint in 1969 about Portuguese incursions into Zambia including the destruction of the Luangwa bridge which carried 92 per cent of the country's supplies of fuel.[45]

If Zambia is the most notable example of destabilisation, Botswana is one of the most recent. A series of protest notes by the Botswana government following several border incidents in 1981 elicited little or no response from the South African government beyond flat denials that the incidents ever occurred. In an interview at the end of 1981, President Masire disclosed that his government was increasingly concerned at indications that the South Africans were fabricating evidence of border incursions as a way of justifying counter-reprisals by their own forces.[46] The incidents which have been so far recorded include border violations, exchanges of fire between Botswana and South African forces, particularly near the Caprivi strip; as well as the smuggling in of arms to facilitate armed robberies and other actions.[47]

The evidence uncovered by the EEC Commission of Enquiry merely reinforced the proposals which the EEC Commission in Brussels sent the Council of Ministers in May 1981 and which formed the basis of its position at the meeting of the seven Western powers at Ottawa shortly afterwards. The Commission's report made it quite clear that of all the industrial countries, Western Europe was most pre-occupied with the domestic security of its main raw material markets; and that such devices as the Lomé Convention were precisely designed to maintain 'stability' in neighbouring regions.[48]

Angola's application to join the Convention in the company of Mozambique, paralleled by the Community's decision to fund a large part of the SADCC's costs, has forced the EEC to become (in the Commission's own words) 'directly involved in the development process right up to the frontiers of apartheid'.[49] What this may mean in security terms is suggested by a tentative French offer to replace Cuban troops in southern Angola, a proposal originally made during a visit to Cuba by Jean Asseuil, the head of the Africa Department of the *Quai d'Orsay*.

The day when European troops may be stationed in Southern Africa to deter the South Africans from attacking neighbouring states may be a long way off, but not as long as South Africa itself may believe. The deployment of European troops would raise the political threshold South Africa would have to cross in pursuance of its strategies. An attack on railway installations protected by French or British soldiers would be tantamount to an attack on South Africa's relations with Europe which, after all, are of more continuous and supreme economic importance to its survival than its own relations with Mozambique.

A military presence would also protect the major investment which needs to be made if the SADCC is to succeed; $800m alone in respect of Mozambique's communications system. It would also protect the growing number of European engineers and technicians who are likely to follow in the wake of such large capital injections. Last, but not least, it would significantly contribute to Mozambique's non-alignment and the further reduction of Soviet influence. Ever since Machel's speech at a mass rally in Maputo in November 1981 in which he severely attacked the defence force and the security police for violations of the constitution,[50] it has become clear that this criticism was also leveled at the army's main trainers and advisers from the Eastern bloc. Asked after an agreement had been signed with Portugal for logistic military assistance whether such dealings with a NATO country would not compromise Mozambique's socialist integrity, the Defence Minister Alberto Chipande responded:

> We are not going to be prevented from cooperating with the Portuguese merely because we are a socialist country. They left infrastructures and equipment here that could be used for military objectives. We cannot spend millions and millions of

dollars merely because we do not want to buy a part from a country that is a member of NATO.[51]

All this suggests that far from growing closer together, NATO and South Africa are likely to find themselves in conflict quite soon. Given South Africa's willingness to launch raids into Angola and Mozambique in the face of diplomatic *démarches* from the Western powers, NATO has been put in an impossible dilemma. Since the MPLA attaches such importance to the Cuban presence for its own security (2000 more Cuban troops were airlifted in the wake of Operation Protea) it will have to find some way to alleviate Angolan fears after the Cubans have departed. And the same will hold true for an independent Namibia which will certainly expect a better guarantee than its word that South Africa will not intervene in the future. Unfortunately, it has very little leverage over Pretoria. There are no arms sales which can be cut off, no military sanctions that can be taken.

It can always be argued, of course, that it is precisely the powers who can act as intermediaries who have most influence, the best intermediaries being, not those with the least bias, but with the most leverage.[52] But precisely because this is true, the West is likely to find itself in some difficulty. It is not the West's bias which is likely to tell against it, as many African critics think, but the fact that the arms embargo has robbed it of any influence over the use of South African forces.

Part II

7 The Warsaw Pact and Africa, 1959–83

Ever since the intervention of Cuban troops in Angola, the West has tended to see Africa as a vast chessboard on which the Soviet Union can move its own pieces at will, whether Cuban or East German soldiers. Yet although Soviet global designs continue to claim our attention, it must be wondered whether we place too great an interest on Soviet strategic intentions and too little on the interests of its East European allies. Seemingly persuaded of the traditional threat, we often overlook the East European connection, or dismiss it as unimportant, or recognise its importance only to reduce the East Europeans to the status of surrogates of the Soviet Union.[1] Too often we forget that the latter have economic interests of their own. Nowhere is this diversity more apparent than in Eastern Europe's relations with Africa; equally, however, nowhere is the coincidence of interest more real.

This is not to deny the importance of the Soviet Union's strategic interest in Africa, any more than it is possible to deny the interest of the United States which, in strict geopolitical terms, may have little to do with the economic rationale for West European involvement. Soviet commentators frequently draw attention to the West's dependence on the continent's resources as well as the importance it attaches to the Cape route.[2] But to many East Europeans these strategic analyses often seem much more ambiguous. The Soviet Union, like the United States, has allies whose interests must be taken into account. It too has to confront the responsibilities as well as the limitations of its power. Its own interests in Africa and those of its Warsaw Pact allies may not be the same.

Their interests and those of Western Europe are in many respects, very similar. Both are concerned about access to the non-renewable resources of the continent, and even more its reserves. Global security is no less real for the Warsaw Pact than it is for the Atlantic Alliance; strategic minerals policy is discussed no less frequently in the Pact's Political Committee than it is in the NATO Council.

EASTERN EUROPE AND AFRICA'S MINERALS

To understand the importance which Eastern Europe attaches to Africa, we must first turn to the raw material problem which the Council for Mutual Economic Assistance (CMEA) has faced since 1972. The extensive mineral resources of the Soviet Union have always been crucially important, not only in terms of its own economic growth, but also that of its partners. Despite the existence of vast domestic reserves their commercial viability began to look doubtful by the end of the 1960s. The Soviet Union began to encounter difficulty in meeting its own domestic needs in the light of the problems that kept production down to certain minimum levels – geographical inaccessibility, the high capital overheads of mining and the ever spiralling costs of transportation.[3]

These constraints were not new. Although the Russians would have preferred to supply their allies themselves, even in the 1950s they recognised that this would not always be possible. Early in 1956, a research group funded by the Soviet Academy of Scientists proposed that Eastern Europe should begin to import raw materials directly from Africa. Ever since it has not felt able to rely exclusively on Soviet supplies. Not only are its own resources completely inadequate; falling production within the Soviet Union has continued to set back the development of its own natural resources at the very time that economic growth has continued to fuel domestic demand.

Generally speaking, the interest of the East Europeans centred on the possibility of deriving the twin advantages discussed by the Polish economist Ignacy Sachs in 1961:

> Economic relations with Africa hold out the long term prospect of obtaining scarce raw materials cheaply in exchange for capital and consumer goods . . .
> Economic relations with the socialist countries of Europe will

strengthen the bargaining position of the less developed countries in their relations with the imperialist powers.[4]

Of course, the import of raw materials was not especially significant in the 1960s. Indeed, raw material imports fell as a percentage of CMEA imports from Africa, from 77 per cent in 1955 to 40 per cent fifteen years later.[5] In Sachs's own country, Poland, the share of Africa in its commodity exports to the developing world was more than a quarter, while the same share on the import side was less than 0.3 per cent.[6]

Nevertheless, the continent began to play a prominent role in Polish imports in certain raw material categories. Poland's main interest in this period was phosphorites and petroleum even though the conditions under which they were sold (for free currency) severely limited the country's import potential. Africa accounted for 100 per cent of Poland's phosphate imports in 1970. Commodity imports from the two phosphate rich markets: Morocco and Tunisia accounted between them for 31 per cent of all Polish imports. That was one of the reasons why imports from north Africa increased three times in the 1960s while its import bill from central Africa remained largely static.

Even more interesting as an illustration of how East European attitudes significantly changed between 1961-70 is Hungary's attitude to Guinea. On the invitation of the government, a Hungarian team looked at the technical problems of production at the Kassa Island mine in 1962. Guinea's largest bauxite mine at Kindia, which produced at one time 2.5m tons a year, was originally established with Soviet assistance. Yet repeated requests for CMEA assistance were not taken up.

As the two CMEA countries possessing a highly developed aluminium industry, Hungary and the Soviet Union both looked for imports from outside Africa even though a Soviet geological team mapped out Guinea's reserves, and even though Hungarian geologists prospected for bauxite in Ghana, Mali and Malagassy on behalf of the United Nations. The main disincentive to relying on Guinea was largely political in nature: compared with the other major suppliers, India, Turkey and Yugoslavia, its political stability looked very fragile.[7]

All this changed very suddenly when it became clear that the Soviet Union itself could no longer be relied upon to supply Eastern Europe with all its bauxite needs. The CMEA Secretariat began looking at Guinea very seriously in 1970. Once Eastern Europe found itself facing the prospect of competition with the West on the open market, its policy towards Africa began to take on a very different dimension and to present challenges of a very different order from those which had been traditionally discussed.

These fears, too, had their genesis in the 1960s. One Czech economist contended that economic cooperation with Africa's recently independent states had 'great significance for an industrially developed country with an insufficient energy base' such as his own.[8] Czechoslovakia was quick to seize upon the independence movement as a threat to Western monopoly control, taking heart from the loss of Western military bases in Libya and Morocco[9] and was one of the first countries to recognise the Algerian Provisional Government in March 1962. Ever anxious that the Western Multinational Corporations (MNCs) might exploit their control of the continent's resources to deny its allies access to them, the Soviet Union accused the Western powers of deliberately under-developing new reserves as part of a neo-colonial conspiracy to perpetuate Africa's under-development.[10]

It was the extent of Western control over minerals during this period that was of such concern to the CMEA. Since 1945 a very considerable proportion of the raw material market had been concentrated in a handful of large companies. Seven leading corporations, for example, controlled 88 per cent of the oil market. Six companies controlled about 85 per cent of the world's smelting capacity in aluminium. In other areas they managed to maintain control over foreign sources of supply by using vertical integration, long term contracts and monopsony arrangements.[11] Even when the Soviet Union itself was involved in the export of commodities in which multinational capital predominated such as petroleum and aluminium, it rarely, if ever, challenged the rules of the market. In aluminium it coordinated its sales with that of the Western leaders; in oil it carefully shaved its prices, reducing them only enough to secure the necessary market penetration.[12]

It was no wonder then that Eastern Europe spent the period up to 1973 urging the developing nations to take greater control over their own resources. At the 21st Session of the UN General Assembly (1966), the Polish delegation played a leading role in drafting the resolution on 'Permanent sovereignty over natural resources' which enshrined the right of all developing countries to own, fully or partly, all companies operated by foreign capital. Six years later the resolution was revived in a motion adopted at the fourth meeting of the non-aligned countries in Algiers which provided the ultimate rationale for the OPEC embargo of 1973:

> The efforts undertaken or intensified by (the Third World) are evidence of a deep movement, . . . which indisputably contains the seeds of a complete overthrow of the marketing system for the natural resources of the poor countries.[13]

Nevertheless, the realisation that the Soviet Union could no longer be relied upon to meet its material requirements in the 1980s, appears to have had less immediate impact on Eastern Europe than the measures which the CMEA itself adopted to meet the crisis. In 1972, the Plan for Multilateral Integration required the East Europeans to bear the costs of further exploration in the Soviet Union. Three years later the Council pegged commodities at the prevailing market price once a year instead of every five. The following July, every member was obliged to increase its contribution to the General Investment Fund, with the exception of the Soviet Union and Cuba, its only net recipients.

Nineteen seventy two was a crucial year, for after it the East Europeans moved with great speed to develop Africa's resources. For, with all the variations which a more detailed account would highlight, two facts became incontrovertibly clear. First, on the advice of the Soviet Union in the 1960s, many countries had already signed formal protocols with mineral rich African states which largely lay dormant until the mid-1970s. Secondly, the main incentive for taking up these agreements in earnest arose from the increasingly exacting demands that the CMEA had begun to make of its own members. In some cases the Council's pricing mechanism had added 15 per cent more to the cost of raw materials than the price they would have reached on the open market. As a result, the disproportionate price differentials between manufactured goods and the raw materials for which they were exchanged had made the terms of barter exchange extremely unattractive.[14]

It is worth, perhaps, citing two examples in some detail to illustrate how raw material imports began to play an ever increasing role in Eastern Europe's trade with Africa.

Bulgaria

In the 1960s, most Bulgarian technical assistance agreements had taken the form of contracts for civil engineering, or medical assistance – service contracts which earned Sofia hard currency and yet called for a few extended lines of credit. By the mid-1970s the pattern had changed as geologists went out by the score to Congo-Brazzaville, Mauritania and Somalia. Sofia even set up a special state enterprise – Bulgargeomin – to coordinate mining operations in the developing world.

If Bulgaria's trade with Africa was not entirely negligible in the 1960s, its demands and operations had been quite limited. Indeed, trade with Ghana and Mali was actually discontinued for no less than a decade after the fall of Keita and Nkrumah. Sofia eventually concluded its first treaty of economic cooperation, not with the three 'progressive states' of West Africa – Guinea, Ghana and Mali – but with Angola and Mozambique which both became independent after 15 years of struggle against the Portuguese.

The case against Bulgaria is especially illuminating in the light of the new spate of joint economic commissions (one of the hallmarks of trade between Third World states and European centrally planned economies). In several cases, the commissions were not established until interest in exploiting the resources of the countries concerned had first taken root; often several years after trade and cooperation agreements had been concluded: four years in the case of Congo–Brazzaville (November 1970–August 1974); 13 in that of Ethiopia (September 1964–March 1978) and 17 in that of Ghana (October 1961–November 1978). Obviously, in Ethiopia Sofia had a vested interest in underwriting a Marxist–Leninist regime; in that respect, the decision to set up a commission can be explained as the result of deliberate political calculation. Indeed, joint commissions with Angola and Mozambique followed only upon the signing of trade and cooperation agreements with both countries. And it was not long before Bulgargeomin began operating in Mozambique, most notably in 1981 when it took over the operation of a new phosphate mine at Kindonakasi which had an annual production capacity of 15 000 tons.[15]

But the same explanation can hardly be applied to Ghana during Nkrumah's ill conceived experiment in socialism, or to Congo-Brazzaville during Marie Ngouabi's brief flirtation with

Marxism–Leninism in the mid-1970s. Neither country rated very highly until the CMEA began making demands on Bulgaria's capital resources. Sofia did not even consider it worthwhile signing a trade and cooperation agreement with mineral-rich Zambia until November 1977, the very month that it also set up a bilateral commission.

Romania

Even today Bulgaria only registers commercial transactions with two countries in sub-Saharan Africa – its volume of trade with the rest being too marginal to merit specific mention. So far Romania has seen fit to publish data for only eight African countries despite the fact that it trades with the continent more extensively than any other East European country. In this respect, the similarities with Bulgaria are no less illuminating than the contrasts.

Once again the volume of imports is far less important than the time that elapsed between the signing of the initial protocols and the subsequent decision to follow them up. Its cooperation agreement with Gabon, concluded in 1972 – the year the Soviet Union issued its warning about future shortages of supply – lay dormant for seven years until the production of a long term forecast of uranium requirements pushed it into negotiating an agreement to import 150 000 tons a year with delivery commencing in 1986.

In other words, Romania like most other East European countries turned to Africa when energy shortages began to figure in central planning. Having evinced little interest in the visit of Kenya's Minister of Natural Resources in June 1972, the Romanians decided to re-open negotiations two years later, which ended in the signing of a formal protocol between the two countries in September 1975. The fact that Bucharest rekindled interest after the Africans had lost interest themselves is a central reality most analysts tend to omit from their explanations of East European behaviour.

The Romanians did not allow ideological affinities to stand in their way. As Angola's Minister of National Planning discovered during a visit to Bucharest in 1978, Ceausescu was much less interested in funding the country's agro-industrial development than in exploiting its offshore reserves of oil. Since Romania had been the most outspoken advocate of diversifying energy imports to escape exclusive reliance on CMEA's multilateral exchange arrangements, it is not surprising that it became the first CMEA country to import crude oil from Africa (in this case Gabon) in June 1978.

Apart from oil, Romania signed an agreement two years later to purchase 3m tonnes of iron ore from the Belinga deposits. Through its own mineral import-export company it held 5 per cent of the shares in the company *Societe des Mines de Fer de Mekambo* (Sonifer) and began importing 150 000 tonnes of manganese per annum (7 per cent of production).

CMEA SHORTAGES

By the end of the 1970s a new problem had begun to tax the East Europeans which, in its implications, was far more serious than the increase of prices within the CMEA. The Soviet bloc had to face the prospect that only iron ore and natural gas would increase their share in the world output while most other commodities including copper, bauxite and phosphates were likely to experience a significant fall. In the case of coal, for example, the share of the European CMEA countries (principally Poland and the USSR) in world exports was expected to fall by 12 per cent by the end of the century.

TABLE 2: *Capital stock used in resource extraction as a % of total capital stock*

	1970	1980	1990	2000
Developed mkt economies	1.05	1.56	2.31	2.88
Centrally planned econs	2.45	5.37	5.36	6.63
Developing countries	3.67	5.02	4.69	8.36

SOURCE: W Leontif (et al) *The Future of the World Economy: a UN Study* (Oxford University Press: 1977) p. 48

Investment in mineral industries in the CMEA has been much higher than investment in the developing world (which has been mostly the recipient of Western finance capital). But this concentration of capital in the CMEA has fuelled a substantial rise in real costs as the frontiers of expansion have shifted at an accelerated pace to marginal fields. The CMEA is now faced with the real possibility, not of short term shortages of the kind which confront the Western economies as a result of cyclical factors – whether unexpected international crises or protracted strikes – but of long term supply shortages arising from a structural deficit, a problem which is much more difficult to live with. In the past, the CMEA has experienced shortages of a number of important commodities, most notably aluminium and coking coal, despite an oversupply on the world market. The increased difficulty of obtaining supplies within the socialist community, coupled with limited hard currency purchasing power in world markets looks set to create a sustained regional disequilibrium between demand and supply.[16]

Even the existing supply of minerals is beginning to prove, if not prohibitively expensive, more expensive than ever. The Soviet Union continues to sell its CMEA partner's natural resources at a much higher price than it sells manufactured goods: the export prices of raw materials between 1975–77 rose at a faster rate than the export prices of machinery and consumer goods.[17] Indeed, the rise in the price of fuels imported by Eastern Europe, relative to the price of East European manufactured goods exported to the Soviet Union, will probably continue to rise until the mid-1980s as the intra-CMEA price setting formula begins to reflect the near trebling of world energy prices between 1979–81.[18]

It is perfectly fair to point out that the expansion of trade with Africa since 1972 has not proved quite the solution to its energy and raw material problems that Eastern Europe originally hoped. Although Romania's trade with the developing world amounts to 28 per cent of its foreign trade, the highest percentage of all CMEA members and second only to that of the Soviet Union in value, its economic penetration has already run into serious difficulties. Ceausescu even disclosed in 1978 that some of his advisers had urged him to reduce trade with the Third World since there was no real prospect of marrying Romania's planning with that of its African trading partners.[19]

It is one matter, however, to explain why the Romanians have begun to despair of ever improving the planning of Third World countries, quite another to postulate that they will be able to rely more than they do at present on exchange mechanisms within the socialist bloc. While it is true, for example, that Romania's present Five Year Plan (1981–85) calls for a greater expansion of trade within the CMEA as a way of escaping market instability outside it, this objective is intended to be reached at the expense of trade with the West, not with the developing world. Trade with the latter will probably remain for the forseeable future at 30 per cent.[20]

For better or worse, Romania will have no alternative but to exploit the contacts it has established since 1972, not least because the supply of raw materials from the Soviet Union is beginning to enter a period of crisis. Some of the most recent CIA reports paint a gloomy picture of raw material deficits over the next 10–20 years, particularly in the lead and zinc industries.[21] Even the Soviet Union has been forced to enter into several long term agreements with African countries, doubling its imports of bauxite and alumina in 1977, with the result that it now depends on foreign alumina for half its requirements.[22]

It is in the field of non-ferrous metals, however, that the Soviet Union's own deficiencies may well prove most telling. These industries have performed lamentably in the past few years because of delays in plant modernisation, increasing labour shortages and critical transportation problems. The slow development of advanced methods of mining, smelting and metal rolling have added to the problem.[23] There is certainly no guarantee that any of these factors will have been successfully resolved by the end of the present Five Year Plan (1985).

It is true, that import dependence so far exists only for bauxite and aluminium, tin, antimony, tungsten, barium and molybdenum,[24] but there is already evidence that this situation, far from remaining static, is getting considerably worse. Imports of titanium and vandium are increasing; the costs of mining ore have in some cases overtaken the costs of importing it.[25] Also significant may be the relatively low levels of Soviet manganese reserves and the progressive exhaustion of higher grade ores, as well as an apparent decline in exports of chromite (from 1.20m tons in 1970 to 0.74m in 1978). The fact that exports to the CMEA increased from 0.22m to 0.39m tons in the same period should not be allowed to detract from the seriousness of the situation: that only by reducing and, in some cases, terminating the supply of minerals to its CMEA partners will the Soviet Union be able to remain self-sufficient in certain basic raw materials into the 1990s and beyond.[26] And there can be no doubt that self-sufficiency will remain, for the forseeable future, a major objective of Soviet policy.

The impact of the quest for self-sufficiency on its export decisions may well be profound. Soviet self-sufficiency in aluminium is a possibility, though not a certainty, in the event of a termination of all exports, including those to Eastern Europe. Indeed, in 1980 it halted the shipment of all primary aluminium to the West. Whether the Soviet Union moves clearly into the independent or dependent area will largely depend on consumption decisions in the future. If, for example, the military use of titanium continues to grow, the recent high level of demand for aluminium by the Soviet military may decrease.

Similarly, while the USSR clearly remains quantitatively self-sufficient in chromite, it must be stressed that the quality of ore has fallen precipitously, as has the percentage of total production which it has exported. The Soviet Union's rapid downturn as a primary international source for chromite, has been matched by a rapid upturn in its interest in foreign chromite including imports from Rhodesia long before the creation of the Zimbabwean state. In the late 1970s, the Russians turned on at least two occasions to African sources of cobalt, buying 2000 tonnes in 1980 from Zaire and Zambia. While it is not clear how much was stockpiled and how much consumed, Soviet requirements cannot keep pace with production. The substitution of nickel for cobalt is possible in some areas, but not in high technology areas such as jet engines. With the continuing military buildup it is likely that cobalt demands will stay at present levels if nothing else.

These examples could be multiplied. Shortages of raw materials including iron ore have on several occasions forced Soviet blast furnaces to work well below capacity.[27] With these and other ore problems it is not surprising that the Soviet Union fell several million tonnes short of the original Tenth Five Year Plan target. Investment in lead processing plants has also lagged behind schedule, a complication which prevented the Soviet lead industry from attaining its annual quota.[28] But it is the manganese industry which has suffered most of all. High grade manganese exports to the West were for all practical purposes terminated in 1977; although even as early as 1975 86 per cent of all Soviet manganese exports were sold to Eastern Europe.[29] The Soviet manganese industry may consequently be in a critical position. If domestic production is to increase, large new deposits must almost certainly come into line. To date, there are few indications that the Soviet Union has located such sources much less brought them into production. As one authority writes:

> Soviet estimates maintain that planned rates of production will deplete known reserves within 30 years, but given current production problems it is likely that the targets will not often be met. Indeed, in 1979 production fell 5 per cent short of target. It may then be safe to conclude that the USSR may either curtail its manganese exports to Eastern Europe, or itself become an importer of what has hitherto been regarded as a mineral in more than adequate domestic supply.[30]

But what of those minerals which are not likely to run short, where demand within the CMEA will probably grow faster than in the free market? Joint investment in projects such as the iron ore mines in Dneprovsk, Mikhailovsk and Stoilensk; the Kingiesepp phosphorous mining plant and seven different ferro-alloy plants dispersed throughout the Soviet Union offer a chance for Eastern Europe to ensure itself a continued and secure source of basic raw materials while offsetting the infrastructure costs of extraction and transportation. Joint ventures involving deliveries of machinery and equipment in return for the repayment of products at a later date, together with the transfer of capital through the Common Production Fund, may help offset the increased prices which the Soviet Union has charged since the mid-1970s. As Alan Smith has written of energy costs:

> World oil price changes accelerated this process by giving the East European countries a greater interest in cooperation in joint investment projects, but simultaneously gave the USSR the wherewithal to alter prices to effect resource transfers without destroying Eastern Europe's economic interest in the projects.[31]

Unfortunately, neither Eastern Europe, nor the Soviet Union have the resources to develop the minerals both of them need. Investment in the Soviet Union is not being generated fast enough[32] which explains its continuing interest in Western finance. The Soviet Union cannot meet the costs on its own. The steep rise in marginal production costs require an offsetting need for development capital at a time of modest increase in national income. It cannot expect much assistance either, from its CMEA partners. At a time when the intra-CMEA terms of trade have changed in its favour, it has had to provide more credits to net resource importing countries. Unfortunately the CMEA's Long Term Material and Energy Programme was drawn up in 1978 in a one-sided demand approach which took insufficient account of Eastern Europe's financial resources.

Even if this were not the case, joint investment schemes would still be extremely unpopular with most East European planners. All but a few of the projects are located in the Soviet Union. Most East Europeans have no particular wish to see Soviet control extended over their own economies, with a corresponding reduction in any future leverage in their trade negotiations with the Russians. The investment remains in the ownership of the country in which it is situated, with very little joint participation in ownership or management.[33] A country like Czechoslovakia would rather invest capital in modernising its own industry, partly because it has not been able to meet its existing planning targets as a result of too little capital investment in new plant and equipment. It has even been forced to reduce energy imports from the Soviet Union. This may not be a vicious circle, but it is obviously a situation which has severely limited Czechoslovakia's economic options.

Moreover, when many joint ventures were originally set up, very little attention was paid to the respective opportunity costs for each partner. Quite often the East Europeans were not even told the prices that were to be used to calculate the costs of each project, or the value of output which would be used to repay the credits which had financed them.[34] Often the participating countries had to buy equipment from the West and to divert some of their hard currency resources to borrow on the international money market at high rates of interest. The gap is increasingly widening between rates on the international market and the usual rates available to CMEA countries.[35] This largely explains why investment has been so low. The energy programmes in 1976–80 absorbed only 4 per cent of all productive investment in Hungary; 3 per cent in the GDR; 2.9 per cent in Bulgaria and only 2.4 per cent in Poland.[36] Nor is it particularly surprising that the number

TABLE 3: *Tonnage and value forecast for 1990 for commodity imports by European CMEA countries from the developing world*

Commodity	Quantity ($m)		Price ($/ton) 1977	Volume ($(1977)/ton)	
	Variant 1	Variant 2		Variant 1	Variant 2
Petroleum	80–100	65–70	265	21 200–26 000	17 200–18 500
Copper	100	80	2300	230	180
Bauxite	4–6	3.5–4.0	33.9	130–200	115–30
Iron Ore	30–40	25–30	25.0	750–1000	625–750
Phosphate Rock	15–20	15–20	38.0	520–700	520–700

Variant 1 = unsuccessful demand limitation policy
Variant 2 = successful demand limitation policy

SOURCE: *Economic relations between the European CMEA countries and the developing countries and their role in development* (UNITAR Research Project: Budapest 1980) p. 91

of new projects adopted in the following Five Year Plan (1981–85) was considerably smaller than the previous one.

The country which invested most in these joint ventures has been the most outspoken critic of CMEA cooperation.[37] The direct dollar content of joint investment projects by Hungary amounted to 54 per cent of the total, an astonishingly high proportion.[38] Even at the time, Hungarian economists complained that the production of uneconomical but local (and therefore 'secure') raw material sources had limited the scope of real growth. One senior member of the Institute for World Economy in Budapest contended that although there was no absolute shortage of raw materials within the CMEA, the feasibility of their extraction was remote. The possibility of increased cooperation could only be turned into a reality by implementing the same economic reforms which had been broached in the mid-1960s but never carried out. In the absence of more efficient planning he did not believe that the CMEA could justify massive new expenditure on the development of Soviet resources.[39] By the late 1970s, many of his colleagues were openly talking of 'reverse import substitution' whereby Eastern Europe

TABLE 4: *Estimated value of invested capital, assets and turnover in CMEA companies in the developing world 1978 ($m)*

Principal activity	Invested Capital	Fixed Assets	Total Assets of companies	Turnover
Marketing	10.8	29.7		256.8
Manufacturing	36.0	202.5		472.4
Resource Develop	172.8	3576.4		
Financial Services	13.2	0.9	671.0	
Transport Services	28.8	62.0		
Other Services	8.8	30.8		
Total	270.4	3902.3		

SOURCE: *East–West Project* (Institute of Soviet and East European Studies, Carleton University, Ottawa 1979)

could obtain from outside the socialist community, primary commodities which it had previously obtained from within it. For better or worse Hungary in company with the other East European states has been forced to look to Southern Africa.

8 The Warsaw Pact and Southern Africa, 1974–83

Political events in Southern Africa after 1974 were crucial in shaping East European perceptions of the prospects for importing raw materials. Trade within the CMEA itself had failed to expand up till then, largely because of deficiencies of central planning. The East Europeans now hoped to apply the lessons they had learned in trading with each other to the not dissimilar problems they had begun to encounter in trading with the developing world.

In November 1976, as Dr Kissinger embarked on the second round of shuttle diplomacy in Rhodesia, a conference of economists and African specialists convened in Budapest to discuss the new options open to them. Although several questions were left unresolved one met with general agreement. As one of the transcripts of the proceedings made clear:

> It was decided that it should be proposed to the government organisations responsible for international economic relations and also to the Secretariat of CMEA that economic relations with developing countries, including the drawing up of joint agreements, should be coordinated more precisely. The participants considered it to be expedient to expand the relevant part of the CMEA's Comprehensive Programme ... to lay down general outlines of their common principles; to itemise programmes for individual developing countries; to elucidate the special interests of the different socialist countries; and to outline the system of implementation of the detailed programme.[1]

Two themes in this thinking should be clearly distinguished – first, the interest in joint planning and economic cooperation which went beyond, but also took account of multilateral forecasting, came at a time when the issue was already under discussion in the CMEA. In coordinating their respective national plans for 1981–85 with the Long Term Cooperation Programme in the Fuel, Power and Material Industries which had been adopted to discuss the possibility of bringing the developing world directly into their own central planning.[2]

When Budapest came to draft its Five Year Plan for 1977–81 the economic planners were instructed to take into account, where possible, the central planning of countries in the developing world and to assist the countries concerned to implement their own plans. In fact, only after radical improvement could they ever be coordinated with those of the European centrally planned economies.[3]

Several East European countries have assisted Algeria, Libya and Guinea-Bissau in drafting their respective Five Year Plans – notably East Germany which reached agreement with Algeria in 1978 on an exchange of information between their planning bodies. The GDR hoped that in these circumstances its trading partners in Africa would be able to take into account its own energy needs before drawing up their own production targets. For its part the Council would be able to 'schedule purchases several years in advance in keeping with plans for the development of the national economy'.[4]

This brings us to the second theme. In each case socialist thinking has honed the prism through which Eastern Europe looks at the world. Despite differences in interest and focus, the East Europeans share a remarkable identity of views about the nature of the international economy and the dilemmas and challenges which have arisen from their own participation. Nothing has been more disconcerting for them than the fact that they have had to trade with countries in which central planning is, at best, inefficient, at worst non-existent. The Polish economist Jerzy Prokopcnk is not alone in his opinion that countries such as his own have only profited from foreign trade when it has been conducted with countries of socialist orientation, 'progressive', if not fully fledged Marxist–Leninist states, who have already taken 'decisive steps to radically change their international economic relations by introducing a new economic order'.[5]

Until 1974, the East Europeans laboured under two separate constraints. In the first instance, extensive economic relations with most African states were inconceivable until substantial changes had taken place in planning. In the second instance, until the political systems had also changed, radical improvements in planning were not to be expected. As a Hungarian economist noted in 1976, for the moment 'neither were on the socialist agenda'.[6]

What changed, of course, after 1974 was the apparently 'authentic' Marxism–Leninism of Angola and Mozambique, and later Ethiopia and Benin. This development was, of course, welcomed by countries such as East Germany which had invested much money and effort in supporting national liberation movements in the 1960s in the hope of gaining preferential access to the resources of Southern Africa.[7]

After 1974 every East European country, with the single exception of Czechoslovakia, concluded inter-party agreements with FRELIMO and the MPLA. Their willingness to sign treaties of friendship and cooperation did not, in fact, mark a departure from the practice of concluding them only with socialist parties. In the same year that Sofia put its signature to a treaty of cooperation with Angola (the first it had entered into with any African country), it also played host to delegations from all but one of the continent's Marxist–Leninist states: from the Ministry of Agriculture in Angola; the Politburo of the People's Party of Benin; the Provisional Military Council of Ethiopia; and the Ministry of National Planning from Mozambique.

It soon became clear, however, that although the East Europeans were agreed on the advantage which they had gained with the success of Marxism–Leninism in Southern Africa, they agreed on little else. The Soviet Union hoped that the MNCs in Angola and Mozambique would be brought under 'proper state regulation and political guidance';[8] most other CMEA members recognised that their contribution was still important, possibly critical to the development of the countries concerned.

The East Germans, like the Russians, often seem more inclined to compete with the West, rather than cooperate with it. East Germany's contribution to the debate on foreign trade contains several recurrent themes which accurately reflect the extensive support it has given the Soviet Union in Southern Africa. In the early 1970s, its ability to supply the Russians with high precision instruments otherwise available only in the West enabled it to meet the cost of importing nearly all its energy resources other than oil.[9] When the price of these commodities rose sharply, Berlin managed to escape relatively lightly by playing a leading role in Soviet policy in Africa.[10] The service which the East Germans have rendered Angola and the role they have played in coordinating Warsaw Pact policy as a whole (a theme to which we shall return in the next chapter) reflects the importance they attach to preserving a preferential relationship with Southern Africa's more radical states.

Given its awareness of the broader political dimensions of Marxism–Leninism in the region, it is not altogether surprising that the GDR has consistently condemned non-barter trade as incompatible with socialism;[11] criticised Hungary for questioning 'the advantages of economic cooperation with third world socialist countries';[12] and remained steadfast in the support it has given the CMEA Secretariat in coordinating the planning of socialist states even to the extent of arguing that Mozambique should be made a member.

Exactly what it hoped to gain from Mozambique's membership of the CMEA is in part a matter of academic speculation. The clue seems to lie, however, in its own energy requirements. Although 70 per cent of the GDR's total primary energy needs are covered by domestic sources of brown coal, the cost of developing and mining this particular energy source rose at least 50 per cent between 1973–78.[13] The environmental costs of mining brown coal also became more burdensome in the 1970s as development was increasingly concentrated on four centres, Cottbus, Halle, Leipzig and Dresden. This may have been one reason why East Germany has shown greater unity of purpose and consistency of interest in Mozambique than anywhere else in Southern Africa.

Although the country's coal mining industry, for example, was one of the first sectors of the economy earmarked for nationalisation, the East Germans persuaded Machel, President of Mozambique, to leave the Moatize fields in private hands until they had time to train their own technicians so that they could take over the management themselves. With 700m tons of reserves, Moatize was of obvious interest to a country which had placed an increase in energy production at the very centre of its 1981–85 Plan and which attached particular significance to boosting coal imports. The fields were eventually nationalised in April 1978 following the visit of Klaus Siebold, the East German Minister of Mines.

During the visit of the Economics Minister, Gunter Mittage

ten months later, a whole range of other mining ventures were also discussed, in some of which the Germans expressed an interest in participating; and in others – such as the Marita copper mines – of taking over direct control. These programmes have broadened in scope in recent years – in September 1982 the GDR joined the Soviet Union in a tripartite agreement on coal and tantalite exploration.[14]

But perhaps, the most trenchant illustration of the advantages the GDR gained from the revolution in Mozambique is provided by the story of Lonhro's Edmundian mine. Lonhro originally set up operations in 1976 with the intention of reinvesting the profits recouped from the pilot scheme. These plans were abruptly scotched when the government insisted that its employees would have to be paid the national minimum wage, notwithstanding the fact that like most other mining companies, Lonhro provided housing and other facilities at its own expense. To escape operating at a loss, the management pulled out.

When the East Germans were asked to take over the management by the National Planning Ministry, they immediately undertook an exhaustive investigation into the reasons for the mine's financial losses. On determining that administrative overheads and labour costs were disproportionately high, they promptly cut wages below the national minimum. In an ambience less self-evidently Marxist, the case might well have generated discussion about the extent and implications of the close working relations between Berlin and Marcelino dos Santos' Ministry of Planning. Instead, it was written off as one of the many difficulties of trading in a socialist country, similar in many respects to the problems Lonhro had already encountered in neighbouring Tanzania.

In view of these genuine economic interests, it would not be surprising to find the Warsaw Pact every bit as concerned about events in Southern Africa as NATO itself, though for different reasons.

SOUTHERN AFRICA: THE LOOKING GLASS WORLD

The proposition that the Soviet Union intends to deny the West access to Southern Africa's resources and interdict its shipping at the Cape is not self-evident merely because the case is so persistently argued. The real threat may come from quite a different quarter: genuine commercial competition from Eastern Europe. As long as Southern Africa remained a Western sphere of influence, resource denial was largely a matter of strategy, not economics. Now that both sides have begun to rely on the same market for supplies, economic competition has become more direct and potentially more disruptive both in terms of its impact on regional stability and its implications for superpower relations.

Political leaders in the West often exaggerate the Soviet Union's freedom of manoeuvre, or see no reason to emphasise the constraints within which it is often forced to act. Obviously, as the most important member of the Warsaw Pact, the Soviet Union largely articulates its aims and defines its interests. That much is not in dispute. Yet, it must be asked whether we place too much emphasis on Soviet strategic interests and too little on the commercial interests of its allies. In their preoccupation with the Soviet threat, many Western analysts either overlook the East European dimension entirely, or dismiss it as unimportant, or dismiss the East Europeans themselves as surrogates of the Soviet Union.

The Cape route

Ever since the Soviet Navy appeared in the Indian Ocean in 1968, the West has been preoccupied by the threat to the sea routes around the coast of Africa, particularly the Cape. Every year 30 000 ships, some 1500 of them tankers, travel the sea routes which are so important to the economy of the West – through the Indian Ocean, through the Suez Canal and Bab-el-Mandeb Strait, around the Cape of Good Hope and on through the Straits of Malacca. On average two tankers pass through the Straits of Hormuz every hour; 40 ships a day pass through the channel between Mozambique and Madagascar. Oil is the most valuable commodity transported; minerals the second. In the late 1970s, by far the greatest proportion of the region's trade was with Western Europe (33 per cent) well ahead of Japan (19 per cent) and the United States (13 per cent). By comparison, the percentage of trade with Eastern Europe and the Soviet Union seems very small (5 per cent).[15] In these circumstances the Soviet

Union might well be able to interdict shipping without risk to its own. Its own internal lines of communication, for the most part, lie overland while those of the West extend across thousands of miles of ocean, through narrow seas adjacent to areas of endemic instability.

This has always been a distorted picture, however, one which took almost no account of Soviet or East European trade. In its strategic planning, the Soviet Union may take much less note of its allies' interests than the United States takes of those of Western Europe, but it is in no position to ignore them entirely. In a much quoted article in *New Times*, Dmitry Volsky found himself asking whether the strategy of interdiction had a future:

> There is, of course, no denying the importance of these routes to the West. It is by these routes that the capitalist world gets a large part of its oil, . . . but these routes are also vitally important for the developing countries . . . which depend on imports of manufactured goods and equipment from Eastern Europe.[16]

In a subsequent article, he went on to point out that the Cape route also carried a substantial percentage of East European trade which was at constant risk of interdiction from the West.[17] NATO may fear an attack along the Cape route, but the Warsaw Pact faces a threat at the Cape itself – it has no doubt as to whose side South Africa will align itself in the event of war.

The closure of the Suez Canal posed a major problem for all the CMEA nations, but in particular for the Soviet Union. The distance from the Black Sea to the Indian Ocean was 9000 miles round the Cape; but only 3000 for the shipping which used Suez. The Soviet Union's main line of supply to Hanoi during the Vietnam war ran from Odessa to Haiphong, a distance of well over 7000 miles. The trip took anything up to a month using its largest and fastest cargo ships of the Belitsk class. On average 47 ships reached North Vietnam every month.

After the closure of the Canal in 1967, the supply route was extended to more than 14 000 miles; a round trip now required nearly five months and the number of ships arriving at Haiphong fell to an average of 25 a month.[18] Looked at in this light, it is possible to understand why the Soviet Union is as much concerned with events in the Middle East and the Horn of Africa as the Western powers.

Far from promoting offensive designs in the region, the Soviet Union is only too aware of the need to defend its own shipping as well as that of its allies. The Soviet Navy, of course, has many missions but it is worth remembering that Admiral Gorshkov lists the protection of 'state interests' as the first of its peacetime roles. While it is unlikely that threats to the shipping lanes or shipping lines will in themselves determine Soviet policy, both may well influence it.

Poland's shipping lines have been so competitive in East Africa that at one point in 1980 it looked as though the East African Shipping Line (EASL) might be forced out of business. There continues to be speculation that it may yet be forced into liquidation by the low freight rates of Polish shipping.[19]

Most maritime nations have attempted to regulate freight rates by joining appropriate conferences for the major trade routes. Soviet shipping in East African waters is so lucrative that the Russians have not been very enthusiastic to join the North Western Europe–East African Conference, or to accept conference rate structures – unless it is on their own terms. They have made known they would only be prepared to join if they were to be given 24 of the originally planned 55 sailings from Hamburg. They found themselves in a particularly strong position in the period 1982–83 having launched no fewer than 31 sailings on the East African route in 18 months.[20] Even in 1977, the Soviet maritime fleet (Morflot) carried 10 per cent of Europe's East Africa trade.[21] That percentage has continued to rise ever since.

In West Africa where the Soviet Union operates a shipping line jointly with Poland and the GDR, its interests are even greater.[22] It is interesting that the Soviet Navy has shown especial interest in the waters off Cape Verde where up to 18 per cent of its merchant shipping is to be found at any one time.[23] It is also important to recognise that West Africa is one of its major fishing grounds, and that the Soviet fishing industry supplies no less than 9 per cent of all food output. The importance of fisheries to the food industry and the large domestic requirements for fishery products require the Soviet Union to have direct access to stocks, 64 per cent of which happen to be located off the coastal areas of developing countries, including West Africa where the Russians have negotiated bilateral agreements with a score of African countries including Sierra Leone, Guinea-Bissau and the Gambia.[24]

To some extent these patterns also apply to the Soviet Union's allies, most importantly Poland. West Africa offers Poland its largest area of operations in the developing world both for its dry bulk and general cargo carriers; and a look at Table 5 (p. 171) will bear out that it is also a not unimportant route for raw materials and liquid fuel.

But above all, of course, it is the presence of the Soviet merchant fleet which is crucial to any understanding of Moscow's own pre-occupation with the safety of its shipping and the security of its own trade routes. During the post war years, the merchant fleet grew from a modest, mainly coastal enterprise to numerically the world's largest fleet. In terms of tonnage since 1960, it has risen in world rank from fourteenth to sixth, increasing its volume six-fold in the process. Ninety per cent of its ships are less than 20 years old. Today, Morflot has 60 commercial lines and trades with more than 120 countries. In 1982, the Soviet Union added more tonnage to its merchant fleet than any other of the top ten maritime states except Panama. As of April 1983 it had 107 dry cargo ships on order, nearly twice as many as any other country, and 22 container ships, the fourth highest total.[25]

All in all, Morflot carries 50 per cent of Soviet trade, substantially more cargo from freight owners of non Russian origins, and earns more foreign currency than any other operation after the export of oil and arms. Given the scope of these operations, it would be surprising if the Soviet Union were not anxious about the security of its shipping. Its concerns are no less real than the West's; indeed, in some respects they may be greater. It should always be remembered that its merchant fleet constitutes the third most important element in the international network for the movement of raw materials, complementing its rail and pipe line systems, and that the fleet has helped reduce its hard currency trade deficits with the West. In 1966, for example, Morflot's earnings covered 45 per cent of its deficit on commodity earnings.[26] That figure is probably much higher today.

Yet, it is in the area of fuels and raw materials that Morflot's future role is likely to prove most intriguing, paralleling as it must Western patterns and preoccupations. At present, the Russians are increasing their tanker fleet to supplement or replace their existing vessels with those of the new Marshal Vasilievski class

TABLE 5: *Polish seaborne foreign trade by area and major commodity groups 1980 – in tons*

Area	Total	Ores	Fertilisers & raw materials	Liquid fuels	Grain	Rolled goods
IMPORTS						
Baltic	1 533 560	1 071 637	–	–	135 876	5 010
Western Europe	4 170 174	831 798	–	7 147	2 490 965	117 879
Mediterranean	213 295	42 294	–	–	–	7 560
Black Sea	305 085	–	–	301 074	–	–
Barents Sea	1 524 541	720 358	728 300	–	–	–
North Africa	1 589 814	–	1 207 704	339 279	–	–
West Africa	455 058	68 723	109 690	129 500	–	–
East Africa	9 419	–	–	–	–	–
Asia	3 497 631	607 567	295 974	1 887 083	204 657	23 176
North America	5 888 656	–	876 088	–	4 910 143	575
Central America	157 401	10 067	–	–	–	–
South America	3 866 532	2 747 295	–	–	818 850	–
Australia and Oceania	98 842	–	–	–	33 505	–
Antarctic	38	–	–	–	–	–
TOTAL	23 310 046	6 099 739	3 215 756	2 664 083	8 593 996	154 201

Area	Total	Coal and coke	Sulphur	Liquid fuels	Cement	Rolled goods
EXPORTS						
Baltic	9 515 029	7 866 896	77 921	399 071	112 306	79 078
Western Europe	11 251 270	8 478 512	1 067 739	650 856	34 675	175 046
Mediterranean	2 757 706	2 376 395	318 520	–	–	32 461
Black Sea	145 567	–	145 059	–	–	–
Barents Sea	–	–	–	–	–	–
North Africa	593 924	–	319 337	–	–	44 241
West Africa	1 338 740	–	–	–	755 828	19 255
East Africa	20 229	–	–	–	–	8 221
Asia	1 704 569	492 014	60 945	–	321 414	360 005
North America	562 517	317 700	–	–	–	91 221
Central America	381 471	–	126 969	178 931	40 637	9 888
South America	1 097 678	961 350	33 181	–	–	18 438
Australia and Oceania	10 638	–	–	–	–	–
Antarctic	136	–	–	–	–	–
TOTAL	29 379 474	20 492 867	2 149 671	1 228 858	1 264 860	837 854

SOURCE: *Shipping Statistics Yearbook 1981* (Bremen: Institute of Shipping Economics 1981) p. 121

with a capacity of 65 000 tons. The latter may play an important part in carrying supplies of Middle East oil and African minerals to their East European allies.[27] In this light, it is difficult to objectively evaluate who represents the greater threat to the other: NATO or the Warsaw Pact.

Denial of minerals

The West's second cause for concern is the competition for strategic minerals. It has become very much an *idée reçue* in recent years that the Soviet Union poses a threat to Western access to Southern Africa without which its economies would not survive for long. This is not a perspective shared by Eastern Europe, nor for that matter the Soviet Union.

In recent years, three themes whose accents are quite new have begun to emerge from the work of Soviet political analysts which were briefly touched upon in the past, but never fully developed. The first is that the West has begun to devise 'various subtle and often underhand means of retaining its neo-colonialist economic and political hold'.[28] Secondly, and more to the point, its reasons for doing so appear to differ significantly from those advanced by so many Soviet writers in the past:

> It should be noted that the imperialist monopolies are now making direct capital investments in oil and mining industries in Africa, not so much to make big profits . . . as to retain the possibility of importing from the continent fuel, ores and concentrates of non-ferrous metals . . . which they need very much.[29]

Thirdly, the East Europeans, as well as the Russians, have a fear of political instability in the region that almost mirrors that of the West in this curious looking-glass world. Their attempts to coordinate planning and to control, if not circumscribe the activities of the MNCs, represent an attempt to find an answer to the extraordinary volatility and discontinuity of political behaviour in so much of Africa, as well as to come to terms with the palpable gap between what so many African Marxists claim to believe and what they really stand for. As one East German writer recently conceded, political reverses are not even inconceivable in

Mozambique and Angola 'because of their weak social base, inconsistencies in thinking . . . and, not least of all, on account of the strong economic position and ideological influence over which imperialism continues to dispose'.[30]

The first theme was raised at the Budapest conference in 1976 which met in the wake of Dr Kissinger's first shuttle to Southern Africa. The cardinal aim of Western diplomacy, one observer later wrote, was to ensure that Africa did not escape from Western control. It was a policy, he argued, predicated upon 'preserving the positions of neo-colonialism, blocking the roads to non-capitalist development and ensuring Africa's pro-Western orientation in the international arena'.[31] To explain the Soviet threat to Western interests as essentially the product of the West's predominant position in the region may seem perverse, but at least this interpretation explains why the Warsaw Pact and not Cuba has been most active of late, and why the Pact has taken an increasing interest in African affairs at precisely the moment that the continent has begun to appear with greater frequency on NATO's security agenda.

From the perspective of the Warsaw Pact, Southern Africa is entirely at the mercy of international capital. Indeed, in its eyes the present threat from the West looks far more alarming than the putative Soviet threat appears to the West. Far from losing their influence the MNCs appear to have become more assertive than ever. The de-nationalisation of *Union Minière* in Zaire followed closely by the de-nationalisation of the phosphate companies in Mauritania in 1978 appears to give the lie to the claim that Africa has been in most respects independent since the early 1960s. Looked at from an East European perspective the system is still closed. As one Soviet commentator noted, the extent of British and French neo-colonial control explained why only 50 per cent and 40 per cent respectively, of new investment went in the new mining sectors; and why the non-colonial powers, the United States and West Germany, had invested 75 per cent of their capital in new ventures.[32]

Even the Russians are now acutely sensitive to the dilemma of Marxists whose countries are so closely tied to the capitalist economic order, and so severely circumscribed in what they can and cannot do, that they do not feel themselves to be fully sovereign. This was the despairing conclusion of Vassilev Solodnikov, the former ambassador to Zambia:

> A specific feature of the development of the socialist orientated countries in Africa is that even after their choice of the non-capitalist way, they are still in the orbit of the world capitalist economic system.[33]

These constant re-interpretations of African socialism, which date back to when Solodnikov was Director of the Africa Institute, represent somewhat forlorn attempts to draw some reassurance that history is on their side, and they themselves are in its van. Africa however, has in some respects changed very little since the mid-1960s. The pessimism which has set in in recent years is not the least significant aspect of their relations with the continent. In 1978 Hungary's Foreign Minister, Frigyes Puja, returned from a visit to Africa with the impression that the West's demand for minerals would continue to impede its chances for 'progressive development' for many years to come.[34]

The Warsaw Pact's second concern — that the competition for finite resources will grow even fiercer — is even more real. There is, in fact, a remarkable similarity in the composition of Africa's trade with the CMEA and the European Economic Community (EEC). Raw materials are exchanged for manufactured goods. Trade is largely concentrated on a few 'sub-imperial' states. African–CMEA relations are no closer to those of the New International Economic Order than those between Africa and the EEC. Both are compatible with the traditional picture of economic imperialism.[35]

The situation from the East European perspective, however, is particularly worrying for two reasons. First, the high oligopolistic pattern of the past — the high level of company concentration on the supply side — is increasing, not diminishing. In the 1960s fewer than ten companies were responsible for producing 60 per cent of the non-socialist world's output of all minerals. Nationalisation and state control may have reversed that trend, but it has done very little to reverse the trend of vertical integration. The quest for greater security of supply has produced two notable changes in the marketing of minerals: an increase in long term supply contracts (some of which are now 20 years in duration); and a declining share of free market sales in the trading of some major commodities. As one Hungarian economist has pointed out:

> Currently 75–80 per cent of international trade in non-fuel

minerals is transacted in 'closed' markets (within the framework of intra-company turnover and long term supply contracts). The proportion of free market trade in non-ferrous metals is only 10–15 per cent.[36]

Obviously, this closed market system is a threat to CMEA access.

It is a threat for three reasons, most of which have received remarkably little treatment by Western analysts. Eastern Europe, to begin with, is likely to find itself even more disadvantaged than in the past, by multinational corporations which command strong positions and substantial experience in key branches of the extractive industry. Closed markets obviously represent a threat to those countries outside the Western economic system, notably the GDR, which have already embarked on political initiatives to circumvent what they see to be the economic constraints imposed by the Western powers.

Secondly, Eastern Europe is likely to have to live with increasing political and economic risks if it too, enters into long term agreements of 20 years or more in duration. Even if it is able to negotiate secure access, like the West, it will still risk suffering the same economic dislocations with all their attendant political implications. This may mean it will have to take out political insurance as the West has done, another reason, perhaps the most trenchant, why the East European dimension of Soviet policy can no longer be ignored.

Finally, and perhaps the most serious of all, is that these are exactly the same concerns as Western governments, a fact which has not escaped the attention of East European economists.[37] The East Europeans too, need stable, long term contracts with major African producers. The consequences of instability for a country like the GDR were shown all too clearly in 1979 when after the cancellation of its contract with Iran, it experienced serious oil shortages which forced it to purchase oil on the very expensive Rotterdam spot market.[38] Unfortunately, their needs are precisely parallel to the requirements of all other nations dependent on the import of fuel or non-fuel minerals in hard currency puts them at a clear comparative disadvantage even with states such as East Germany with a relatively high level of technology.

On balance, many East European countries do not believe that the West will secure its position indefinitely, but they do maintain that the West's wish to retain its comparative advantage helps

TABLE 6: *The degree of oligopolistic firm concentration*

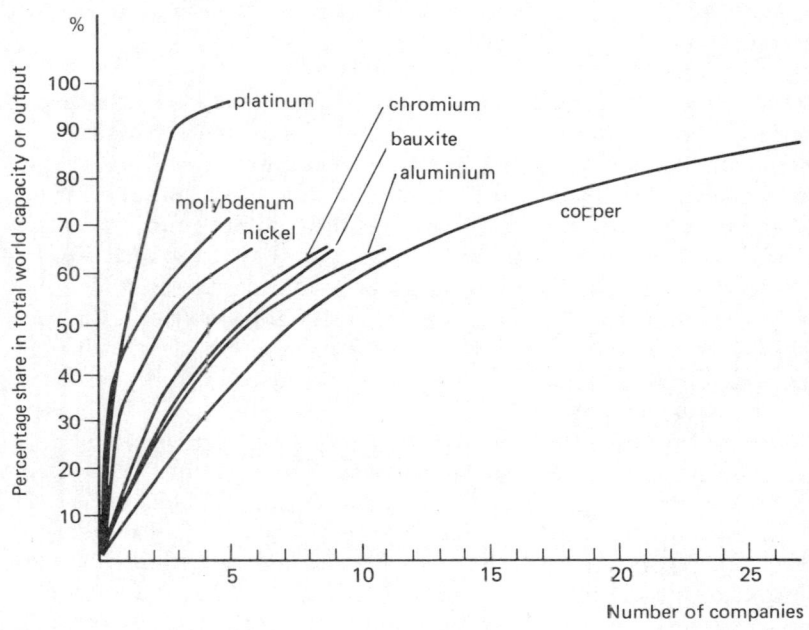

NOTE: Bauxite: output in 1976; aluminium: capacity in 1974; copper: refining capacity in 1974; chromium: mining capacity in 1974; nickel: metal output in 1976; molybdenum: mining capacity in 1974; platinum: metal capacity in 1974.

SOURCE: I Dobozi, 'Projected trends of World raw material and energy markets until 2000' *Studies on Developing Countries* No 110 (Budapest: Institute for World Economics: 1982) p. 19

explain the 'aggressive action' and 'imperialist interference' since 1976 – exemplified by Dr Kissinger's shuttle diplomacy and incidents such as the French parachute drop at Kolwezi. Soviet writers are constantly pointing out that NATO's dependence on one or another raw material resource has been used 'to justify the use of gunboat diplomacy or armed intervention';[39] that the loss of its privileged position in South Africa would be fatal to its interests; and that the West has a stake in 'condemning' Africa to a state of continuing stagnation in order to exploit its resources more ruthlessly than ever.[40]

It is no wonder that the Western threat is as potent in the East as the Soviet threat is in Western Europe. Many East European states genuinely fear that, should they ever be denied access to Southern Africa by military action, including action against Marxist–Leninist Angola and Mozambique, raw material shortages may prevent industry from meeting its targets. The future may hold out an unhappy prospect of reduced growth, rampant inflation and undue delays in planning with possible adverse consequences for consumer spending.

If we forget Soviet geopolitical goals, however, and look only to East European interests, the Soviet threat looks far less formidable. Eastern Europe needs to compete with the West, not to exclude it altogether. The price of doing so would be high; the returns, in all but a few cases, minimal. Apart from the willingness of the Africans themselves to fall in with such schemes there is much to be said for the Hungarian position: that Southern Africa's mineral wealth will only be successfully exploited if the MNCs are coopted, not controlled.

The East Europeans probably wish to assure themselves access as well. Because their real interests are essentially commercial rather than geopolitical, their sights are, in all probability, set much lower. Few think in terms of interdicting Western shipping at the Cape; fewer still of a second scramble for Africa's resources.

The third and final theme of recent East European writing, however, holds out little prospect of reaching agreement with the West. Indeed, it suggests that the Warsaw Pact may well turn to military solutions to deal with a problem which has taxed the Western powers as well; the problem of political instability. Its distrust of the West – and the extent to which it holds the West itself responsible for Africa's continuing political instability – is nowhere more in evidence than in political writings which try to make intelligible the endlessly changing pattern of political allegiances in the continent. Nowhere does socialist progress appear more uncertain, or more likely to meet with serious setbacks.[41]

It is hardly surprising, in these circumstances, that the Soviet bloc is not at all reassured by the self-professed Marxism of Mozambique's leadership. It is not at all sure it will not be coopted into the Western camp. The expansion of Western trading links has already highlighted the inefficiency of many East European managers. Within a few years of taking over the management of the Motaize coalfields, Maputo decided to dispense with the services of 60 East German technicians.[42] In Angola the failure of successive East European attempts to revive the country's ailing railway system prompted the government to ask the Portuguese back. Under East German management the port of Luanda became one of the most congested in the world. When invited back, the Portuguese harbour masters found only 1 per cent of its forklift trucks in operation. Within six months 40 per cent were in action.

The East Europeans cannot but be concerned that there are now more MNCs in Angola than there were before independence; and that foreign investment has been accorded a far more important role in Mozambique's future development than was the case in Portugal's Third (and last) National Plan (1968–73). The pessimism with which the East Europeans have begun to regard their economic interests since 1980 is not the least significant aspect of its relations with Southern Africa. It has served to narrow their range of choice and restrict their freedom of manoeuvre.

The erosion of the East's economic influence in Southern Africa is only one threat which it now faces. Much more serious is the threat of political destabilisation which, if successful, might exclude it altogether. It is this latter concern that explains the increasing interest shown by the Warsaw Pact, and East Germany working on behalf of its members.

Eastern Europe, like the West, is searching for political stability to assure itself that changes in government to which Africa is all too prone do not put at risk large capital sums which have already been invested in mining – notably by Poland in Angola and East Germany in Mozambique. The Soviet Union and its allies have no option but to block Western attempts to make the region more 'stable' since political stability in the vernacular of the East means nothing less than instability. As the Soviet writer, K. Uralov, reminded his readers in the aftermath of the West's 'rescue mission' in Rhodesia:

What the imperialists fear most of all is a repetition in Zimbabwe and Namibia of what happened in Mozambique and Angola where power was taken by the progressive forces which lead the national liberation movements of their peoples. Back in May 1976 formulating the 'new African policy' of the United States, the US Secretary of State had this to say to the Senate Foreign Relations Committee: 'We have a stake in not having the whole continent become radical and moving in a direction that is incompatible with Western interests'. The policy of the new US Administration as spelled out in the speeches and press conferences of the American leaders, has little new to offer.[43]

The choice before the West is whether to defend what remains of the old order, or coopt and work with the new. For the Soviet Union and its allies the matter is at once more simple, but no less problematic: how to defend the 'progressive' regimes in Southern Africa from counter-revolutionary forces.

9 The Warsaw Pact, East Germany and the Threat of Western Intervention

Since Cuba's intervention in Africa much has been written about its role. That interest is understandable. The presence of 20 000 combat troops and its operations in the Horn two years after the Angolan civil war demonstrated forceably the West's inability to prevent military adventurism in a region of the world traditionally considered a Western sphere of influence.

Cuba's role, however, may already be a passing phenomenon. It has naturally captured the headlines because it seems a typical illustration of the Soviet Union's use of surrogate forces. The Russians, it could be argued, have pursued their interests in Africa with a dazzling lack of hypocrisy – dazzling, that is, to an American public accustomed to scrutinising the covert activities of the CIA or the Department of State. Cuba intervened quite oblivious to criticism. It trained and organised a Marxist–Leninist party (the MPLA) with a consistency of purpose which largely disarmed criticism of its methods.

The involvement of the Warsaw Pact, however, and in particular East Germany, may be far more significant in the long run. The GDR's own presence in Southern Africa can be explained in terms of national interest. Its commitment of financial and military resources seems more pregnant with significance than the support provided by Cuba which one cannot help suspecting has largely served the very limited end of gratifying Castro's *amour propre* – his desire to cut a figure on the world stage and to rediscover the revolutionary roots of his own socialism.

As Castro himself admitted to an American Congressional

delegation in 1976, the greatest expense of the Angolan adventure had not been the cost of military operations (that had been partly, but not wholly, subsidised by the Russians) but the concomitant loss of skilled personnel, particularly doctors and engineers, on indefinite secondment to the MPLA.[1] It is ironic that Cuba's military contribution should continue to pre-occupy the United States since it is not of much concern to its European allies. When Henry Kissinger suggested in a television interview in 1976 that he would not object to the presence of 'several hundred' technicians providing Havana withdrew its troops, he gave little thought to the economic consequences which would have followed a blanket withdrawal.[2] In one respect, the GDR was not being entirely disingenuous when it declared on the first anniversary of Angola's independence that the country's success or failure in solving its economic problems would be determined very largely by how far the Cubans managed to lay the groundwork for its future development.[3]

Dr Kissinger's comments at the time, and those of his successors ever since, reveal a fundamental ignorance about the nature of Cuba's military presence. It is difficult enough to distinguish civilian and military functions since the two are often interchangeable. As the danger of an American invasion receded in the early 1970s, Castro began to place less emphasis on a permanent standing force and more on a military reserve. Reservists drawn from a variety of social spheres have found it comparatively easy to slip into a civilian role, or slip back into a military one whenever necessary. The Cubans have never gone into combat without the presence of reservists, and the latter have never represented less than half, and at times four-fifths, of their combat forces in Angola and Ethiopia.[4]

The deployment of so many skilled and semi-skilled men has added to the net drain on the Cuban economy. It has also helped throw into relief the extent of its technical assistance. Cuba can ill afford to send so many civilian technicians overseas. The long term cost for a developing country, if not insupportable, must be judiciously weighed in the balance of its own development. Its under-development has forced it, when drawing up foreign aid programmes, to place a much greater emphasis on men rather than money, on the expertise to run development programmes rather than the cash to fund them. The Cubans have remarkably little to throw into the development pool.

It seems inevitable that they will not be able to maintain an indefinite commitment without placing an intolerable stress on their economy (which is already heavily subsidised by the Soviet Union as it is). It is also clear that one of the results of providing men rather than money is the need to co-opt other governments, in nearly every case East European, to assist the countries in which their forces are active. In Southern Africa that role has been played largely by East Germany. Since 1978 the GDR has been on subcontract to Cuba (rather than answerable to Angola itself).

GDR AND SOUTHERN AFRICA, 1974–78

By 1978 there were 41 000 Soviet bloc military personnel in sub-Saharan Africa of which 3800 were East Europeans and 40 per cent of these East Germans. After the Soviet Union the GDR was responsible for selling more arms to guerrilla movements than any other country (Czechoslovakia included, whose arms corporation, Omnipol, was the fourth largest in the world). In a rare admission in February 1979, Erich Honnecker announced that East Germany had spent on average $100m a year on military support for nationalist movements in Southern Africa.[5] After meeting Honnecker in Lusaka, Joshua Nkomo, the veteran Zimbabwean nationalist leader, thanked the GDR and the Soviet Union for their extensive military help.[6]

East Germany's association with the region has a comparatively long history. In Mozambique the East German delegation to the Afro–Asian Solidarity Committee took the trouble to journey to Dar-es-Salaam in 1969 to hand over its contribution in person. German teachers volunteered by the score for the Mozambique Institute, FRELIMO's school in neighbouring Tanzania, which had been so concerned about accusations of 'cultural imperialism' that it had earlier refused an offer of scholarships from the Ford Foundation. After the assassination of its founder, the party's new leader Samora Machel visited East Berlin for the 8th rally of the East German Communist Party (SED), an honour reciprocated five years later when the SED and CPSU were among the principal foreign guests at FRELIMO's third party congress.

These contacts were not restricted to Mozambique. In 1961 *Deutsch Aussenpolitik* was the first East European journal to publish the MPLA's party programme, four years before the movement was recognised by the Soviet Union. Its founder, Angostinho Neto, enjoyed consistent German support throughout the struggle against Portuguese rule, in contrast to the Soviet Union which on more than one occasion considered transferring its support to his chief rival on the central committee, Daniel Chipenda.

Early in 1972, the *Neues Deutschland* congratulated the MPLA for being the only nationalist movement in Southern Africa possessing 'a foreign policy which clearly orientates itself to cooperating with the socialist world'.[7] Fully alive to the ideological import of the Angolan revolution, Berlin described the MPLA's proletarian internationalism as 'a remarkable expression of the changed balance in the international arena'.[8]

The East Germans played a limited, though not unimportant, role in the Angolan civil war, sending what Radio Berlin euphemistically called 'solidarity freight' – MiG-21s rather than men at the height of the fighting. The South African newspapers at the time presented conflicting accounts of the number of military personnel in the field – from 'a great number' according to *Die Vaterland*, to 'several hundred' according to the *Windhoek Algemeine Zeitung*, although the best informed West German source could only trace one officer from East German state security as late as November 1976.[9]

Several years later in the course of periodic offensives against UNITA strongholds in the south, East German pilots gradually began taking the place of their Cuban opposite numbers in flying MiG-21 sorties. French intelligence sources close to Savimbi, head of UNITA, maintained that the East German government had established a special command centre at the former Portuguese army base at Henrique de Carvalho where it had begun to train Cuban and Angolan soldiers.[10]

There were several explanations for this East German activity before 1979. The most telling was that the GDR's ruling elite hoped to buy Soviet support by acting on behalf of Soviet interests. Its attitude to the struggle in Zimbabwe seemed to bear this out. The East Germans were largely instrumental in maintaining almost uniform support for Nkomo's movement (ZAPU) until the very eve of the Lancaster House conference. The Soviet Union had never put its trust in Robert Mugabe because of his earlier sympathy for China. ZANU, like the PAC and SWANU, was always excluded from the nationalist summits sponsored by

Moscow, to which movements such as ZAPU, SWAPO and the ANC were always invited. As late as February 1979, Mugabe told a reporter from the Western press that, apart from Romania, he expected no significant assistance from 'the rest of the socialist bloc'.[11]

Although Julius Nyerere arranged for ZANU's entire central committee to visit Eastern Europe in November 1978, the GDR prevailed upon its Warsaw Pact allies to continue withholding arms. It also dissuaded Castro from interceding despite three separate visits he held with Robert Mugabe in almost as many months. In the event, West Germany, and not the GDR, was invited to Zimbabwe's independence celebrations in April 1980. By resolutely supporting the Soviet line, the East Germans gratuitously denied themselves an excellent opportunity to discomfort the West German government.

Yet it is the West German connection which provides another explanation for East German involvement, one which makes it questionable to dismiss its role as that of a surrogate of the Soviet Union. To characterise its role in such terms is to subsume its national interests in a dubious collective identity which obscures the real interests the two states share. Because we still insist on discussing the politics of Southern Africa in terms of a contest between the Superpowers, we often fail to take account of the fact that special circumstances in one area of the world may well produce special interests in another.

After 1972 the GDR began calling itself a 'socialist nation', removing by intellectual *legerdemain* the name Germany from its vocabulary and conceding the right of the other German state (the Federal Republic) to call itself the German nation. From 1972 on the GDR, tended to look upon itself as a strictly political entity whose political legitimacy stemmed from a social order superior in every respect to that which prevailed in the West by virtue of its Marxist–Leninist values.[12]

Not only did the ideology become vitally important, but its participation in the revolutionary struggle in Southern Africa compensated the East German citizen for the revolutionary sclerosis which had set in within the GDR itself. This was especially noticeable in the support which its mass movements gave Mozambique: the *Frei Deutscher Gewerkschaftsbund*; the *Freie Deutschjugend*; and the *Demokratischer Frauenbund Deutschland*. Each gave substance to the cultural agreements signed in August 1978 by the East German ambassador and the Secretary-General of Mozambique's Ministry of Education.

The East Germans did not hesitate as well to take advantage of West Germany's links with the surviving white state. Their attack was first launched at an anti-apartheid conference in East Berlin (May 1974) at which the South African–West German 'axis' first came under the scrutiny of the United Nations. The 'axis' represented the 300 firms with subsidiaries in the republic; another 6000 which maintained direct, or indirect links with South Africa; and the support which the Federal Republic's investment insurance corporation extended to companies investing in the Republic's public sector: from steam generating equipment provided to SASOL 2 (South Africa's oil shale project) to the turbo-compressors supplied to its uranium enrichment plant at Pelindaba.

It was not only in the sphere of economics that the Federal Republic found itself at a disadvantage. The GDR was one of the first countries to condemn South Africa's Bantustan programme when it began to take shape in the early 1970s. It even described Gatscha Buthelezi who had resolutely refused independence for his own homeland, KwaZulu, as 'a white man's stooge'.[13] Five years later it seized upon the invitation extended to the President of Lebowa from the Essen Chamber of Commerce as evidence of West Germany's interest in investing in the homelands while officially disassociating itself from the homeland policy.

Having renounced its German nationality, the GDR was not averse to drawing upon Germany's Nazi past for analogies with recent South African history likely to embarrass the government in Bonn. The laws forbidding inter-racial marriage for example, were frequently compared with the Nuremberg laws of the mid-1930s which had prohibited the marriage of Aryans and Jews.[14] The success with which it exploited West Germany's links with South Africa undoubtedly helped it to maintain a pretence of inter-racial solidarity in its pursuit of less disinterested goals.

But it was above all in furtherance of their economic interests that the East Germans pursued an active policy in Southern Africa during this period. In June 1978, economists from the Humbolt University in East Berlin arrived in Luanda to set up a special Institute of Planning and Administration. Their presence soon became so marked that it aroused acute disquiet among their Angolan hosts. One of the main reasons for Lope do Nascimento's sudden departure from the Ministry in December was his over-reliance on East German advice and the disturbing presence of so many East German advisers within the administration. After his dismissal, Neto warned of the need to guard against 'the action of certain forces within our country which had pretended to make our party follow an orientation which is not our own' . . .[15] Although he refrained from mentioning East Germany by name, the Secretary of the MPLA felt constrained to reassure Berlin that Nascimento's dismissal did not mean that the country was beginning to drift away from the socialist bloc.[16]

In Mozambique, the presence of a large contingent of East German advisers in the Ministry of Planning enabled Berlin to assume control over a number of mining ventures, including the Moatize mines. They also helped run the peoples militia and the National Bureau of State Security thus underwriting Machel's position and contributing decisively, according to *The Voice of FRELIMO*, to 'the material base of scientific socialism'.[17] Anxious to exploit the country's mineral wealth, the East German advisers weaned it away from revolutionary Marxism to more Leninist principles of economic management. The *grupos dinamizadores* lost control of management in the interests of 'democratic centralism'. When they were called in by dos Santos' Ministry (later to be reorganised into the National Planning Commission) they ensured that political education classes were held in the workers' time, not the mines'. Not long afterwards, production quotas began to make an appearance. Not long after that the workers began to complain that they were being forced to conform to 'bourgeois working methods'.[18]

GDR AND THE WARSAW PACT SINCE 1978

The number of East German forces which are at present in Africa is not known for certain. Analysts have to rely on information from Western sources, mainly from the West German Ministry for Inter-German relations. There are no figures available for the number of officers of the East German National Peoples Army (*Volksarmee*, NVA) who are currently posted in Africa. Some Western press reports speak of 2500 to 5000 German troops training SWAPO guerrillas in 1981,[19] and 1500–2000 military personnel in Libya.[20]

Such evidence is difficult to verify. A lot is South African disinformation, particularly the 1979 reports of German soldiers in Eritrea. Other sightings cannot be verified. President Mobutu claimed that most of the equipment captured from the Katanganese rebels in May 1978 originated from East Germany, but the claim was never confirmed by the West German government.[21]

Since Germany's military assistance is classified information, any overall view of the GDR's military role must be pieced together from fragmentary intelligence reports, and regular visits of East German military delegations. The East German government normally denies most Western claims. In 1978 Honnecker described as 'a fabrication' a story which appeared in the *Guardian* based on supposedly 'informed sources in Johannesburg' about the presence of several hundred troops from the GDR encamped only 50 miles from the Namibian border.[22]

What we do know is that most NVA officers instruct their African counterparts in techniques of information gathering, interrogation and infiltration of dissident groups. There are a number of radio communications experts in Mozambique: and training brigades seconded to SWAPO in camps in southern Angola. All in all, the East Germans probably have 5000 men in Southern Africa, the great majority in Angola and Mozambique.

The key year seems to have been 1978, a year which saw the visit to Angola and Congo-Brazzaville of a military delegation led by the Defence Minister, Heinz Hoffmann. It was that year too that the military authorities confirmed that German military aid was 'on the increase'.[23] In June, a delegation also visited the Angolan military bases at Luso, Texeira de Sousa and Henrique de Carvalho. On this occasion Hoffmann was accompanied by the Angolan Minister of Defence, Teles Carreira.

The most significant development was the establishing of an extensive air defence system around the major southern towns of Lubango and Mocamedes, the scene of recent South African incursions. At one point in 1978, a senior East German party official explained that support for the forces of national liberation was nothing new. What was new, however, was the military assistance that East Germany now intended giving the Front Line States to deter attacks from outside, an eliptical reference to South African raids which began in that year to become more frequent and more devastating.[24]

East Germany's intervention is interesting because it seems to represent an overall Warsaw Pact strategy which was formulated in 1978. During the meeting in November of the Pact's Consultative Committee, aid to the liberation movements in Namibia and South Africa was specifically discussed in the context of aid to their main patrons, the Front Line States. The Pact appears to have guaranteed Angola and Mozambique from South African 'aggression' and to have provided itself with a role at the same time. Although most African states were well aware that the solution to the region's growing insecurity lay not in the multiplication of treaties but in redressing the situations which necessitated them, South African intervention appeared to offer them no alternative.

It seems clear that General Hoffmann represented the Warsaw Pact as well as East Germany during his second visit to the region in 1979 since his tour coincided with an important meeting of the Military Council in Budapest at which all the other Defence Ministers were present. His own absence clearly revealed where the priorities of the group lay. Given the fact that the GDR is second only to the Soviet Union in importance, it seems probable that it has taken upon itself responsibility for coordinating a military strategy which has the express backing of its Warsaw Pact allies.

This view was further reinforced by the Shaba 2 invasion the same year. In May the *Observer* carried a report that at the 9th SED Congress in 1976 the GDR had been allocated the role of destabilising Zaire and thus reducing its support for the FNLA guerrillas. The congress had been attended by an Angolan delegation led by the governor of Huambo province and a member of the central committee of the MPLA.

On behalf of the other Pact members, Berlin had agreed to two courses of action: first, to provide the FNLC guerrillas with military equipment including a strike capacity against the Zairean air force so that the movement could mount a lightning thrust against Dilolo, Lubumbushi, Bukama and the military base at Kamina; secondly, to create 45 separate pockets of 'permanent revolution' in Shaba, supported with arms from Angolan military bases. In the course of 1977, a large number of Czech heavy duty military transports were delivered to the FNLC, who also received training from 100 German experts. It seems that this programme was deliberately kept separate from Cuban support; and that it was clearly understood that the GDR would not get involved directly even at the cost of military failure.[25]

It is not surprising that, given its economic interests in Southern Africa, the Warsaw Pact should have become directly involved in 1978. Recent developments within the Pact suggested that out-of-area operations could not be excluded. The Political Consultative Committee gained in importance in the Brezhnev years. To facilitate the better coordination of foreign policy, meetings of the Foreign Ministers had been convened regularly since 1969, and in 1976 a Committee of Foreign Ministers was added to the Pact's formal command structure.

The Soviet intervention in Angola merely highlighted an issue which had reportedly appeared in Warsaw Pact deliberations in the past: the possibility that the East Europeans might be called upon to render some form of military assistance in support of Soviet objectives beyond Europe. Despite the stipulation in the Warsaw Treaty that mutual defence obligations are limited to an 'armed attack in Europe', it has been widely rumoured that Soviet leaders twice issued such a call – in 1969 at the time of the Sino–Soviet border clashes and in 1979 during the Chinese invasion of Vietnam. The need to deter both the West and its supposed 'clients', South Africa and Zaire, from challenging the new political order in Angola may well have constituted a third case.

The defence of the Front Line States has continued to exercise the Pact's attention. Five years later at the summit meeting at Hradcany Castle the focus of debate was once again directed at 'recent acts of aggression committed by the *apartheid* regime against the progressive peoples of Southern Africa', a reference to continued South African raids into Angola and Mozambique.

By this time the raids were beginning to have a direct effect on their own economic interests. Back in 1977, attempts to pump out the Chipanga 7 coal mine in Moatize after an instance of severe flooding had been prevented by continued Rhodesian attacks on the railway which, in turn, had stopped the import of diesel fuel for the pumps. At the time the mine was under East German management.[26] Five years later the East Germans stood by helplessly as attacks by South African financed MNR guerrillas brought to a halt the renovation of the Condo–Derunde railway, causing a bottleneck on the line to the Moatize fields where more than a year's production was already stockpiled.[27] Such attacks have encompassed countries other than the GDR – in August 1983, 14 Soviet geologists were captured in an MNR raid on a tantalite mine in the central province of Zambezia.

Where does this leave East Germany and the Warsaw Pact? It was Richard Löwenthal who argued some years ago that the Soviet Union had begun to move from old-style anti-imperialism to a new concept – that of counter-imperialism

> a strategy of fighting Western imperialism by using the familiar imperialist methods of establishing zones of political and economic influence linked to the Soviet Union by firm ties.[28]

One need not subscribe to Löwenthal's model to accept that the Warsaw Pact has pursued, whether intentionally or not, a policy of counter-imperialism with increasing success since 1978. This has proved a particularly successful strategy against the West's attempts to shore up its position in the aftermath of the Angolan civil war, a development which has alarmed the East almost as much as Soviet intervention in Angola originally alarmed the Western powers.

As Erich Honnecker told a conference in East Berlin in October 1980, the support given to national liberation movements by the Warsaw Pact had 'nothing in common with the export of revolution', but was aimed solely against the export of counter-revolution by the West.[29] East European efforts to discredit the Anglo–American initiatives in Zimbabwe and the Contact Group's discussions on Namibia were intended to counter a NATO directed 'offensive against the national liberation forces in Africa', a theme which was taken up in earnest by Honnecker during a visit to the region in 1979. During his tour he warned his hosts about the extension of NATO's field of activity to Africa.[30] In a communiqué published at the end of his visit to Mozambique, the two countries pledged themselves to oppose NATO's attempts to transform the area into an 'international crisis centre'.[31]

This counter-revolutionary strategy has also been dictated by the alarming prospect of a clash with South Africa. Indeed, so potent is the threat that the GDR has been particularly reluctant to honour its treaty with Mozambique. So far, the bilateral treaties between East Germany and Mozambique have remained precisely that. When the Warsaw Pact's Political Committee delegated responsibility for its interests in Southern Africa to the GDR in 1978, it did so in the hope of limiting NATO activity in the region, not provoking NATO intervention by pursuing adventurist policies of its own.

Of the three separate treaties of friendship between the GDR and Africa's Marxist–Leninist states, only the one with Maputo contains an agreement to go to the other's assistance in time of war. So far, however, the East Germans have failed to honour their commitments. In 1979, General Hoffmann promised Mozambique that its armed forces would become 'one of the most modern and efficient in Africa in their ability to confront the threat of imperialism',[32] yet Berlin's reluctance to provide an adequate air defence system against South African air strikes contrasts rather embarrassingly with the Soviet Union's promise of a massive military aid package to Zambia after the first Rhodesian raids on Lusaka. Much of the equipment that has been supplied to Mozambique is, by contrast, defensive in nature and dated in technology. Its MiG-17 fighters are first generation aircraft, a poor match for South Africa's Mirage IIIs which were supplied by France in the 1970s. Even the missile defences outside Maputo and Mapai are so old that they can offer very little protection despite the fact that they have been recently improved by the installation of anti-aircraft radar tracking and guidance systems.[33] Even the visit of two Soviet warships in February 1980 in the wake of the South African strike against Maputo only served to reinforce the fact that the deterrent against such raids was very much at the Soviet Union's discretion, and was neither fixed nor irrevocable.

Neither the Soviet Union nor the GDR could possibly have forseen the scale of recent South African raids. Nor could they have predicted the impotence of the West in the face of actions which have so patently conflicted with its true interests and which have contributed more to regional insecurity than the much vaunted Cuban presence. What does seem clear is the restraint with which the GDR has acted. Recent intelligence reports indicate that it is opposed to any idea of replacing Cuban troops in Angola for fear that it will become involved in a military stalemate in difficult terrain with the possibility of a clash with South African forces.[34]

Ironically, it is probably because the Warsaw Pact believes that, in the final analysis, South Africa is a surrogate of the West,

rather than an independent actor, that it no doubt believes that a
conflict with Pretoria would be seen by NATO in a very different
light than intervention against a non-Western power such as
Cambodia or Afghanistan.[35]

Indeed, for the moment it seems that neither the Soviet Union
nor its partners wish to challenge the West's position; only to
underwrite political stability which in this curious looking glass
world means the centrally planned economies of Southern Africa,
not the existing capitalist order. In this respect, the East Germans
are probably quite sincere when they refute suggestions that
'thousands of members of the National Peoples Army are
allegedly spreading world revolution in Africa and blocking the
raw material sources of the capitalist industrialised nations'.[36]

Many East European governments have no wish to deny
Western capital a role in the region. They may wish to bring it
under state regulation, but they have few illusions that new
reserves can be developed without Western assistance. Since the
mid-1970s some have begun to sub-contract major parts of
development contracts to Western corporations in order to reduce
the spiralling overheads of mining operations.[37] In their choice of
partners, more often than not, they have turned to companies with
whom they have already established close links in Eastern Europe
itself. In Africa, Dunlop and Pirelli have both benefitted from
their prior association with the Hungarian state trading organisations, Chemolimpex and Taurus. The East German organisation
Unitechna brought Krupp into Ethiopia in 1980.

On the East European side, it is the countries with the most
flexible and decentralised structures that have been the most
eager to enter into tripartite ventures in Africa, with Hungary
leading the field, followed by the GDR and Poland. This
cooperation has grown out of years of cooperation between the
partners during which both sides have come to understand what
each can offer the other.[38] Such understandings could well be put
at risk by a crisis between the superpowers occasioned wholly or in
part by the pursuit of strategic interests which have little or no
economic content. The East Europeans learned at first hand,
what the invasion of Afghanistan meant for further joint venture
cooperation in Eastern Europe. Any further restriction of these
operations would have an immediate bearing on their own
position.

CONCLUSION

The Warsaw Pact's intervention in Southern Africa has been one of the most important developments of recent years. Indeed, one of the conclusions reached at the Budapest summit in 1976 was that political cooperation within the Soviet bloc had reached a more developed stage than economic cooperation. To many people this may not appear surprising. One would expect the Soviet writ to run more extensively in the political sphere than the economic. Nevertheless, the picture is not quite so simple. National foreign policy goals have begun to influence the framework of Soviet policy. However much East European governments may defer to Moscow, the Soviet Union has been forced to take into account the interests of its allies. The latter have already influenced the content of Soviet policy. Indeed, the presence of so many East German soldiers in Africa has given Berlin importance at the point of execution, if not command; and this, in turn, has had some influence on the commands that have been given.

It is hardly surprising that the Soviet Union has made out a strong case for a concerted effort on the part of its allies. In the first place, it probably wishes to prevent a clash of interests from arising within the Warsaw Pact; in the second, it probably recognises that the Pact's involvement in Africa may provide a continuous point of reference for its members in their relations with one another.

What does seem certain is that the Warsaw Pact will intervene more frequently in the future. Its distrust of the West, and the extent to which it holds the West responsible for regional instability is nowhere more in evidence than in political writings which have tried to make intelligible the endlessly changing pattern of political alignments in Africa. Not even Angola or Mozambique seem to have escaped from the permanent cycle of political regression which opened, for most African countries, immediately after independence.

Marx himself once called Germany of the necessary but impossible bourgeois revolution of the mid-19th century 'the comedian of a world order whose real heroes are long since dead'.[39] This phrase seems particularly apposite for the new Marxist–Leninist states of Southern Africa which are about to enter their second decade of independence without any sign of developing political institutions which might, at the very least, assure the political stability for which their friends in Eastern Europe are looking.

Part III

10 Africa, the Western Alliance and the Soviet Challenge, 1961–78

Once they became independent most post-colonial societies were interested in their own stability and economic development. These preoccupations also extended to the sphere of foreign relations, where the new states were reluctant to become involved in squabbles which had nothing to do with themselves. None wished to be tied too closely to the military blocs, especially NATO. If the choice of non-alignment appeared to be anti-Western it was because Africa was tied in almost every other respect to the Western world. In the aftermath of independence, most states found themselves enmeshed by a web of interests and sympathies which bound them closely to the former metropolitan powers. As Kwame Nkrumah admitted, Africa could not cancel out 100 years of history overnight, and history had brought Africa and Europe into close communion. The signs of dependency were much the same: limited resources, inadequate bases of political support, in the majority of cases close military, financial and political ties with Europe.[1]

The weakness and instability of much of Africa was not in dispute, but its causes often were. Their experience in the immediate post-independence years prompted many Africans into anguished introspection. Many searched for an explanation of their predicament in neo-colonialism. Whatever their chosen vocabulary or terms of reference, whether Marxist or socialist, anti-communist or anti-capitalist, African politicians usually treated the past as a story whose depressing end was implicit from the beginning, picturing their own countries as the weak and divided rump of the capitalist world, a continent adrift in a world of competing ideologies and military blocs.

Non-alignment was born of a complex mix of interests and aspirations, an incompletely resolved dilemma whether to pursue the politics of virtue – non-alignment, or to face up to the challenge which had confronted their Asian *confrères* in the 1950s when the United States, in an effort to align the Third World into collective security pacts modelled on the North Atlantic Alliance, had withheld economic assistance from countries who had often been expressly opposed to Western policy.

For most Africans non-alignment offered a much more convincing prospect of peace than contracting agreements with more powerful patrons who were likely to demand in return bases, defence agreements and overflight rights. It was not only that Africa wished to avoid becoming an arena of competing ideologies: alignment with one or other of the military blocs seemed unlikely to affect the issue of international peace one way or the other:

> ... when we in Africa survey the industrial and military power concentrated behind the two great powers in the cold war we know that no military or strategic acts of ours could make one jot of difference to this balance of power, while our involvement might draw us into areas of conflict which so far have not spread below the Sahara.[2]

For Nkrumah and the first generation of African leaders, Africa lacked either the power or resources to play an independent role in the increasingly hostile world in which they found themselves. They tended to judge countries and the alliances they represented by a simple but telling yardstick: the extent to which their policies advanced or impeded their own independence. Non-alignment was a natural choice for the new states. The reasons which had impelled Asia to opt for neutrality in the 1950s proved even more compelling for Africa in the 1960s. The Africans saw in the policy as adumbrated by the founding fathers of pan-Africanism their only hope of realising the social and economic promise that nationalism held out, even more the political independence which they had so recently won.

To have aligned themselves with the Western Alliance would have meant aligning themselves with states with quite disproportionate resources and different aims. It would have produced a relationship of inequality and subordination which would have been to the obvious disadvantage of the weaker partner. Association with either bloc, as Sylvanus Olympio of Togo commented in 1961, would have brought in its train a new bondage.[3] The independent states of Africa were sensitive to the question of sovereign rights, both jealous and more assertive of their independent position. Most wanted to avoid obligations which might subsume their national interests in collective defence. None were willing to submit themselves to the military judgments of states from whom they had just won independence, or to defer to the judgment of others on matters they did not consider vital to themselves.

As long as they recognised NATO was a regional defence pact limited by treaty to operations north of the Tropic of Cancer, most Africans did not see it as an aggressive alliance. For the same reasons, of course, many saw no reason to be concerned about the Warsaw Pact. They objected to NATO only to the extent that it had taken an equivocal position on Algeria, and continued its tacit support of Portuguese rule in Southern Africa. They approved of the Warsaw Pact only to the extent that its members provided the liberation movements with arms and equipment without which they would never have been able to mount a serious challenge to Portuguese rule.

There were many countries in NATO, however, who paid little attention to the arguments, almost as little as the Soviet Union who believed that the culture, history and commerce which bound Africa to Europe made non-alignment suspect. Like Nkrumah, they maintained that the independence granted in the 1950s had been false because the colonial powers continued to control the economies of their former possessions, and to an extent their security as well; that neo-colonialism represented not only the highest stage of imperialism but far worse because, in contrast to the period of direct rule, it allowed for the exercise of power without responsibility.[4]

The West took these radical critiques at face value and often chose to ignore what preoccupied the Soviet Union so much: the ties which bound Africa and Europe so closely. Nevertheless Africa's very dependence on the West reinforced the impression that non-alignment must be implicitly anti-Western. Africa's complaints, after all, were directed at the countries with whom relations were so close rather than the countries with whom relations were few.⁵ Kenneth Kaunda, the President of Zambia, reminded the non-aligned conference at Lusaka:

> We threaten no power and have nothing against the powerful states. All we want is to make sure that our political freedom, economic and social progress are secure in our hands, and are not subject to manipulation to benefit other nations against our interests.⁶

Nyerere's analysis of the structure of dependency revealed a political world very different from what most Western leaders imagined. He was insistent that the security of Africa when and if it was threatened, should be looked at within the framework of African politics, not the East/West balance. He denied that questions of strategic principle were important in shaping the political actions of the Western powers, finding a more convincing explanation in their self-interest and commercial ambitions. Most strategic questions raised by the Alliance seemed empty rhetoric employed to serve the immediate and personal interests of Western politicians.⁷

Nyerere and Kaunda were not oblivious to Western concerns, especially after the appearance of the Soviet Navy in the Indian Ocean, but they both believed that Western interests were threatened only to the extent to which the problem of racism in Southern Africa was left unresolved. They believed that the cold war lobbyists would be better advised to turn their attention to colonialism and apartheid which bred impatience and discontent among African powers, which the Soviet Union so assiduously exploited. They criticised the West for lacking the will to tackle the problems posed by white supremacy, for taking refuge in simple strategic arguments which provided a quite inadequate framework for understanding developments in the region.

NATO was, perhaps, fortunate in these years that some of its members, notably Canada, were able to win the confidence of the African powers. Nkrumah actually stated the case for Ghana's non-alignment at a joint session of the Canadian Parliament in 1958, a time when non-alignment did not have America's support and was equally offensive to France and Britain. The Canadians later replaced some of the British officers and training facilities phased out in 1961. A briefing paper produced by the Ghanaian Foreign Ministry the following year, specifically referred to

Canada's special role in NATO as one of the factors which made its military support acceptable to a non-aligned country.[8] The Canadians, indeed, turned down a British suggestion that their army mission should merge with the remaining British air wing because they felt it would prejudice their independent position.

Africa's acceptance of Canada was based, in part, on its perception of its unorthodox NATO role. Within the Alliance itself Canada was often seen as an unreliable partner wedded through the Diefenbaker government to nuclear disarmament. The Cuban missile crisis had shown it to be a less than enthusiastic member of the NATO–NORAD continental defence system.[9] Its military assistance to Ghana in the Nkrumah years and to Nyerere's Tanzania after its *rapprochement* with China confirmed America's suspicions of Canada's role. Those very suspicions, of course, reinforced Canada's independent image. Its stand on nuclear disarmament was shared by most African countries, particularly Nigeria.

After 1962 (the year which saw the abrogation of the treaty with Britain) Nigeria joined Canada on an 18 nation Commission for Disarmament. The two countries shared similar views on the comprehensive Test Ban Treaty, the non-proliferation of nuclear weapons and the liquidation of foreign military bases. Canada was openly sympathetic when Nigeria broke diplomatic relations with a fellow NATO member, France, over French nuclear tests in the Sahara. Perhaps the most symbolic manifestation of Canadian policy in these years was its military assistance agreement with Tanzania. Interestingly, Canada was initially extremely reluctant to enter into any such undertaking and only agreed to do so under pressure from Britain and the United States who wanted to keep Nyerere in the Western camp.[10] This was possibly the first time that both powers had found Canada's independent position politically useful.

It was soon found to be difficult, if not unwise, to play politics in this fashion. The Canadian military mission was embarrassed not by the presence of the Russians (they had pulled out in mid-1965) but by that of the Chinese training team. The agreement was plagued with misunderstanding from the beginning. It was eventually cancelled in 1969 when Ottawa refused to arm Tanzania against external aggression which was likely to come from only one quarter: from Portugal – one of its own NATO partners. The Trudeau government's somewhat equivocal position over Portugal's presence in Africa undermined the good press it had previously enjoyed and which it recovered briefly in 1971 when it opposed British arms sales to South Africa and even tightened up its own restrictions.

By 1974, therefore, the Atlantic Alliance found that by its ambivalent attitude towards the Southern African question, it had already undermined much of the trust and mutual confidence that its responsible behaviour had produced in the 1960s. The NATO allies doubtless reflected that they were blamed for sins of omission rather than commission, even so the crisis in Southern Africa eventually loomed even larger in allied thinking for reasons that no-one could have foreseen. In the 1960s NATO had come to rely on non-alignment to shore up its southern flank. But while Africa's commitment to non-alignment was sincere, and deeply held, its strength was only as good as the reluctance of both blocs to intervene. It was, in part, reluctance on the part of the Warsaw Pact which accelerated Europe's strategic disengagement from Africa in the 1960s. But the part of the equation rarely discussed, and upon which non-alignment was contingent, was the situation in Africa itself which threw up few opportunities for the Soviet Union to intervene directly. The collapse of Portuguese rule in 1974 shattered Africa's complacency and opened up a debate which, to all intents and purposes, had been put to rest in the mid-1960s: whether, in view of the fact that the Africans were quite incapable of defending themselves, NATO should take a more active part in Africa's defence.

BASES AND BASE RIGHTS

Nothing aroused more suspicion of the North Atlantic Alliance than the continued presence of European forces. Most European powers dismantled their bases very soon after independence, not soon enough, however, to meet the objections of one Guinean official who believed that there was no problem or crisis in Africa which could not be accounted for by 'the presence of continuing British and French forces'.[11] However eccentric his interpretation, such sympathies and antipathies were of the stuff of African politics, whether they affected many powers or only a few. In trying to satisfy those who looked forward to their complete departure without offending those in their own ranks who did not, the Europeans vacillated too long, clinging to a role which had lost any meaning once their colonies had won independence.

The Russians found it useful to sketch the conflict between East and West in simple broadbrush strokes – to show that the Western powers were as much a threat to Africa as they had been in the 19th century. By painting this picture they could project themselves as the apologists of non-alignment, a picture that, though manifestly false, the Alliance found difficult to challenge while its members continued to maintain garrisons in West Africa.

The Africans, for better or worse, saw the presence of foreign bases as a threat to their independence. Indeed, some believed that the presence of foreign troops had originally set back their efforts to secure self-rule. Recourse to history introduced as many questions as it answered. In addition to using their own bases at Kamina, Kitona and Albertville during the Congo emergency, the Belgians had also airlifted forces from the American airfield at Wheelus Field and the neighbouring French stations at Pointe Noire and Brazzaville. As the representative of Mali told the UN Committee on Colonial Peoples in September 1962: 'there was a connection between military activities and colonialism . . . and the presence of military bases as . . . an impediment to the process of decolonisation'.[12] His concern was echoed by most African leaders for whom the experience of colonialism was still fresh. It was difficult for them to believe that the former colonial powers would not intervene in their affairs whenever instability seemed likely to threaten their vital interests. On this matter, as on so many others, the Europeans tended to be rather diffident.

It was not surprising, therefore, that the Anglo–Nigerian defence pact of 1960 became one of the first casualties of nationalism, an early victim of the suspicion and distrust which characterised the early post-independence years. The Nigerian Minister of Defence confessed in 1962 that the government had had to abrogate the pact because of the agitation of ambitious opposition politicians anxious to discredit the Federal government by putting it abroad that it was an agent of the Atlantic Alliance.[13] Ironically it was conservative African leaders, not the Europeans, who were most profoundly affected by the network of defence agreements and basing rights which enmeshed the continent in the European orbit.

By the late 1960s the threat of direct intervention by the European powers had begun to fade, but the threat that the mere presence of foreign bases might involve Africa in the wider anti-communist struggle made them even more unacceptable. Despite repeated assurances from the Europeans, including France, about the importance they attached to Africa's neutrality, their actions continued to arouse suspicion. At the Addis Ababa conference in 1963 which acted as midwife for the OAU, a resolution was passed obliging all members 'to bring about by all means of negotiation the end of military occupation of the African continent, the elimination of which constitutes a basic element of African independence and unity'. Its members were invited to renounce all agreements they might have negotiated with the metropolitan powers or any other non-African states by virtue of which foreign bases or military personnel still remained on African soil. It is difficult to escape the conclusion that the timing of the proposal and the publicity surrounding it compelled many Europeans to reassess their own position.

The difficulty of fulfilling the obligation to the letter, nevertheless, became demonstrably evident by the time the Council of Ministers met in Lagos in February 1964. The resolution on non-alignment, in fact, was so considerably watered down that the reference to military bases disappeared from the text altogether. In its place appeared a vague promise to remove any 'commitments' which would militate against a consistent policy of non-alignment, a somewhat indeterminate promisory note for the future.

In view of the importance the French attached to bases, together with their often stated desire to draw Africa into the European orbit in matters of defence as well as trade, it is understandable that Europe did not take kindly to the OAU proposals. But whether it identified itself with the goals or not, French forces were asked to leave Mauretania, Cameroon and Niger, and most notably of all, the Malagassy Republic in 1973. Even so it would be wrong to suggest that the Europeans were thrown out of Africa. France itself was quite sensitive to African criticism and in the case of Algeria relinquished control of the huge naval base of Mers-el-Kebir in February 1968, seven years ahead of schedule.

There was, of course, rather more to the OAU's efforts than the eradication of bases on the mainland. The organisation looked beyond, to the Indian Ocean as well. In much the same way that French nuclear testing in the Sahara in the late 1950s had sparked off a proposal for an African nuclear-free zone, so Soviet naval deployment in the Indian Ocean and the swiftness of the West's response prompted Africa to endorse Sri Lanka's call in 1968 for a zone of peace. Adopting Resolution 2832 (XXVI), the General Assembly called upon the great powers to halt the further escalation of their naval forces and to eliminate all existing bases and military installations in the area. At a time when the need to unite on the issue seemed plain, the local powers hoped that, where individual protests had fallen on deaf ears, concerted action might succeed.

The declaration owed its origin to the Lusaka summit which had been anxious to reaffirm one of the fundamental principles of the non-aligned movement: that its own members should not opt for membership of alliances or pacts conceived in the context of the cold war. The term 'Afro–Asian ocean', which was used for the first time at the conference, signalled the growing sense of responsibility which the states in the region were beginning to feel for their own political destiny as Asians or Africans, a dimension which the West had only just begun to take into account and of which the Russians hoped to take advantage. In fact, the Soviet Union was determined when it first despatched ships to the area to avoid the mistakes of the Western powers. It was well acquainted with the problems which had beset, as well as the precedents which had been set by the West – that is why it was so quick to propose the demilitarisation of the Indian Ocean as the prelude to its own entry, to exploit the fear that there would be a race to fill the vacuum left by Britain when the local states doubted whether a vacuum actually existed.

In September 1971, the Foreign Ministers of 54 non-aligned countries who had gathered for the 26th session of the General Assembly reaffirmed the Lusaka Declaration and agreed to take concrete steps to implement it. By then the situation appeared to be more urgent than ever with Britain's decision to renew the sale of arms to South Africa. On 1 October, the Tanzanian representative addressed a letter to the Secretary-General requesting that the issue be placed on the agenda. A week later, on the recommendation of the General Committee, the General Assembly instructed the First Committee to consider the matter more fully.

During the 26th session the General Assembly failed to reach agreement whether the matter should be referred to the Committee on Disarmament or discussed directly with the major powers. It did agree, however, to set up an *ad hoc* committee of 15 members which included four African countries: the Malagassy Republic, Mauritius, Zambia and Tanzania (and later Kenya and Somalia) to study the proposal's implications. When the *ad hoc* committee met in 1973, it even agreed to draw up a factual statement detailing, as precisely as information allowed, the naval dispositions of each of the powers, a report which was subsequently criticised by the Superpowers, neither of whom showed any inclination to enter into consultation with each other.

There the matter rested until 1974. It was evident that while the Africans themselves were still committed to the demilitarisation of the Indian Ocean, they were uncertain how best to proceed. They were not all agreed on the use of the United Nations as a forum; some doubted whether the UN could be used at all. Although there was near unanimity on the principle of demilitarisation doubts about the feasibility of the zone of peace as a concept prompted some countries to abstain from participating in the voting in the First Committee and subsequently in the General Assembly as well.

The *ad hoc* committee, in fact, never defined precisely what it meant by the concept, its scope or delimitation, or the obligations and responsibilities of those called upon to honour it.[14] Inevitably its recommendations lacked clarity of thought and its actions consistency of purpose. At the first meeting of the committee it was agreed that the passage of warships need not be restricted unless they remained in the area indefinitely. But the proposal that the Superpowers might be allowed to transit the Indian Ocean instead of maintaining permanent bases was unlikely to appeal to NATO. The Europeans had already discovered that the Montreux convention which allowed Soviet submarines to transit but not remain in the Mediterranean had not prevented them from remaining for months at a time before proceeding to their final destination.

The discussion of the zone of peace also led to misunderstanding on the part of the Soviet Union. The zone defined by the *ad hoc* committee would not have applied to the French Navy and its bunkering facilities in Réunion and Comoros. Was the inclusion of France likely to advance its achievement or to create more problems than it resolved? Even if France's NATO partners had no reason to expect that they would automatically have first claim on its allegiance, in Soviet eyes a zone which preserved the military bases of any of the 'imperialist' powers would put the Soviet Navy on an unequal footing.

In short, the zone of peace proposal which emerged between 1971–74 obscured more than it revealed about its authors' intentions. It is true that it represented a bold and imaginative attempt to limit cold war competition, and even to proscribe it. It offered a prescription for the future, as well as a description of the danger in which Africa would find itself if the naval build-up continued. Yet its provisions were not thought out clearly.

In their efforts to have the Ocean declared a zone of peace, the Africans saw Diego Garcia most of all as a symbol of all that they most disliked. Suspicion of the United States had always figured prominently in their attitudes to NATO despite the fact that the Americans had always been punctilious, almost to a fault, in not trespassing on African sensibilities. As the Prime Minister of Mauritius, one of the most vociferous critics of the base, reminded the non-aligned conference at Colombo:

> With the exception of Diego Garcia there is no problem in the Indian Ocean – it gives free access to all major powers. It is a free ocean not free to freebooters, but to those who want peace and harmony and wish to make it a zone of peace . . .

The role played by Mauritius reflected its own image of itself as the spokesman of the Indian Ocean powers. Africa's deepening political and economic crisis, and the constant threat of domestic disorder made it particularly sensitive to initiatives which were likely to make the Indian Ocean an area of conflict.

Nevertheless, it would be a mistake to assume that African opinion was unanimous. Widely held though such sentiments were, they were not held by all. From private conversations conducted with a number of African countries, none of whom were particularly vocal in their public support, the State Department concluded that the response was far more restrained than expected. Indeed, where it had not been given outright support, it had become clear that some countries would have been far more upset if the Americans had not decided to match the Soviet presence.

TABLE 7: *Survey of Reaction Towards US Proposals to Expand Diego Garcia*

	Official	Press/Public
South Africa	Favourable	Favourable
Malawi	Favourable	No reaction
Malagassy	Negative	Negative
Tanzania	Balanced	Balanced
Kenya	No reaction	Negative
Somalia	No reaction	Negative
Ethiopia	Favourable	Balanced
Zambia	No reaction	No reaction
Sudan	No reaction	No reaction
Egypt	No reaction	No reaction

SOURCE: *Proposed Expansion of US Military Facilities in the Indian Ocean.* Hearings before the Committee of Foreign Affairs, subcommittee on the Near East and South Asia, House of Representatives 1975, p. 45.

The controversy excited by the Diego Garcia issue provides one of the few cases where differences of opinion divided the African powers. Although the build-up of naval forces was a cause of growing concern to the 36 countries in the region, and to the Africans most of all, opinion tended to divide along predictable lines, with one group hoping that the Indian Ocean would soon become a zone of peace, the other apparently resigned to the fact that, admirable though such aspirations were, the most that could be hoped for was a 'balanced' presence. To a large extent, though with notable exceptions, these conflicting positions tended to mask the pro-Western and pro-Soviet sympathies of the countries entertaining them.

Several countries, for example, who were sympathetic to the United States accepted America's contention that the expansion of Diego Garcia would not eliminate the possibility of arms control talks in the future. They were inclined to go along with the argument that the facility was not in itself likely to fuel naval competition, that America had the right to protect its legitimate interests in the area and that, in the circumstances, neither the Soviet Union nor Africa need feel threatened. They were also of the opinion that if progress was to be made in the field of naval arms reduction it would have to win the acceptance of the powers directly concerned, and that it was both unrealistic and possibly misguided to imagine that the Superpowers could be restrained without their consent.[15] There was no evidence at the time that either of the powers were anxious to enter into arms limitation talks, but quite a lot to indicate that the process would not be brought any nearer by blanket condemnation of NATO designs or American ambitions.

Yet the truth of these general propositions was disputed by the majority. Few African countries were as fair-minded as Madagascar in proposing that the whole matter of naval arms limitation talks would be more fittingly handled by the Conference of the Committee on Disarmament based in Geneva.[16] Tanzania spoke for the main body of African opinion when it accused NATO of being 'an aggressive military machine' which had failed to make any concessions to African aspirations. In October 1973, the Tanzanian government returned to the attack by expressly rejecting 'the reason advanced by the US authorities that if the Russians increase their fleet in the Mediterranean, then the Americans must increase their fleet in the Indian Ocean'.[17] This reasoning seemed to be untenable because Tanzania doubted whether the United States would have used the same argument to send aircraft carriers to the Baltic Sea. It was the weakness of the African countries which explained why the USN was in one sea and not the other.

The Tanzanians did not see why the matter should be the subject of discussion between the blocs at all since Africa, not the West, was under threat, and since the Western powers were more of a threat than the Russians. 'The colonial powers have said not a word on that subject', argued one African representative on the Committee of 24:

> indeed they have used a completely different vocabulary: strategy, crisis, *détente*, security, etc. The Committee is faced with a totally different philosophy. Strategic interests must not be permitted to take precedence over the interests of the colonial peoples.

In the face of such criticisms NATO could be forgiven for often dismissing non-alignment as a catchphrase which was at best self-deceiving, at worst self-serving. Africa was too weighed down by the burden of history to communicate its underlying concern. It was not the appeal for a zone of peace which rankled with NATO, but the apparent bias of those most eloquent in putting it forward.

When the question of Diego Garcia arose in the early 1970s, the

Western powers were not surprised to find the Soviet Union playing the old theme in apparent confidence that residual fears of Western imperialism would more than offset African concern about its own presence in the Indian Ocean and its base facilities in Berbera. In the absence of confidence and mutual trust between the Western powers and Africa, the Russians were listened to more readily than NATO.

After 1974, and particularly after the Soviet invasion of Afghanistan, the African states expected very little to come out of the intermittent naval arms limitation talks between the Superpowers. As the Tanzanian delegate to the UN Committee on the Indian Ocean observed in June 1981:

> When it comes to matters of mutual benefit the Superpowers are quite willing to talk; but when it is in their interest to disagree they do so at the expense of others.[18]

That most African states should still have felt that the West was a greater threat than the Soviet Union to their own security is not all that surprising in the light of the build-up of the US presence. As Alexander Haig told the Senate Foreign Relations Committee in September 1981:

> our broad strategic view of the Middle East recognises the intimate connections between the region and adjacent areas: Afghanistan and South Asia; North Africa and the Horn; the Mediterranean and the Indian Ocean.[19]

This conception of strategic unity represented for the Reagan Administration what Zbigniew Brzezinski had termed 'an arc of instability'. The build-up of the RDF brought Kenya and Somalia into what President Carter termed 'a cooperative regional security framework' for the Indian Ocean. Most other states in the region derived little confidence from it.

The Indian Ocean's geographical assymetries gave the West a preponderant influence at its four points of entrance and exit: Suez, the Cape, the Straits of Malacca and the Australasian–Indonesian passages. After 1979, American strategy sought to expand these advantages by negotiating rights of entry to several more African ports to counter the slim advantage the Soviet Union derived from access to airfields in the immediate hinterland. The balance of advantage undoubtedly lay with the United States. While in time of war the Soviet Union might be able to airlift its forces into Africa, in time of crisis the United States could seal off and harass all shipping including, of course, all shipping involved in intra-Ocean trade. This was even more so after the extension of the Suez Canal in 1981 to ease the passage of American aircraft-carriers.

The local states made very little headway in promoting the idea of a zone of peace, mostly because of American opposition. In the late 1970s, the Malagassy Republic began to use its influence with left wing governments or parties in Mauritius, Réunion and the Seychelles to press for demilitarisation. It even tried to set an example by rejecting the presence of any foreign naval vessels and undertaking in 1977 to close its ports to all great powers including the Soviet Union. The Seychelles followed suit after the *coup* of 1976 which brought a socialist administration to power anxious to mend its fences with the Soviet Union. Despite reconciliation between the two countries, the government declined to open its ports to foreign naval shipping. This strictly non-aligned posture, however, did not prompt the government to ask the United States to give up its satellite tracking station on the island of Mahé which was quite clearly used for military purposes. Remaining negotiations were only concerned with increasing American payments.

By this time Diego Garcia was also beginning to loom large in African thinking. By 1977, the year President Carter spoke of the complete demilitarisation of the Indian Ocean, there were already 1400 American troops on the island. Its importance as a centre for military surveillance always made it likely that it would be retained whatever else might be decided in the negotiations. With the expansion of the RDF, Diego Garcia took on a role fulfilled by no other base in the region: the projection of offensive power. In the summer of 1981, the Americans finally obtained British approval for building airstrips that could take B-52 bombers with a nuclear delivery capability.

A year earlier the OAU had unanimously demanded the return of Diego Garcia to Mauritius, claiming that the continued American presence represented an unacceptable 'threat to African security'.[20] The United States remained largely unmoved. As the former Under-Secretary of State, David Newsom, had told the Senate a few months earlier 'in all countries there are images and political clichés about past colonisation and intervention which come to the fore when a Western country talks of securing or establishing bases'.[21] The fact that Diego Garcia far eclipsed the Berbera base at the height of Soviet influence in Somalia was something which American military planners too easily forgot, or conveniently ignored.

BRITISH ARMS SALES TO SOUTH AFRICA

British arms sales to South Africa proved to be the most divisive of all the issues which divided Africa and the Atlantic community even though the sale was a purely bilateral matter between the British and South African governments. Despite the arms embargo Western Europe provided the largest source of imported arms and equipment. In addition, it was the predominant source of the sophisticated weaponry which South Africa could not manufacture itself. The success of the embargo in this context was critically dependent upon the policies of the Western powers.

In the 11 years it had been in operation, the arms embargo had failed to have much effect. The Africans constantly called for tougher measures; the British government in June 1970 questioned whether it was worth imposing sanctions at all. Inevitably, its decision to press ahead with the sale of helicopters and frigates to assist the South African Navy's (SAN) operations in the Indian Ocean excited greater suspicions of British motives than those of its allies, including the French. The OAU mission under Kenneth Kaunda, although rebuffed in London and cold-shouldered in Bonn, was well received in Paris. Indeed, France was 'sincerely thanked' for promising to reduce arms sales to South Africa despite the fact that, at the end of the day, France was left supplying as broad a range of military equipment as the British hoped to supply themselves. And as the South Africans were quick to point out, the small arms and light armoured vehicles the French had promised to withhold were already being produced in the republic under French licenses, using French capital investment.

Although France and West Germany had also been singled out for special criticism at the OAU heads of state conference five months earlier, at the Commonwealth Conference at Singapore, Britain figured most prominently. Obviously, the British government in 1970 was not prepared to accept constraints on its sovereign right to sell arms as it wished and as it saw necessary for its own security; equally clearly, the Africans believed that the embargo had a moral sanction which overrode all other considerations, including those of strategy.

That the controversy did not wreck the Commonwealth Conference was due almost entirely to the initiative of Canada – the only other Commonwealth member that was also a member of NATO. Had it not been for Canada's support from the outset, Zambia and Tanzania might never have attended. Strategic necessity had its place in a political context, but the Canadian government was particularly incensed with Britain for devaluing the Commonwealth connection and paying too little regard to African opinion on matters which it believed were of concern not only to the Commonwealth but also, contrary to what the British claimed, to the Western Alliance.[22]

In a personal letter to Edward Heath, Trudeau urged full consultation with the Commonwealth before embarking on a policy which was bound to bring it into conflict with so many of its members. His personal initiative coincided with a decision to tighten up the Canadian embargo. In November 1970, Ottawa announced the termination of the continued sale of spare parts for military planes which had been sold to South Africa prior to 1962. In December, Trudeau personally intervened again by sending a special emissary to Kaunda and Nyerere to persuade them to attend the forthcoming Commonwealth Conference in Singapore. Later, during Mr Heath's visit to Canada, he persuaded the British government not to press the issue before it had given its Commonwealth partners a chance to reach a consensus.[23]

The nine day meeting itself was memorable for the acrimony which marked the debate. The British succeeded in convincing enough of the delegates that they had not fully understood the implications of the Simonstown Agreement and won a respite by placing the whole matter in the hands of a study group made up of eight members including Canada and two African states, Nigeria and Kenya. It was generally assumed by the members of the study group that Britain would defer selling arms to South Africa until the group had produced its report. But the decision to go ahead with the sale of seven helicopters before its members had a chance to meet ensured that it never met at all.

In the aftermath of the debate, relations between Britain and

Africa reached their lowest point in over a decade. Lines of communication with the Commonwealth were more strained than at any time since Britain's refusal to use force against Southern Rhodesia in 1965. The Africans went away from Singapore not in the least reassured that Britain's case was 'legitimate', or that the arms supplied to South Africa would not be used against the civil population. A few years later Edwin Ogebe Ogbu, the chairman of the Special Committee on apartheid, summed up the general feeling:

> We cannot ignore military cooperation with the South African regime even if it is said to be for defence. What that regime seeks to defend is the oppression of the African people – and any assistance to that regime constitutes direct or indirect complicity in that oppression.[24]

Even if the British were taken aback by the extent of the reaction, they showed no inclination to back down. That was to come later with evidence of public hostility in Britain itself, and representations on the part of its NATO partners. Far from retreating, the British government was confirmed in its resolution by expressions of support from several African countries, including the two most likely to be affected by its decision. President Banda told the Parliament of Malawi that he would rather see arms sold to South Africa than 'the body of water between Gibraltar in the West and Bombay in the East become a private swimming pool of a hostile nation'. To this voice was added another in Britain's support: that of the Foreign Minister of Mauritius who believed it would be quite wrong to expect Britain to look after the defence of the Indian Ocean and then deny it an opportunity to bring South Africa over to its side.[25] In the circumstances, it was natural that the two countries in the best position to defend the sea routes should reach some understanding. The price of living with each other was the price of living with the problems too.

Indeed, neither the Malagassy Republic nor Mauritius felt able to criticise Anglo–South African cooperation as long as NATO showed no interest in taking over Britain's responsibilities in the area – an argument that the British themselves employed in justifying their actions. Both countries looked aghast at the open competition for advantage between Britain and France manifested most notably in the pressure the French put on the government of Madagascar to revoke the agreement which allowed British aircraft to use the Majunga airfield to patrol shipping in the Mozambique Channel. The persistent refusal of the French to allow the USN access to Comoros and Réunion also appeared to reflect disunity within the Alliance, and open disagreement among its principal members which left Britain dependent on South Africa until the situation improved.[26] It was precisely because such countries felt themselves to be seriously disadvantaged by such behaviour that they were ready to come to terms with what, even for Britain, was only a second best solution.

But to the great majority of Africans, the Soviet naval threat was not very real.[27] They did not deny that Britain had interests in the area which needed to be defended. They also recognised that as a major trading power, the defence of the sealanes was a matter of some concern. But they insisted that such interests were common to Africa as well and that African interests would not be served by re-arming South Africa. The case was put most cogently by Britain's old protagonist, Julius Nyerere. Like many others, he was happy to meet Britain's objections half-way: to agree that in time of war Britain would not be able to pick and choose its allies. But in peacetime Africa had a right to expect Britain to march to a different set of priorities:

> Before any nation adopts another as an ally it is as well for it to consider whether this new alliance means becoming involved in other separate conflicts which are irrelevant to its purposes. It is the total situation which matters, not one new ally for a possible future conflict.[28]

Nyerere continued to argue, up to and beyond the Singapore conference, that the only conflict in progress at the time was taking place in Southern Africa, and that the conflict there was not between communism and capitalism but between racialism and freedom, a conflict in which the Africans hoped to have NATO on their side. Britain's Commonwealth partners maintained that its agreement to sell arms to South Africa could be interpreted in one light only: that Britain preferred to throw in its lot with apartheid rather than rely on what Nyerere termed 'the friendship of the young and free nations bordering the Indian Ocean'.

Though Kaunda looked upon himself as Africa's principal spokesman, Nyerere played the central role at Singapore. It was

Nyerere whom Heath invited to London in October 1970, who was approached by Trudeau in the run-up to the conference and who put forward the most persuasive arguments against the renewal of sales to South Africa once the conference had convened. In a private paper which circulated among the delegates on the opening day, he rested his case not on a strategic assessment of the Soviet naval presence, which he considered open to interpretation, nor the legal implications of the Simonstown Agreement which continued to be in dispute, but on what, for most Africans, was the only irrefutable fact in the whole case:

> You can trade with people you dislike, you can have diplomatic relations with governments you disapprove of, you can sit in conference with those nations whose policies you abhor. But you do not sell arms without saying in effect *we anticipate that in the last resort, we will be on their side in case of any conflict.*

The suspicions entertained of Britain, and by association the Alliance of which it was a member, persisted long after the debate had fizzled out. The arguments advanced by Nyerere and others in 1970 brought to a head apprehensions about NATO which had been entertained for many years, in particular the suspicion that South Africa and the Western Alliance were partners in all but name; that NATO was opposed to national liberation because of concern that its success might deny it the use of military bases in the area. Few appreciated how responsive Britain's allies had been in the face of changing security conditions within and outside the continent or the fact that most members of NATO including the United States considered the Anglo–South African connection a grave embarrassment to the Alliance made no less so by the fact that in exploiting the image of its own indispensability, South Africa had made its dispensability superfluous by collaboration.

AFRICA AND PORTUGAL

The impunity with which the poorest member of NATO and the most underdeveloped country in Europe, underpowered and undermanned to wage a long colonial war, nevertheless managed against all the odds to do so, inclined many to blame the North Atlantic Alliance for the tenacity of Portuguese rule. Those whose attitudes had been transformed by the bitterness of the colonial wars in Southern Africa were increasingly ready to implicate Portugal's allies in what they interpreted as a conspiracy against self-determination. By 1970, NATO's attitude to Portugal's continued membership of the Alliance became for many a test case of its own sincerity; for others who were sceptical of NATO's position from the beginning, Portugal's allies appeared to be paving the road to hell with rationalisations of self-interest.

In 1961, a few months after the Angolan revolt, Nkrumah had placed the blame for Portugal's obstinacy firmly at the door of the Atlantic community:

> Portugal is only able to wage a colonial war because fundamentally she has the backing of NATO. If this backing were withdrawn tomorrow and Portugal was excluded from NATO Portugal's colonial rule would collapse the day after.[29]

However unfair the diagnosis and unrealistic the prescription, both ran with the grain of African opinion. It seemed impossible that Portugal could maintain control of a territory 20 times its size and over a population 50 per cent greater than its own unless it had the support of more powerful allies. Speaking to a university audience in Toronto eight years later, Nyerere agreed that the Western alliance might not be able to bring peace to Southern Africa by expelling Portugal from its ranks, but it was the West, not Africa, which had to make a choice between peace and war, for the question was not whether the Western powers could coerce Portugal, but whether they were willing to do so. Upon the answer to that question would depend the future of Southern Africa for years to come.[30]

Most Africans held fast to this analysis well into the 1970s. At the first session of the Security Council ever held in Africa, Zambia's Foreign Minister called upon NATO to follow the example set by Norway which had, in the first instance, publicly disassociated itself from Portuguese policy and, in the second, discontinued selling arms. The call for a complete suspension of arms was taken up in earnest by Kenya and Tanzania who invited the Alliance to join the struggle against colonial oppression by discarding considerations of purely short term interest. The Nigerian Foreign Minister warned of the implications that would result if matters were not resolved quickly, advancing the opinion that, but for its membership of NATO, Portugal would never have carried its war of repression into open aggression against its neighbours – a reference to the 'invasion' of Guinea in 1970 which had led the government of Seké Touré to call upon the assistance of the Soviet Union. Colonial rule in Portuguese Guinea posed a challenge, not just to nationalism within the country, but to the survival of neighbouring Guinea as a nation-state.[31]

The strong current of opinion which ran against the Atlantic Alliance for most of the period, a mood of frustration expressed in occasional rhetorical attacks and a reluctance to take its professions of support for self-determination at face value, emerged most forcefully in 1973 during a conference sponsored jointly by the United Nations and the Organisation of African Unity. Among the participants, who included the UN Council on Namibia, the Committee of 24, and the OAU's own special Committee for the Liberation of Africa, the NATO allies were conspicuous by their absence. The United States, Britain, France and West Germany took no part in drafting the Final Programme of Action which was later adopted by the OAU Council of Ministers the following month and which eventually formed the basis of the Secretary-General's report to the General Assembly. Their absence seemed to represent a studied indifference towards African opinion. It also explained the enthusiasm of the delegates for condemning NATO by name, in proposals 10 and 12 of the Action Programme:

(10) A warning should be given against any extension of the activities of the North Atlantic Treaty Organisation to the south Atlantic and the Indian Ocean as this would be regarded as a threat to the peace and security of independent African countries and an act of direct support to Portugal and South Africa.

(12) Members of the North Atlantic Treaty Organisation which refuse to supply arms to Portugal should take joint action within the Council of Ministers to bring an end to the Organisation's support for Portugal's colonial wars.[32]

As it happened, very few delegates accused NATO of deliberately supporting Portugal – the sins for which they blamed it were those of omission rather than commission. In its preoccupation with a conflict between communism and capitalism in Africa which had yet to take place, the organisation had allowed the present conflict to be almost completely obscured. The voices heard on this point were all but unanimous. Torn between the costs of continuing the war on the one hand, and the need to satisfy the military on the other, the Caetano government was unable either to opt out or reconcile itself with African nationalism. Perhaps its expulsion from NATO would have tipped the balance. We simply do not know. Less than a decade since the end of the revolt (and two since its outbreak), the matter is still open to speculation, historically unrewarding though interesting to ask.

In the concluding session Herbert Chitepo, the chairman of the Zimbabwe African National Union (ZANU), spoke on behalf of all the liberation movements represented at the conference when he explained:

> We have commented very adversely on such institutions as NATO, not because they are themselves evil, but because they allow their member countries or have not used their influence sufficiently against their member countries, when they misuse their weapons to carry out wars and support policies of oppression and exploitation of the people of the Portuguese territories.[33]

Since 1961 opposition to NATO had been expressed quite frequently, but it had never been as sustained or significant as it was in 1973. As a representative of one liberation movement (PAIGC) reminded the conference, Portugal's predicament had reached a point where the immediate cessation of arms could tip the balance. In Mozambique an army base had almost been overrun because the local commanders had not had enough helicopters in the area to fly in ammunition to the beleaguered garrison.[34] In Portuguese Guinea, 11 planes had been shot down by surface-to-air missiles only two weeks before the conference convened, a rate of attrition which could only be met by continued sale of planes by its NATO allies.[35] Here was a direct challenge to the Alliance on a matter that was no longer open to debate. While the costs of intervening had increased the costs of non-involvement were beginning to increase quite substantially.

It was not the first time, of course, that NATO had been held accountable for selling arms to one of its own members. Back in 1959, the use of American equipment in Algeria had been branded an affront to the whole Arab world by its self-appointed spokesman, Abdul Nasser.[36] In August of the same year, the conference of independent African states, meeting in Monrovia, had formally appealed to the Alliance to suspend all arms sales to France. Gone were the days, however, when the Alliance could be impervious to outside opinion. The UN–OAU conference represented the end of a long journey. Not all the NATO members had travelled along it, but on the way they had all come to recognise some obvious truths – first and foremost, that it faced suspicions of its motives in Africa which its association with Portugal had done nothing to dispel; secondly, that the experience was best avoided in the future.

In asking why the Western powers lacked the will to expel Portugal, most Africans looked no further than the East–West struggle. The evidence, as they saw it, was that NATO had made a choice a long time ago to put strategic self-interest before the principles of self-determination embodied in its charter. Since their own perspective was shaped so forcefully by very different considerations, it is not surprising that they were over-sanguine about Soviet aims and intentions, deaf to the warnings which emanated from Brussels. At a time when NATO's alleged collusion with Portugal and South Africa preoccupied them so much, it never seemed very likely that NATO would communicate its own concern about Soviet aims and intentions.

FRANCO–BELGIAN INTERVENTION IN SHABA, 1978

It is fair to say that no event generated more discussion of Western intervention in Africa than Shaba II. No event better illustrates Africa's ambiguous relationship with the Western Alliance. Calling in foreign diplomats a month after the French and Belgian parachute drop, Nyerere deplored what he saw as an unbridled attempt to reassert European domination under the pretext of defending the continent against external aggression. He deplored particularly the tendency of the West to treat Africa as an appendage of the North Atlantic Alliance, an area of the world which fell within its own sphere of operations and in which indigenous powers were denied the right to challenge Western control or elect regimes unsympathetic to Western interests.[37]

No event generated a much longer, more searching, more self-revealing appraisal of Africa's attitudes towards NATO.

Some of the criticism was justified but much of it betrayed an unwillingness to come to terms with Africa's predicament. Most African polemics focused hardly at all on the striking consistency with which the Alliance had come to terms with African nationalism. Anyone listening to the debate for the first time might have been misled into thinking that the Alliance had still not come to terms with it at all.

These attitudes found expression at the OAU Heads of State meeting in Khartoum in July 1978. From the outset the OAU divided into three camps, with the more radical members, including Guinea-Bissau, Benin and Congo-Brazzaville, strongly criticising Western intervention, and particularly the parachute drop in Zaire. Given their historical perspective, their line of attack was predictable, but nonetheless forceful for that. It was expressed most cogently by the President of Mozambique, Samora Machel:

> At the time of the conquest and partition of Africa the colonists tried to divide us and to buy us with trinkets and mirrors. Now to divide us they use concepts such as Francophone, Anglophone and even Lusophone. They play with promises of aid, with bribery and corruption; they promise expansionism, chauvinism, and wars of conquest. When this fails imperialism instigates, finances, and promotes those who it considers moderates and realists, moderation meaning subordination to the interests of imperialism, realism implying the surrender of principles, the sacrifice of the fundamental interests of Africa and our peoples ...
> Mental colonisation, mental subservience, which some have in relation to their former metropoles, often leads to the definition as 'foreign to Africa' only that which is anti-colonialist and anti-imperialist, that which implies a rupture with the models of economic, cultural and social dependence on the former colonial powers ...
> Within this mode of thinking ... the weapons which don't come from NATO member countries, especially those countries which enslaved Africa, are foreign. According to this logic only the bases, military pacts and agreements, troops and instructors which don't come from the former colonising power are considered foreign, against the interests of Africa and in violation of non-alignment.[38]

One lesson Machel drew from the crisis was that the Europeans would continue to treat Africa as part of their own sphere of influence as long as Africans were divided among themselves or continued to break ranks and call in outside forces to sustain themselves in power.

The countries in the second camp, including those who had contributed to the successful outcome of Shaba I – Morocco, Senegal and Egypt – took the view that Soviet expansionism would only be countered if the Western powers took a direct hand in the matter. In an interview with an American newspaper a month after Shaba II, Leopold Senghor, President of Senegal, insisted that the East only had the edge because it had definite objectives and was prepared to commit very efficient, modern and expensive means to attain them. So far the presence of 40 000 Cuban troops in Africa, largely sustained and supported by the Soviet Union, had not been challenged.[39]

Senghor hoped that the Kolwezi operation would encourage the Western Alliance to abandon its previous strategy of appeasement and put its trust once again in containment:

> The Americans want to have things both ways. They want Africa to resist the East's offensive but will not help it do so. They want the end without the means. They refuse to supply us with the modern weapons we need to defend ourselves . . .
> At the same time NATO was meeting and proposing an annual increase of 3 per cent in its defence budget. So the West adopts the necessary measures to assure security but the West thinks that Africans can defend themselves empty-handed against attacks from outside. That is not a consistent attitude: it is contradictory. We are asking our Western friends simply to help us in the same way the Marxist–Leninist states are helped by their friends.[40]

In posing the question: would the Alliance be prepared in future to act directly in Africa, Senghor felt its implications too keenly to carefully weight the different answers. For the majority of OAU members, however, merely to pose the question was not enough. Both Tanzania and Nigeria rejected the notion that Africa's security was of legitimate interest to NATO. They were well aware of the West's concern about Soviet and Cuban penetration of the continent, but they considered that, for the most part, it was grossly exaggerated. To the extent that any African country could be called 'communist', the West often had only itself to blame. 'The fact of the matter', Nigeria's President insisted:

> is that Africa was colonised by Western powers and not the Soviets. In the struggle for independence and freedom the only source of effective support was the Eastern bloc countries. The Soviets were therefore invited into Africa for a purpose and that purpose was to liberate the country to which they were invited from centuries of cruelty, degradation, oppression and exploitation . . .
> The Cubans are, of course, a newcomer to Africa. Their presence has the same background as the Soviets. In every case where Cuba's intervention was established they intervened as a consequence of the failure of Western policies and on behalf of legitimate African interests.[41]

This interpretation of Soviet activity in Africa contrasted markedly with that volunteered by the defence ministers in Brussels. The endemic instability of the continent threw up more and more opportunities for foreign intervention every year. Only a few years earlier those opportunists had been exploited largely by the Western powers. This was no longer true now that the reach of Soviet military power was not restricted to territories neighbouring or not far beyond the Soviet Union. The advice Obasanjo offered the Africans was that they could hardly ask the great powers to leave them alone, while in most cases their own actions provided them with an excuse to intervene. To the Russians and their allies, he advised that, having been invited to Africa to assist the liberation struggle, they should not overstay their welcome.

Nevertheless, Obasanjo went on to remind the Western Alliance why for so many countries in Africa, his own included, its actions raised more acute concern; why, in presenting a general case against foreign intervention, Shaba II rather than Angola or Ethiopia confirmed their diagnosis that, but for the existence of economic and strategic interests, the great powers would not intervene so often. Their concern was prompted largely by their own historical experience and that experience in turn derived largely from recent history:

> To the Western powers I say that they should act in such a way that we are not to believe they have different concepts of independence and sovereignty for Africa and for Europe. A new Berlin style conference [a reference to the NATO summit in Washington and follow-up meeting in Paris] is not the appropriate response to the kind of issues thrown up by the recent Kolwezi incident. Paratroop drops in the 20th century are no more acceptable to us than the gunboats of the last century were to our ancestors. Convening conferences in Europe and America to decide the fate of Africa raise too many ugly spectres which should best be forgotten both in our and Europe's interests.

Obasanjo's remarks must be placed in the context of the debate which continued to divide African opinion: whether the threat from the Soviet Union was more serious than European economic predominance. Most Africans were opposed to Western Europe's economic domination of the continent, as they were to military intervention by the Soviet Union. Neither Nyerere nor Obasanjo questioned Zaire's right to ask the French for help. Both accepted that there were many countries in Africa in which the government, despite broad-based support, might be threatened by forces quite unrepresentative of majority opinion. In Africa's present state of development, outside assistance might well be needed. But despite conceding this, Nyerere rejected the principle that the Western powers had a right to maintain in power governments that had lost popular support, 'Africa cannot have its present governments frozen into position for all time by neo-colonialism or because there are cold war or ideological conflicts between big powers'.

Here was the very nub of the question and as usual Nyerere identified it clearly. Was not the West guilty of double standards? Why had NATO at its summit meeting in Washington refused to discuss France's occupation of Mayotte or its intervention in Chad which had earlier been condemned by Denmark and Norway? Until NATO appreciated Africa's point of view it would continue to invent plausible reasons for shifting the focus of East–West conflict to Africa instead of looking to where Soviet tanks really did present a threat: central Europe.[42] At Khartoum, Nyerere reminded his colleagues that the threat to security came not only

... from nations in the eastern bloc. The West still considers Africa to be within its sphere of influence and acts accordingly. Current developments show that the greater immediate danger to Africa's freedom comes from nations in the Western bloc.

Eventually this view won the day. The resolutions drafted by the Council of Ministers at sessions held concurrently with those of the Heads of State affirmed that Africa's defence and security were its own responsibility. External assistance could only be considered within the context of the principles enshrined in the OAU Charter.[43] A second resolution on military intervention expressed concern that foreign assistance might create or perpetuate conflicts and artificial divisions.[44] Like most of the resolutions that emerged from the conference, as opposed to many of the speeches by the Heads of State, these statements made up in rhetoric what they lacked in realism. The only real ground for hope remained that which had inspired the original signatories of the OAU Charter – that African states would avoid calling in outside help and preferably avoid precipitating situations in which it would ever become necessary. Many commentators in the West found these resolutions grounded in that curiously Manichaean view of the world which had always bedeviled the non-aligned movement. Foreign intervention, whatever form it assumed, was invariably presented as an appalling denial of self-determination, a denial not simply because force was likely to be unjustly and irresponsibly applied but applied under the cloak of strategic necessity with no regard to Africa's interests. The fact was, of course, that the means, safeguards and actions needed to rescue societies in the developing world from external threats were more varied and complex than many African leaders were often willing to admit. Inevitably, therefore, NATO military planners, while perceiving Africa's international predicament in the same stark terms, tended to draw radically different conclusions.

AFRICAN ATTITUDES TO THE SOVIET INTERVENTION IN ANGOLA

The events of 1975 did not immediately alter this perception. Africa's renewed concern about Western intervention was the result of its past experience as well as further reflection on recent history; also of its continuous struggle to live by the principles of non-alignment. The non-aligned movement needed no reminding that Africa provided over half its 88 members, as well as its anti-colonialist and anti-racist content. As a continent which had suffered from great power rivalry in the past and seemed likely to suffer in the future, its troubles sharpened the demands for a new international order. Africa represented the acid test of the success or failure of the developing world's aspirations. Its emancipation from colonial rule, the ending of racial discrimination against people of African origin, its neutrality and denuclearisation in a world of great powers were not merely regional or continental concerns, but the priorities of the entire non-aligned group.

In an interview five months before the Havana summit, Nyerere set out his reasons for feeling threatened by the West more than the Soviet Union:

> Africa today has a formal relationship with the European Community. We are like appendages to the EEC. We are to Western Europe what Latin America is to the United States. So, for those Africans who feel they need to enlarge their area of freedom the problem is not the Soviet Union. It is Western Europe . . . We are dependent on Western Europe and I know that I don't want to be dependent on anyone else, the Soviet Union included.[45]

As if to underline Nyerere's complaint the former French Foreign Minister Louis Guiringaud affirmed that the policy of *Afrique aux Africains* (Africa for the Africans) meant only that Africans should be able to settle their own problems 'without interference from powers who have no ties to Africa'.[46] Nowhere was the Eurafrica doctrine so tellingly expressed – the belief that where the Europeans could intervene to protect interests of many years' standing, the Russians could not.

As a result, Western warnings about Soviet intentions tended to go either unheard or unheeded. The Western Alliance had little success in persuading the Africans that Soviet intervention in Angola or the Horn might be the opening move in a second scramble for the continent's resources – none at all in tying the use of the words aggression, intervention and destabilisation to the Soviet bloc.

Secondly, Africa's suspicion and distrust of the West was

reinforced by the unwillingness of the Western powers, preoccupied as they were with their own security, to challenge white supremacy in southern Africa. Their failure confirmed what for many countries was rapidly becoming a primary truth of politics: namely that Africa would have to look to its own exertions to advance objectives which were of pre-eminent value only to itself. In this respect, the Soviet Union's intervention in Angola seemed to be no more arbitrary than the West's decision to oppose the MPLA; neither were inconsistent with their past actions:

> ... why countries give arms to the MPLA is a matter which they know and others can only conjecture. What is certain is that the arms were obtained and used for the independence of Angola.[47]

Nyerere remained convinced that had the MPLA not found itself fighting America as well as South Africa the Russians might not have intervened at all. Angola had been attacked by American money, an American equipped army and American mercenaries put in the field with the tacit support of the Western Alliance.[48] As a result, the MPLA had faced a compelling and inescapable context of necessity. Only Soviet intervention had prevented Angola's first 'independent' government from being imposed by international forces over which it had little control. The context of necessity seemed to be reflected in the striking continuity with which the Superpowers pursued their goals during the civil war. In the eyes of many African leaders, the great majority of whom were far from sympathetic to the Soviet Union, the West's support for the FNLA was a cynical tactical response to a crisis which had caught it by surprise.

As a result, many Africans were singularly unimpressed by America's attempts to portray Soviet intervention as 'imperialistic', and to use the vocabulary of non-alignment for its own ends. When Daniel Moynihan warned the United Nations that the Soviet Union had embarked on a second scramble for Africa his warnings were greeted with frank disbelief.[49] When he castigated the Committee of 24 for demanding that South Africa withdraw from Angola without demanding that the Cubans do the same, he was reminded that a threat to Angola's independence (from whatever quarter it might arise) would manifest itself only after freedom had been won, not before.[50]

In asking why the divergence of opinion should have been so profound one need only remind oneself of the West's equivocal attitude to the nationalist struggle in Southern Africa in the period before 1974. Nyerere believed that the Americans had learned nothing from the lessons of the 1960s when their preoccupation with Soviet expansionism had prompted them, perhaps unwittingly, to support the *status quo*. After the Portuguese had left, America's policy in Angola, such as it was, still seemed to be influenced by the moves and countermoves of the cold war.

Nyerere objected to the fact that right up to the end Kissinger had continued to characterise the MPLA as a Soviet puppet without looking to local circumstances or historical influences to explain its association with the Russians. Kissinger seemed prepared to make allowances for the *coup* in Portugal itself. Months after the military coup, he insisted that the United States would have to outgrow the notion that every setback represented a Soviet gain or every problem was the result of Soviet interference; difficulties were more likely to be explained by local circumstances or inadequate responses on the part of the United States.[51] In Angola, by contrast, Kissinger refused to concede that the MPLA might have been less reliant on the Soviet Union but for the West's failure in the 1960s to respond to the challenge of national liberation.

Of course, it would be quite wrong to suggest that African opinion was unanimous on the issue. The OAU not only failed to prevent the great powers from intervening, it also failed to uphold one of the cardinal principles of its own charter: that African disputes should be solved by Africans themselves. In the event, Cuban intervention proved too determined, too resilient and too resourceful. The OAU displayed no comparable energy or fixity of purpose in trying to resolve the internecine conflict between the nationalist movements.

There were many African countries who were deeply suspicious of Soviet intervention, deeply concerned that the supply of arms to the competing factions might internationalise the problem. In his report to the OAU in February 1976, its Secretary-General warned that if matters were not resolved quickly Angola might be permanently dismembered. By then the foreign ministers of central Africa had already condemned all intervention, whatever its origin, taking issue with those outside their own ranks who were not inclined to question Soviet goals, their nature, content or development. Although international circumstances limited Africa's response, not all leaders agreed that Cuban intervention was desirable, even if they were all agreed that it would have been better if the great powers had not become involved at all.

An emergency OAU summit in February was attended among others by 21 countries who had already recognised the MPLA as the legitimate government. In the face of such support, Kaunda sounded a rather belated warning when he argued that whatever assistance the Russians had given the movement in the past could not excuse their present actions. This was the first time in the post-colonial era that thousands of non-African troops had been brought into the continent to install a political movement in power; the first time that either of the Superpowers had intervened directly.[52] For the first time, too, Kaunda showed that, when he wanted to be, he could be a penetrating critic of those in the non-aligned movement who condemned the West, but often remained silent in the face of Soviet 'aggression'.

But the forces of moderation lacked direction and definition and by the time their voice was heard the MPLA's success had already been assured. It was not surprising that many African states, removed from the immediate area or otherwise not directly involved, should have played up South African involvement and played down that of the Cubans. They were traditionally suspicious of South Africa's links with the Western Alliance, traditionally ignorant of Soviet policy. One of the most moderate African leaders, Seretse Khama, President of Botswana, spoke for most countries when he insisted that South Africa's invasion of a neighbouring country constituted aggression of a far different order from foreign intervention or the use of mercenaries.[53]

For whatever reasons, only some of which have been touched upon here, the conference ended in deadlock. It took little more than a month for the issues that could not be settled round the conference table to be finally decided on the field of battle. By the beginning of March, the OAU Council of Ministers resolved by a majority vote to recognise the MPLA as the legitimate government of Angola.

In retrospect, Henry Kissinger may have been right to suspect that the Africans resented Soviet intervention no less than they resented America's covert support for the FNLA,[54] but their resentment lasted only as long as the struggle to keep the Alvor

Agreement afloat. What Africa resented most of all was the Soviet Union's unilateral recognition of the movement at a time when it was trying to persuade all the parties to work together. The Russians invited criticism because they put pay to those attempts not because they chose to support the most avowedly Marxist of the three movements, a distinction which Kissinger failed to grasp in time. Instead, he thought that the Africans should have accepted that a coalition government would be a recipe for disaster. Perhaps they should, but they did not. He thought that the moderates among them should have recognised the constructive aspects of South Africa's intervention and put their anti-racist ideology behind them. But Nigeria's decision to recognise the MPLA 15 days after the official transfer of power and within days of the first arrival of Cuban troops should have warned him that the Africans were not prepared to fight communism with Pretoria as an ally.

11 Conclusion: NATO and the Threat to Africa

Contrary to received opinion, the Atlantic Alliance recognises very well that the Soviet record in Africa is one of failure as well as success and that the Africans themselves do not want Western help at the moment. The Europeans have tried to avoid simplifying the African situation in terms that might make sense to a European or American audience but not to an African audience already suspicious of Western intentions. As the Political Committee of the North Atlantic Assembly reported in 1979, the appeal of the Soviet Union for many Africans, not all of them Marxists, come from several diverse sources, part ideological, part social. The language of Soviet policy – its support for 'non–capitalist development', 'national democratic regimes' and national wars of liberation merely echoes the authentic voice of African nationalism. Ultimately, ideological sympathy will probably count for much less than the fact that the Soviet Union is prepared to finance and equip guerrilla movements, while the West is not.[1] As the Committee had concluded in 1978:

> Undoubtedly Africa is of immense importance to the Alliance, strategically, politically and economically. This does not mean that the Alliance as an alliance should encompass Africa. In fact, such a development could have possibly serious disadvantages of viewing African developments only in the light of the East–West conflict without due consideration for traditional indigenous traditions and developments.[2]

NATO knows full well that Russian support for nationalist movements has rarely paid off in enduring political alliances. The nationalist struggle in the 1950s failed to produce a single

Marxist–Leninist state: the nearest equivalent were the radical socialist regimes of Mali and Guinea. The first avowedly Marxist state, Marie Ngouabi's Congo-Brazzaville, did not appear until the early 1970s, followed shortly afterwards by the three countries which emerged from the *détruitus* of the Portuguese empire in 1974.

These setbacks must not go unremarked. Despite Soviet assistance for the national liberation struggle the Soviet Union's progress has been marked by as many reverses as advances, most of a far reaching nature. Its advances to date certainly do not require the West to station forces on the continent; they require only continuing bilateral and multilateral consultation within the Alliance so that measures to counter Soviet intervention might be taken promptly.

Very little today remains of Khruschev's optimism when at one time it seemed that Africa might be at the beginning of a revolutionary era. As Raymond Aron tellingly reminds us in his study *Peace and War*:

> The African Republics may be converted to the new faith when governed by converts, but it is not subject to the same pressures, exposed to the same sanctions, as the satellites near the temporal and spiritual capital. States which become peoples' republics or socialist democracies in Africa . . . have not been restrained by the Soviet Union and they are not alienated to the same degree from their own autonomy.

Such cautionary reminders are more necessary than ever in the face of demands for a more active Western response.

To say that there has been no formal challenge, however, does not mean that African states are reconciled to their predicament. Many were not at all happy that Angola and Ethiopia had to call upon Soviet assistance. While acknowledging that both countries had a right to call on outside help they would have preferred the problems to have been solved by the governments themselves or, failing that, by other OAU members. The memory of the colonial era has left a strong distaste for the presence of non-African powers in the continent whatever their origin or ideological affinities.

Whatever their private views African states, including the most militant, have publicly repudiated actions and policies which have threatened to make their conflicts part of the larger East–West struggle. This outlook is reflected in the persistent demand that the West should address the problems of racism and colonialism in Southern Africa while there is still time and that the Soviet Union or its allies should not overstay their welcome. The Africans themselves have made their own position unequivocally clear: they will continue to oppose strategic moves by either bloc which will reduce their own independent posture.

Yet in the increasingly turbulent period into which the continent is entering, we may expect to see a growing assymetry in the willingness of Western and communist powers to respond to African requests. In that respect, it matters very little whether the Soviet Union has created opportunites in Africa or taken advantage of them: the fact is their allies are now in Africa and are there in comparatively large numbers. Whatever the origins of their presence, it represents a threat to the West's interest and the long term interests of Africa as well.

In short, though the West is probably right to eschew what Henry Kissinger once called 'the undifferentiated globalism' of American policy – the tendency to view every instance of political instability in the developing world as the effect of Soviet penetration – it may not be able to act entirely on the assumption that Africa can defend itself. Shaba II showed that in certain circumstances the West can act very effectively on its own account. France's striking success in cultivating the Francophone states provides it with a firmer base than most other Western powers to meet threats when and if they arise. Since French intervention has on the whole been sanctioned by its NATO partners, the Alliance may draw important lessons from French policy.

Apart from the threat that we have already discussed in Part II, one other part of the equation needs to be addressed: the question of arms sales to the continent which continue to multiply. Back in May 1978, America's Secretary of State, Cyrus Vance, recognised that it was important to assist Africa to meet its legitimate security needs; that military as well as economic assistance was a vital element in its efforts to reassure African moderates.[3] Nevertheless, the Carter Administration did very little to honour those pledges. Both Botswana and Zambia were refused military assistance although both were the victims of South African attack. American military training for African forces represented only 10 per cent of the world wide total despite an alarming increase in Soviet arms transfers.

By 1980 the Soviet Union alone accounted for 75 per cent of African military imports, a figure which did not include Czech and East German purchases. Although it was argued that Soviet sales were concentrated on a few countries, notably Ethiopia, the Soviet Union was only just behind France in the total number of its military clients in Africa, and was already the sole or predominant supplier of 13 African states, twice as many as any other supplier. In the six major conflicts in 1977 – the Western Sahara, Chad, Eritrea, Angola, Rhodesia and Namibia – the Soviet Union was directly or indirectly involved.[4] It was not surprising, therefore, that in an interview with a French newspaper Leopold Senghor should have complained:

> The Americans want to have things both ways. They want Africa to resist the East's offensive, but will not help it to do so. They want the end without the means. They refuse to supply us with the modern weapons we need to defend ourselves.[5]

In the light of these complaints it is only natural that the NATO powers, and not only the United States, should be concerned in the assymetry between their own willingness and that of the Soviet bloc to respond to African requests. The arguments against selling arms may be compelling, but they are not conclusively so. Not all disputes are susceptible to political solutions. Indeed, an unwillingness to arm a particular country might be taken as a sign that the defence of the country and/or regime is no longer vital to Western security.

In these circumstances, it seems fitting that NATO itself should not get involved, but that Britain and France should respond in a manner most fitted to the defence of their own interests. The case against large scale arms transfers from the United States is rather different. Obviously, the Reagan Administration is committed to arming Africa against Soviet intervention. It has persisted in the view that African solutions are not consistent with Western interests. In its first year in office, foreign military sales increased by 178 per cent with new recipients in the person of Senegal, Botswana and Gabon and substantial increases in the case of Kenya, Liberia and the Sudan. Nevertheless, those who have formulated American policy in such terms might stand back and think again. For against the narrow strategic advantages that such arms transfers might bring must be set the political and diplomatic consequences of competing with the Soviet Union on terms that can never be equal.

One of the most worrying aspects of the arms trade in Africa since 1974 is that most of the arms sold have no longer been surplus, over age and technologically inferior weapons, but high technology, first line weapons which can be found in the arsenals of most advanced industrial suppliers. In the 1960s, aircraft sold to Africa were more often than not ten year old MiG-17s or F-86s, rather than the first line aircraft of the period – F-4s and MiG-21s. Today the latest MiG-23s and F-15s can be found in the inventories of many African countries. Whether it is in the West's interests to compete on these terms, or, more to the point, whether it can, is a moot question.

The examples of the last few years would suggest that the United States, at least, does not have the option. Delivery times for advanced equipment have grown alarmingly. Most of the 300 M60A tanks promised to Egypt have still not been delivered. Chrysler can turn out 40 a month, but needs at least two years from the time the order is placed on the books to the time of delivery. The lead time for the F-16 which was 23 months in 1977 is now three and a half years. When the Reagan Administration promised to rearm the Sudan against a putative Libyan attack in 1981, it found it had to call on front line supplies in West Germany which precipitated a crisis among the Joint Chiefs of Staff. Even so the air defence system which it promised would not have been fully operational for three years.

Because of these problems American arms sales are unlikely to deter the Soviet Union from arming its own clients, or supporting their adventurist policies. They provide no point of departure for tackling Moscow's ability to exploit opportunities that have arisen in the past and may arise in the future. It is not that African solutions are preferable or possible (the OAU has failed miserably to keep the peace in Chad); it is only that the United States and its allies, more often than not, do not have the power to enforce solutions of their own.

If we look at the Soviet Union's own actions, however, the situation is far more encouraging. Their are five points worth making here. First, Soviet military assistance has often been so extensive that it has allowed countries to defeat their enemies quickly and get on with the process of development in which the West has on all occasions played a major part. This was true of the MPLA's victory over its two rivals in 1975–76 and Ethiopia's defeat of Somalia two years later. If this assistance had not been forthcoming, or if Soviet support had been half-hearted (a fact which explains Ethiopia's continuing struggle against the Marxist rebels in Eritrea) both countries would have remained dependent upon the Soviet bloc for very much longer, possibly indefinitely.

Where Western military assistance has continued, or in the case of Angola, where South African operations still force the MPLA to spend 50 per cent of its national budget on defence, economic development has inevitably been set back. Indeed, South African targets are mostly located precisely in those sectors of Angola's economy which most need Western investment.

Secondly, the era of palace revolutions and rapid military intervention is unlikely to last much longer. The example of Chad is worth pondering. Ten years of direct French intervention solved nothing. In 1983 Mitterrand was far more reluctant to intervene than Giscard or Pompidou before him. The same lesson is likely to hold true for the Soviet Union.

Thirdly, all the evidence of recent years suggests that the Soviet Union and its allies are not anxious to get involved directly. In the summer of 1983, Castro instructed his troops in Angola not to engage South African forces in the south so as to avoid exacerbating East–West tensions at a particularly critical time in relations between the United States and the Soviet Union.[6] In spite of considerable Soviet aid and the presence of 15 000 Cuban troops, Ethiopia has been unable to defeat or contain the many nationalist movements within its empire. For the moment, Moscow cannot afford to extend its commitments above and beyond their present level.

Fourthly, there seems no evidence that the Soviet Union is willing to allow its clients to use the weapons they have been given to challenge the prevailing political order. Most of the 2400 tanks that it has supplied Libya have no crews. Many of its MiG-25s are flown by Russian pilots; all but a few of its Mirage IIIs are maintained by Soviet technicians. Even in Ethiopia jet engines for Soviet built fighter planes are sent back to the Soviet Union for servicing despite the fact that the country's American trained pilots are capable of looking after planes as sophisticated as the

TABLE 8: *Time trend of wars in black Africa, military budgets, arms imports*

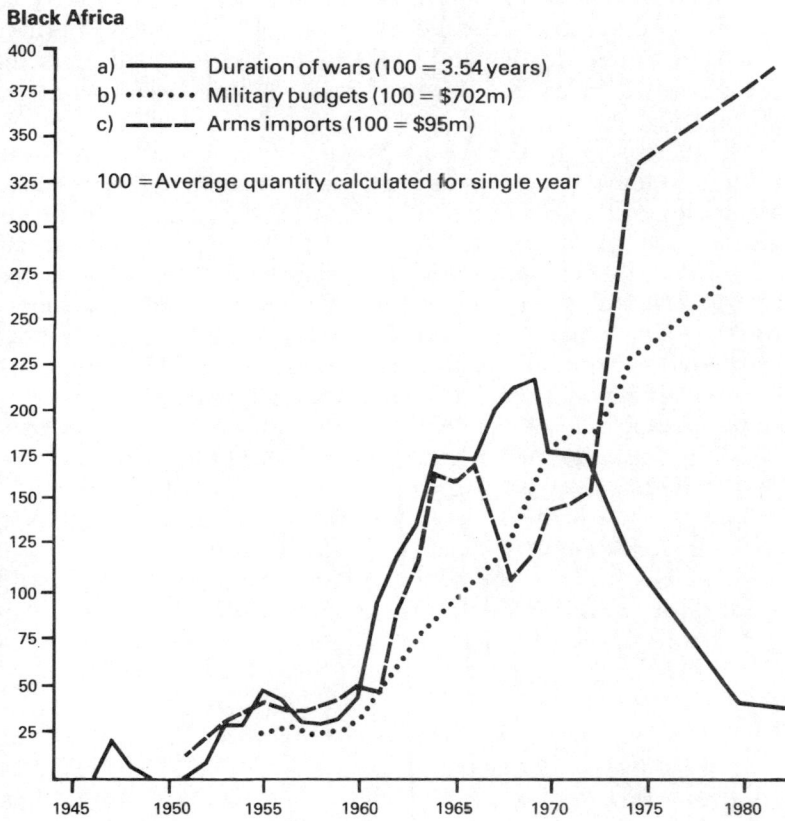

SOURCE: I. Kende 'The post 1945 wars of black Africa and the Middle East' in *Economic relations of the socialist countries and Africa Vol I: Hungarian contributions* (Budapest: Institute of World Economics) p. 133

F-5. The Russians appear to have no intention of offering their African clients open-ended assistance of the kind they offered Sadat in 1972.

Lastly, the confrontation in Africa is not only between East and West; it is also between North and South; even between different cultures Christian and Islamic. Military intervention for both blocs is no longer an answer. At most, both NATO and the

Warsaw Pact can stop each other moving into political vacuums, but such vacuums, as Gerard Chaliand writes, are likely to multiply as the post-colonial and neo-colonial order in Africa begins to break down completely in the late 1980s.[7] It is the prospect that Africa may have no future which is most worrying of all.

Of all regions in the Third World Africa remains the most underdeveloped. It is a continent with a diversity of regimes, ideologies and alignments, with countries varying in size, power and even stages of growth. It is only to be expected that it will continue to be vulnerable to foreign intervention, plagued by divisions within its own ranks. Since Africa still presents a zone of conflict over which the great powers of the 20th century have continued to squabble for advantage as the powers of the 19th century did before them, it is quite understandable why so many states irrespective of ideology should continue to hold to their belief in non-alignment. For its part, NATO should recognise that, whether sympathetic or not to its own values, all but a minority of African states will continue to see the East–West struggle as something foreign to their future as developing nations. For its part, the Warsaw Pact, in the knowledge of the West's continuing influence should not want it otherwise. The indications suggest it does not.

THE ALLIANCE OR THE ALLIES?

In the last few chapters, we have looked at how Africa's national situation has changed in the past 20 years, how the continent figured prominently in NATO's contingency planning in the early 1970s, more so perhaps in the light of the decision by Britain and France to deploy forces outside the North Atlantic area in response to the steady growth of the Soviet blue water navy. These last developments have proved to be the most far-reaching to have come about outside Europe in the long and at times contentious debate whether NATO as an alliance should focus on security matters beyond the Tropic of Cancer. A hypothesis which deserves serious consideration is that the terms of the debate have changed very little since 1952; indeed, that the present reappraisal of the Alliance's role is resonant with themes familiar from the 1950s. In those days when the Soviet Union was in no position to project its military power beyond its own borders and that of its satellites, the United States, Britain and France were often more preoccupied with the communist threat outside Europe than Soviet military power within it. Often the redeployment of forces originally assigned to NATO gave the security of the developing world an unusual prominence in national planning.

The decision to intervene in Shaba was not the first time that burden sharing was discussed in NATO: but it was the first time that France had to admit that it could no longer meet its existing obligations without the assistance of its allies. One would have expected that in an Alliance which is extremely sensitive about the division of labour and which has been deeply divided in the past about the use of military force in the developing world, France's decision to intervene would have raised suspicion, if not opposition. That this was not the case must be taken as evidence that the Europeans, no less than the French, were deeply concerned about events in Africa.

By placing the debate in a historical context we can better appreciate the extraordinary change which has taken place. But for its military weakness in the 1960s, the West might not have strategically decoupled from the continent so quickly after its imperial retreat. To propose strategic re-entry in the late 1970s was, in effect, to acknowledge that these halcyon days had passed down the highway of history, with its baggage train of assumptions following closely behind.

So far, however, the Alliance has failed to translate the consensus that Africa is important into a policy that has the unanimous support of its members. Most Europeans are still sceptical about deploying military forces in Africa, conscious that the extension of NATO's theatre of operations would arouse criticism from the Africans themselves and that such criticism might well be translated into public opposition.

Thus although the recognition of the Soviet Union as a Superpower of the same order of the United States has produced greater unanimity within the Atlantic Alliance, this unanimity has so far stopped short of any constructive suggestions about the contribution the Europeans might make to American operations, the scope of future contingency planning and the thorny, but vital question of French participation.

Indeed, one of the remarkable features of the period since 1974 has been the reluctance of the Western powers to intervene in

Africa despite the unprecedented projection of Soviet military power in a part of the world hitherto regarded as a Western sphere of influence. One explanation for their self-restraint is that they have been unable to reach agreement among themselves. Because the crises which have erupted in the last few years have been so important and the need for agreement so imperative, the Western Alliance has tried to work together and to discourage the United States from acting alone. But beyond reaching unanimity on the need for closer consultation, it has been unable to find any effective way of deterring the Soviet Union.

Of course, an alliance that fails to respond in time to the challenges that confront it must expect to pay the penalty: confusion in its own ranks. NATO fell into disarray in 1973 not for want of consultation. The Middle East had been frequently discussed in the NATO Council, the Political and Military Committees of the North Atlantic Assembly, even the Policy Advisory Group. But none of these discussions carried much weight. Europe and America were seriously divided in their response to the problem of security outside the North Atlantic area; their vision was unclear; their intentions were muddled; their experiences were frequently different.

In 1973 a Committee appointed by the North Atlantic Assembly presented a report which came out in strong support of European–American summits to resolve current differences of opinion. 'European–American summit meetings, if carefully prepared are decisive', it maintained, 'and until the present serious situation is overcome they would give the greatest impetus to solving European–American problems'.[8] In the face of objections that regular meetings even if feasible would devalue ministerial meetings, the committee proposed *ad hoc* summits, as, and when, the situation appeared to merit them.

In fact, instead of taking place inside NATO, the summit meetings have become part of a dialogue within the Western Alliance – a much broader grouping including the President of the European Commission and Japan. The summit process began at Rambouillet in November 1975 when the heads of government of the five NATO powers and Japan met to discuss problems of international trade and finance. For most of the 1970s, discussions were largely confined to economic matters until the first of the non-economic summits at Guadeloupe in January 1979 focussed attention on the security of the Persian Gulf. Guadeloupe, it should be noted, was a one-off affair with the four Berlin powers in attendance (the United States, Britain, France and West Germany), a NATO steering group which met at the behest of the United States so that the Europeans could be briefed on the progress in the second round of Strategic Arms Limitation Talks (SALT 2).

For the forseeable future consultation will probably continue to take place in summit meetings. Discussions of international security matters will, in all probability, continue to precede discussions in NATO. The Western Alliance as a whole is much better placed to develop a global strategy, not only in terms of economic reach but also the instruments at hand to implement Western policies.

A study commissioned by the Atlantic council concluded that the NATO Council or an *ad hoc* grouping within the Atlantic Alliance would not be the best agency for discussing matters of international security. It would merely add another source of tension between the United States and Europe, and quite possibly between the Europeans themselves – between countries who were in a position to act, and those who were not in a position to act at all. Neither the Netherlands nor Norway, for example, would have any interest in seeing the authority of the NATO Council undermined:

> It is with respect to developments elsewhere that NATO members frequently have divergent policies or reluctance to assume responsibility. These external developments are sometimes military, or entail the danger of military action, but they are more usually due to political and economic instability. . . . The political–economic arena is much more confused than the military security coordination area and the sense of common purpose much less.[9]

NATO has suffered too often in the past from clumsy attempts by the United States to impose a political and strategic consensus on its allies; there have been too many periods in its history when Britain and France have struck postures which have been disastrous for the political integration of Europe.

In short, there should be no question of redrawing the NATO boundary. It is neither necessary, nor desirable. The boundary was originally drawn to delineate the area in which an attack on one member would be considered an attack on all. This has not changed. What has changed is that there is now a recognition on the part of all NATO governments that their security is intimately bound up with events outside Europe. Beyond that it is difficult to agree. Even after the invasion of Afghanistan, NATO Council communiqués insisted that policies pursued beyond the Tropic of Cancer were and should remain matters for 'national decision'.[10] Occasionally several nations can agree to act collectively. But the difficulties normally encountered in implementing decisions reached at international summits tend to generate endless debate at ministerial meetings and, more often than not, produce posture statements which are meaningless, if not misleading.

These disagreements, however, are unlikely to be confined to Europe and the United States. They are more than likely to engender inter-European disputes. It is only to be expected that the BENELUX and Scandinavian members will at times disagree with the position of their partners in view of their notably more radical posture on Third World issues. Since the late 1960s, Denmark has provided substantial assistance to the Southern African liberation movements – approximately $3.5m between 1972–76. In 1975–76 alone the Netherlands contributed over $1m to SWAPO.[11] Since 1977 Norway has provided direct support to nationalist movements in Africa, principally to the ANC. In these circumstances it would be foolish to expect them to go along with policies which may seem to conflict with the political priorities they have established since the mid-1970s.

Yet it would be equally erroneous to imagine that their support could not be relied upon in diplomatic negotiations. In fact, quite the reverse. It is precisely because they have supported the initiatives of the larger NATO members, principally the Anglo–American initiatives in Zimbabwe, and the Contact Group discussions in Namibia that their own policies have been denounced as conservative by their more militant African critics. In 1976 the Danish Foreign Minister described the first stage of the Anglo–American plan as being completely in line with America's traditional support for colonial liberation, a support which to most African leaders has always appeared more rhetorical than real.

In October 1976, Norway also endorsed the new initiative on the understanding that the alternative – continued military struggle – was 'too ghastly to contemplate'.

If Britain and American had resisted these trends and chosen to underwrite the *status quo* they would have forfeited the support and sympathy of their own allies with consequences in other spheres of defence that might not have been very welcome. It should always be remembered that even Scandinavian support for the national liberation movements, which so often appears as out of step with British and American thinking, is intended to bolster Western interests. In a statement to Parliament in 1977, the Danish Foreign Minister described his government's support for the nationalists as part of a Western crusade:

> We want to see to it that in any case we, by default, by what we do not do, do not contribute to giving other political systems and powers behind them increased possibilities for influence in Africa.[12]

This alternative strategy is a valuable asset which should not be forfeited in pursuit of a military policy which will never win unanimous support, and which might well fall short of public understanding.

A consensus is unlikely to be achieved by trying to secure ratification for the revision of the NATO Charter to allow forces to be deployed outside the North Atlantic area. It is only to be expected that there will be policy issues on which the Alliance will disagree and on which some of its members will dissent from the majority. The answer is to recognise that such differences of opinion exist and attempt to minimise them, rather than seek total unanimity on every issue. At the very minimum, it may be possible to agree on the facts and their significance, to agree even on the causes of crises and to arrive through discussion at a better understanding of what its members can do on their own account, or collectively, without expecting NATO itself to sanction any particular policy. As a former British representative on the NATO Council has aptly written:

> NATO exists as a forum to pool information, exchange assessments and may be draw conclusions. Action about these situations is then a matter for those members of the Alliance willing and able to do something about them individually or collectively.[13]

To argue that NATO should not deploy forces outside its present defence perimeter is not to argue that forces should not be committed, or that its members should not act collectively; it is only to recognise that the allies and the Alliance are not always the same.

Notes and References

1. THE PAST AS PROLOGUE: THE WESTERN ALLIANCE AND AFRICA, 1949–74

1. Nicholas Henderson, *The Birth of NATO* (London: Weidenfeld and Nicolson, 1982) pp. 72–3.
2. Escott Reid, *Time of Fear and Hope: The Making of the North Atlantic Treaty* (Toronto: McLelland and Stewart, 1977) p. 215.
3. Cited William Roger Louis, *Imperialism at Bay: The United States and the Decolonisation of the British Empire 1941–5* (New York: Oxford University Press, 1978) p. 562.
4. *The Vandenburg Resolutions and the North Atlantic Treaty*. Hearings held in executive session before the Committee on Foreign Relations, US Senate, 80th Congress, 2nd Session; 81st Congress, 1st Session, June 1948/9, Historical Series, August 1973, pp. 143–4.
5. *Foreign Relations of the United States–Western Europe 3 (1948)* (Washington D.C. Department of State, 1974) p. 240.
6. *Events Leading up to the Signature of the North Atlantic Treaty* Cmnd 7692 (para. 5), 1950 (London: HMSO, 1950).
7. *NATO Final Communiqués 1949—74* (Brussels: NATO Information Office, 1974) p. 55.
8. Robert Osgood, *NATO: The Entangling Alliance* (Chicago: University of Chicago Press, 1962) pp. 66–7.
9. E. A. Boateng, *A Political Geography of Africa* (Cambridge: Cambridge University Press, 1978) p. 127.
10. Richard Connolly, 'Africa's Strategic Importance' in Grove Haines (ed.) *Africa Today* (Baltimore: Johns Hopkins Press, 1955) p. 56.
11. John Foster Dulles Speech before the Supreme Lodge of B'nai B'rith, 8 May 1956 cited Rupert Emerson, 'The Atlantic

Community and the Emerging Countries', *International Organisation*, 17:3 Summer 1963, p. 631.
12. For a full transcript of the Committee's report, *NATO Letter* January 1957, p. 5.
13. See Melvin Gurtov, *The United States Versus the Third World: Anti-Nationalism and Intervention* (New York: Praeger, 1974).
14. Cited in Alfred Grosser, *The Western Alliance* (New York: Continuum, 1980) p. 152.
15. Henry Kissinger, *The Troubled Partnership* (New York: Harper and Row, 1965) p. 9.
16. Raymond Aron, 'Reflections on American Diplomacy', *Daedalus*, Fall 1962, p. 728.
17. Ben Moore, *NATO and the Future of Europe* (New York: Harper and Row, 1958) p. 66.
18. Alastair Buchan, *NATO in the 1960s: Implications of Interdependence* (London: Chatto and Windus, 1964) p. 31.
19. Harland Cleveland, *NATO: The Transatlantic Bargain* (New York: Praeger, 1970) p. 176.
20. Norman Padelford, 'Political Cooperation in the North Atlantic Community', *International Organisation*, II, Summer 1955.
21. All forces in NATO are under national command and assigned to the Alliance only in time of war or crisis or during military manouevres. Consequently, governments are permitted to withdraw forces for crises outside the NATO theatre. The British did so for the Malayan emergency; the French for operations in Algeria after 1958.
22. Alvin Cottrell/James Dougherty, *The Atlantic Alliance: a Short Practical Guide* (London: Pall Mall Press, 1964) p. 202.
23. Charles de Gaulle, *Discours et Messages* (Paris: Plon, 1970) pp. 247-8.
24. Wolfram F. Hanrieder/Graeme P. Auton, *The Foreign Policies of West Germany, France and Britain* (New Jersey: Prentice Hall, 1980) p. 106.
25. George Ball, *The Discipline of Power* (New York: Little and Brown and Co., 1968) pp. 64-5.
26. Ian Smart, 'The New Atlantic Charter', *The World Today*, June 1973, p. 240.

2. THE WESTERN POWERS AND AFRICA, 1949–74

1. Philip Darby, *British Defence Policy East of Suez 1947–68* (Oxford: Oxford University Press, 1973) p. 329.
2. Ibid., p. 208.
3. Cited Olasupo Ojedokon, 'The Anglo–Nigerian Entente and its Demise 1960–62', *Journal of Commonwealth Political Studies* 9:3 November 1971. After the treaty's abrogation both governments agreed 'to endeavour to afford the other at all times such assistance and facilities in defence matters as are appropriate between members of the Commonwealth.' (*Commonwealth Survey* 14 August 1962 p. 668). For a comprehensive discussion of Britain's military links with Africa, see Anthony Clayton, 'The Military Relations between Great Britain and the Commonwealth Countries with Particular Reference to the African Commonwealth Nations', in W. H. Morris-Jones, *Decolonisation and After: the British and French Experience* (London: Frank Cass, 1980) pp. 193–224.
4. Cited M. Bell, *Military Assistance to Independent African States*. Adelphi Paper, 15, December 1964 (London: Institute of Strategic Studies, 1964) p. 6.
5. Harold Wilson, *The Labour Government 1964–70* (London: Weidenfeld and Nicolson, 1971) p. 243. 'Three years afterwards when I was asked about mistakes I had made in office I instanced my clinging to our East of Suez policy when facts were dictating a recessional. I was, I said, one of the last to be converted.'
6. For a discussion, see Fred Northedge, *Descent from Power: British Foreign Policy 1945–73* (London: George Allen and Unwin, 1974), pp. 296–301.
7. *The New York Times*, 6 December 1972.
8. *The Times* (London) 2 December 1970.
9. D. C. Watt, 'Britain and the Indian Ocean: Diplomacy before Defence', *Political Quarterly*, 42:3, July–September 1971, p. 312.
10. Speech at the Guildhall, November 1970, cited B. Vivekanandan, 'Naval Power in the Indian Ocean', *The Round Table*, 257, January 1975, pp. 59–73.
11. The US Joint Chiefs of Staff gave the Senate Armed Services Committee the following breakdown of British warships, excluding auxiliary and service vessels in the Indian Ocean

on 12 March 1974: 43 (1968) 33 (1969) 19 (1970) 18 (1971) 12 (1972) 10 (1973). Some of the ships formed part of the Beira patrol which had policed the Mozambique Channel since 1966 to ensure oil supplies did not reach Rhodesia. Similarly, two British Shackletons used to fly from Majunga in Madagascar until 1971 to keep an informal check on South African naval movements and their reports were made available to Tanzania under normal Commonwealth defence arrangements (*Africa Confidential* II: 18 September, 1970).

12. Laurence Martin, *British Defence Policy: The Long Recessional. Adelphi Paper* 61 (London: IISS, 1969), p. 15.
13. Lecture delivered to *Institut des Hautes Etudes de Défense Nationale*, 25 June 1970, *Revue de Défense Nationale*, August–September 1970, pp. 1245–58 (italics mine).
14. General de Monsabert, 'North Africa and the Atlantic Alliance', *Foreign Affairs*, 31: 3 April, 1958.
15. For a discussion of the defence agreements, see Chester Crocker, 'France's Changing Military Interests', *Africa Report*, June 1968.
16. Chester Crocker, 'Military Dependence: The Colonial Legacy in Africa', *Journal of Modern African Studies*, 12:2, 1974, pp. 265–86.
17. Ibid., 275–81.
18. M. Ligot, 'La Cooperation Militaire dans les Accords Passes entre la France et les Etats Africains et Malgache d'Expression Francaise', *Revue Juridique et Politique*, 17, 1963 p. 521.
19. General Revol, 'Commaunaute et Strategie Mondiale', *Centre Militaire d'Information et Documentation Outre-Mer* Document 627G, 1961.
20. James Mayall, *Africa: The Cold War and After* (London: Elek Books, 1971) p. 91.
21. Edgar S. Furniss, *France: Troubled Ally* (Oxford University Press, 1960) p. 162.
22. See Lorna Hahn, 'Last Chance in North Africa', *Foreign Affairs* 36:2 38, January 1958.
23. *The New York Times*, 30 April 1959.
24. Cited Gurtov, *The United States Versus the Third World* op. cit., p. 221.
25. William Attwood, *The Reds and the Blacks* (London: 1967) p. 16.
26. Jacques Guillemin, 'L'Importance des Bases dans la Politi-

que Militaire de la France en Afrique Noire Francophone et Madagascar', *Revue Francaise d'Etudes Politiques Africaines*, August–September 1981, p. 38.
27. Colonel Guillemin, 'La Politique Militaire francaise Outre-Mer *Centre Militaire d'Information et de Documentation sur l'Outre Mer*' Document 693G, 1967, pp. 21–22.
28. Michel Debré, 'La France et sa Défense', *Revue de Défense Nationale*, January 1972, p. 15.
29. Ibid., p. 20.
30. Jean Touscouz, 'La Normalisation de la Cooperation Bilaterlale de la France avec les Pays Africaines Francophones', *Etudes Internationales* 2:2 June 1974, p. 217.
31. In 1974 the Chairman of the Joint Chiefs of Staff provided the following breakdown of the French naval presence in the Indian Ocean between 1968–74, excluding auxiliary and service vessels: (1968) 3, (1969) 4, (1970) 5, (1971) 6, (1972) 8, (1973) 7.
32. *Africa Confidential* 13:20 1972.
33. *Le Monde*, 27 August 1970.
34. For a typical French view see Admiral Joire-Noulens' 'Quelle marine et pour quoi faire le temps de paix?' *Défense Nationale*, July 1976, pp. 21–42.
35. US Department of State Press Release 605 (October 30 1953).
36. *Department of State Bulletin* 22 June 1950 pp. 999–1002.
37. Rupert Emerson, *Africa and US policy* (New York: Englewood Cliffs, 1967) p. 24.
38. *Report of the Special Mission to Africa, South and East of the Sahara* House of Representatives, Committee on Foreign Affairs 84th Congress, 2nd Session July 1956, pp. 148–49.
39. Waldemar Nielsen, *The Great Powers and Africa* (London: Pall Mall Press, 1969) p. 368.
40. *Ethiopia and the Horn of Africa*. Hearings before the Committee on Foreign Relations, Subcommittee on African affairs, US Senate, 1976, p. 36.
41. John H. Spencer, *Ethiopia, the Horn of Africa and United States Policy* (Cambridge, Mass. Institute for Foreign Policy Analysis, 1977) p. 22.
42. Colin Legum, *The Fall of Haile Selassie's Empire* (London: 1975) p. 22.
43. The USN had originally made arrangements to use 16 different ports in Africa; by 1973 these had been reduced to

three. See *Special Study Mission to Africa, South and East of the Sahara*. Hearings before the Committee on Foreign Affairs, Subcommittee on Africa, House of Representatives, July 1965, p. 149.
44. Statement of James Noyes, deputy Assistant Secretary for Defense and Adam Elmo Zumwalt, Chief of Naval Operations, *Proposal Expansion of US Military Facilities in the Indian Ocean*. Hearings before the Committee on Foreign Affairs, subcommittee on the Near East and South Asia, House of Representatives, Washington 1976, pp. 57, 139.
45. These doubts have persisted to the present. In May 1978 the deputy Chief of Naval Operations told the Naval War College that 'every country in the area is accessible from the sea, but local sensitivities dictate that we do not put a permanent presence ashore, that the visibility of our forces be carefully controlled and that we be prepared to assist not replace the forces of allies when and where help is needed'. *The New York Times*, 18 May 1978).
46. Statement by Adam Moorer, *Implementation of the US Arms Embargo against Portugal and South Africa*. Hearings before the Committee on Foreign Affairs, Subcommittee on Africa, 1973, p. 256.
47. *The Indian Ocean's Political and Strategic Future*. Hearings before the Committee on Foreign Affairs, Subcommittee on the Near East, House of Representatives, 1971, p. 72.
48. For the findings of the latter, see 'An Evaluation of US Naval Presence in the Indian Ocean', *Naval War College Review*, October 1970.
49. *The New York Times*, 18 July 1974.
50. Press Conference given by Gerald Ford, 28 August 1974, cited *Africa Report*, January/February 1975, p. 8.
51. *The New York Times*, 20 May 1974.
52. *Africa Confidential* 17:25, 17 December 1976.

3. THE NORTH ATLANTIC ALLIANCE AND SOUTHERN AFRICA, 1949–74

1. For Soviet statements typical of the 1960s see Patricia Wohlgemuth 'The Portuguese Territories and the UN', *International Conciliation*, 545, November 1963, pp. 21–37.
2. Escott Reid, *Time of Fear and Hope*, op. cit., p. 199.

3. Cited Oliver Holmes, 'Portugal–Atlantic Pact Ally', *American Perspective*, Winter 1950.
4. John Marcum, *The Angolan Revolution 1950–62*, Volume I (Cambridge: Massachusetts Institute of Technology Press, 1969), p. 183.
5. *The New York Times*, 29 May 1962.
6. Ibid.
7. Cited 'Origin of Portuguese Military Equipment', *Portugal and NATO* (eds.), S. Bosgra/C. van Krimpen (Amsterdam: Angola Comité, October 1969).
8. Henry Kissinger, *The Troubled Partnership: a Reappraisal of the Atlantic Alliance* (New York: McGraw Hill, 1965).
9. Cited *Complex of US–Portuguese Relations*. Hearings before the Committee on Foreign Affairs, Subcommittee on Africa, House of Representatives, 93rd Congress, 2nd Session, 1974, p. 58.
10. At one time Salazar publicly accused the United States of reducing Portugal's contribution to Europe's defence by refusing to sell arms which would have brought the rebellion in Angola to a speedy end. See Rupert Emerson, *Africa and US Policy* (New Jersey: Prentice Hall, 1967), p. 157.
11. Cited Geoffrey Ripon, 'South Africa and Naval Strategy: The Importance of South Africa', *The Round Table*, 239, 1970, p. 308.
12. Cited *Fact Sheet*, June 1971 (New York: American Committee on Africa).
13. Speech made by Sieste Bosgra at UN Conference on National Liberation in Southern Africa, Oslo 1973, reprinted in Loave Stokke/Carl Widstrand (eds.), *The UN–OAU Conference on Southern Africa* (Uppsala: Scandinavian Institute of African Studies, 1973), p. 33.
14. *The New York Times*, 29 December 1968.
15. Cited *Implementation of the US Arms Embargo* op. cit., p. 84.
16. *Hearings before the Special Subcommittee on North Atlantic Treaty Organisation Commitments*, House of Representatives Committee on the Armed Services, 1972 pp. 13588, 13593.
17. Ibid., p. 13511.
18. Ibid., p. 13510.
19. Letter from Linwood Holton, Assistant Secretary of State for Congressional Relations, *Implementation of the US Arms Embargo*, op. cit., pp. 153–54.

20. Statement of Seymour Finger, US representative on the Committee of 24, *Department of State Bulletin* 62:1609 27 April 1970 p. 558.
21. As late as 1972 the MPLA, the most avowedly Marxist of the liberation movements in Portuguese Africa, agreed to a continued Portuguese military presence in Angola in return for the promise of immediate independence. See Angostinho Neto 'A message to the Angolan people', *MPLA Bulletin* 3/4 1972.
22. For a sympathetic view of the Portuguese argument see Louis Axel 'La Congolisation de l'Afrique de l'Angola: une grave menace pour l'Occident et pour l'OTAN', *Revue Militaire Generale*, October 1961, pp. 393–409.
23. See Neil Bruce, *Portugal: the Last Empire* (New York: Wiley, 1975) pp. 62–70.
24. A full account of the raid is given in the UN's published investigation. *Report of the Security Council Special Mission to the Republic of Guinea Established under Resolution 289 (1970)*, UN Security Council Official Records, Special Supplement No 2 1970.
25. *The New York Times*, 2 December 1970.
26. *The New York Times*, 9 December 1970.
27. *The Washington Post*, 4 April 1971.
28. *The Washington Post*, 16 May 1971.
29. *The Washington Post*, 16 May 1971 (emphasis added).
30. Elmo Zumwalt *On Watch: A Memoir* (New York: Quadrangle, 1976).
31. *The New York Times*, 16 April 1961.
32. Marcum, *The Angolan Revolution*, op. cit., p. 131.
33. Letter from Assistant Secretary for Congressional Relations to Senator Clifford Case, 13 November 1970, reprinted *Congressional Record* 116:30, 8 December 1970, p. 40345.
34. Part of the agreement involved the treatment of Portuguese soldiers wounded in battle in West German hospitals. Only 15 years later the government of the German Democratic Republic (GDR) put its hospitals at the disposal of Cuban troops who were invalided out of Angola fighting the UNITA guerrillas.
35. Cited William Minter, *Portuguese Africa and the West* (London: Penguin, 1972) p. 107.

36. Document published (in part) in *Wehrdienst*, 9 December 1968.
37. Sietse Bosgra, 'Territories under Portuguese Administration: Proposals for Action', in Stokke/Widstrand, *The UN–OAU Conference on Southern Africa*, op. cit., p. 86.
38. The charge against NATO did not stop at arms and equipment. In 1961 Holden Roberto, leader of the FNLA, one of the three nationalist movements in Angola, accused the Alliance of supplying Portugal with napalm 'to let her participate in defence of the so-called free world'. (Marcum, *The Angolan Revolution I*, p. 224). As it happened, the Portuguese produced their own napalm but imported herbicides from America which, according to Francisco Gomez, the commander in Angola in 1971, were used on quite an extensive scale (*The Washington Post*, 4 April 1971). Ironically, the Portuguese agreed to use defoliants instead of napalm in response to criticism from their NATO partners. In the first two years of the Nixon Administration the sale of herbicides quadrupled. Explaining the increase, the State Department claimed that at least two of the varieties sold had been withdrawn from the official munitions list in December 1970, though it was the first to admit that both had been used in Indo–China (*Implementation of the US Arms Embargo*, p.81).
39. Cited *Africa Contemporary Record 1970–1* (London: Rex Collings, 1971) pp. C44–7.
40. Cited Robert Emerson, *Africa and US Policy* (New Jersey: Prentice Hall, 1967) p. 72.
41. Dean Acheson, 'Fifty Years After', *Yale Law Review*, 51, Autumn 1961, p. 9.
42. *US Security Agreements and Commitments Abroad: Spain and Portugal*. Hearings before the Committee on Foreign Relations, Subcommittee on US Security Agreements and Commitments Abroad, US Senate, March/April 1969, July 1970, 91st Congress, 2nd Session, pp. 2404–7.
43. Department of State, 'Guidelines for Policy and Operations: Portugal' (Washington DC: Department of State, 1963), p. 1.
44. Maxwell Taylor, 'US Policy towards Portugal and Republic of South Africa', Memorandum for Secretary of Defence from Joint Chiefs of Staff, JCSM 528–63, 19 July 1963, p. 1.
45. Statement of Alexis Johnson, Undersecretary of State, *Execu-*

tive Agreements with Portugal and Bahrein. Hearings before the Committee on Foreign Relations, US Senate, 92nd Congress, 2nd Session, February 1972, p. 49.
46. John Marcum, *The Politics of Indifference: Portugal and Africa, A Case Study in American Foreign Policy* (Ecuardo Mondlane Lecture, 1972) (Syracuse University, 1972).
47. The *Guardian*, 31 March 1971.
48. Marcum, *The Politics of Indifference*, op. cit., p. 22.
49. For the text of the Azores Agreement, see *US Security Arrangements and Commitments Abroad*. Hearings before the Committee on Foreign Relations, Subcommittee on US Security Arrangements, US Senate, Part 2, Parts 5–11, 91st Congress, July 1970, p. 2405. The economic package in the 1971 Treaty not only exceeded the loans that America had extended to the whole of Africa over the previous 25 years, but also all previous allocations to Portugal itself.
50. Alastair Buchan, *NATO in the 1960s: Implications of Interdependence* (London: Chatto and Windus, 1964), pp. 119–20.
51. Arnold Rivkin, 'Lost Goals in Africa', *Foreign Affairs*, 44:1, October 1965, p. 148.
52. John Marcum, *The Angolan Revolution, Volume 2: Exile Politics and Guerrilla Warfare 1962–76* (Cambridge: Massachussetts Institute of Technology, 1978) p. 421, n. 422.
53. Alvin Cottrell/James Dougherty, *The Politics of the Atlantic Alliance* (New York: Praeger, 1964) p. 231.
54. Cited Clyde Sanger, 'What does Canada care about Africa?' *Africa Report* 15:4 April 1970 p. 15.
55. Paul Ladouceur 'Canadian Humanitarian Aid for Southern Africa' in D. Anglin (ed.) *Canada, Scandinavia and Southern Africa* p. 89.
56. Cited Kenneth Grundy, 'We're Against Apartheid . . . But: Dutch Policy Towards South Africa' *Studies in Race and Nations*, 5:3 1973–4.
57. Ibid.
58. Cited *Africa Contemporary Record 1978–9* (London: Rex Collings, 1979), p. A92.
59. At the time of Portugal's accession one observer noted: 'So far as Lisbon and Washington are concerned, the less notice taken by public opinion of the collaboration between these two particularly incompatible governments the better'.

(Oliver Holmes, 'Portugal – Atlantic Pact Ally', *American Perspective*, 4:1, Winter 1950, p. 45).
60. Sietse Bosgra, 'Territories Under Portuguese Domination: Proposals for Action', in Olave Stokke/Carl Widstrand, *The UN–OAU Conference*, op. cit., p. 37.
61. *NATO and Portugal* (Amsterdam: Angola Comité, 1969).
62. Ritchie Ovendale 'The South African Policy of the British Labour Government 1947–51' *International Affairs*, 59:1 Winter 1982–3 p. 45.
63. Cited Amy Vandebosch, *South Africa and the World: The Foreign Policy of Apartheid* (Lexington: University Press of Kentucky, 1970) pp. 131–2.
64. See G. R. Laurie, 'The Simonstown Agreement: South Africa, Britain and the Commonwealth', *South African Law Journal*, 85:2 May 1968. Laurie wrote 'South Africa's relations with the West in general are now the important factor in her role and it should be recognised that this factor today requires ties with all the NATO powers, and not just a special tie with Britain alone.'
65. Cited James Barber, *South Africa's Foreign Policy 1945–70* (Oxford: Oxford University Press, 1973) p. 82.
66. M. A. Fitzsimons, *The Foreign Policy of the British Labour Government 1945–51* (Notre Dame: Indiana, 1953) pp. 164–5.
67. *The Simonstown Agreement* Cmnd 9520 (para 2.3) (HMSO: 1955).
68. Cited Gail Cockram, *Vorster's Foreign Policy* (Pretoria: Academia, 1970) p. 65.
69. Laurie, 'The Simonstown Agreement' op. cit., p. 168. This also explains some of the palpable discrepancies in the agreement – why neither country could involve the other in war, or even come to its defence; why provision was made for South Africa's obligations in a war in which South Africa herself might not take part, yet why the treaty was silent on the question of a war in which the United Kingdom was not involved. Since the memorandum referred to a further conference these matters might very well have been ironed out, but when Erasmus and Lord Mancroft met to arrange when it should meet, they found that the differences which had emerged at Nairobi in 1951 were if anything more marked.

70. Typical of South African official thinking was the statement made by the Defence Minister at a party rally in Vereeniging in June 1963. Erasmus reminded his audience that within three weeks of the outbreak of hostilities there would be 2000 ships in the south Atlantic or Indian Ocean seeking facilities that only South Africa was in a position to provide. Cited Denis Austin, *Britain and South Africa* (Oxford University Press, 1966) p. 123.
71. J. E. Spence, *The Strategic Significance of Southern Africa* (London: Royal United Services Institute, 1972) p. 14.
72. Cited Denis Austin, *Britain and South Africa* (Oxford University Press, 1966) p. 132.
73. Ditchley Park Foundation Lecture 1968. Cited Abdul Minty, 'International Action Against Apartheid in South Africa', *Objective Justice*, 5:3, July/August 1973, p. 50.
74. D. C. Watt, 'The Continuing Strategic Importance of Simonstown', *US Naval Institute Proceedings*, October 1969.
75. Spence, *The Strategic Significance of Southern Africa*, op. cit., p. 17.
76. Cited in 'Simonstown: Bastion of a Free World', *Background*, 1970, January/February.
77. *The Economist*, 30 January 1971.
78. (*The Times*, 9 February 1971). Address at Royal Commonwealth Society, 8 February 1971.
79. *Legal Obligations of HMG Arising out of the Simonstown Agreement* (Cmnd. 4589, 4 February 1971).
80. Among the arms not sold but which at one time were under discussions were the Rapier missile system recommended by the British Aircraft Corporation after it had carried out a survey of South Africa's air defence; new frigates for the Navy despite exploratory talks which opened in April 1971; and the MB 326K advanced military trainers which Rolls Royce hoped to sell in 1973 through the Italian licensed company Aermacchi (see J. E. Spence, *The Political and Military Framework*). Foreign Investment in South Africa Study Project Paper 4. Study Project on External Investment in South Africa and South-West Africa (Namibia). (Uppsala: Africa Publications Trust, 1973), pp. 34–5.
81. *The Times*, 23 July 1970.
82. *The Sunday Times*, 19 July 1970.

83. R. D. Laing, 'South Africa – A Bastion for an Oceanic Association', *Report from South Africa*, June 1969, pp. 18–21.
84. Cited 'Call for an End to Military Cooperation with South Africa', UN Unit on Apartheid, *Notes and Documents*, 18/73, October 1973.
85. See Michael Chichester, 'Whitehall Cover-up; Westminster Exposure', *Navy International*, July 1976, p. 8.
86. J. E. Spence, *The Strategic Significance of Southern Africa* (London: Royal United Services Institute, 1972), p. 47.
87. Cited *Africa Contemporary Record 1970–1* (London: Rex Collings, 1971), p. A79.
88. Laurence Martin, 'The Cape Route', *Survival* 12:10, October 1970, p. 349.
89. *The Security of the Southern Oceans — Southern Africa the Key*. Report of a seminar at the Royal United Services Institute for Defence Studies, 16 February 1972.
90. 'Luns over NATO en de Atlantische Oceaan', Nieuwsbulletin (Zuid-afrikaanse Ambassade Den Haag nr 41, 12 October 1972, pp. 1–2). See also *Angola Bulletin* 10:1, December 1971–January 1972, pp. 7–11.
91. *Congressional Record* 120:13, 3 June 1974, p. 17379; for a general discussion of the SACLANT study see *The Washington Post*, 2 May 1974; *The Observer*, 1 September 1974; R. A. Manning, 'A South Atlantic Pact in the Making', *Southern Africa* 10:3, April 1977, p. 6.
92. Letter from Assistant Secretary for Congressional Relations to Chairman of the subcommittee on Africa Committee on Foreign Affairs, House of Representatives, 17 December 1974, reprinted in *Review of State Department Trip Through Southern and Central Africa*. Hearings before the Committee on Foreign Relations, Subcommittee on Africa, 1974), p. 154.
93. Security Study Memorandum 39, reprinted Barry Cohen/ Mohammed El-Khawas, *The Kissinger Study on Southern Africa* (New York: Spokesman Books, 1975, p. 83).
94. *The New York Times*, 12 July 1970. See also David Newsom, 'The United Nations, the United States and Africa', address before the Chicago Committee of Council on Foreign Relations, 17 September 1970, *Department of State Bulletin* 63:1633, 12 October 1970.
95. *Congressional Record*, op. cit., p. 17380.

96. Interview with Chester Crocker, Washington DC, October 1979.
97. Statements of Ronald Spiers and Robert Pranger, *The Indian Ocean: Political and Strategic Future*. Hearings before the Committee on Foreign Affairs Subcommittee on National Security Policy and Scientific Developments, July 1971, p. 166, p. 171).
98. *The Guardian*, 20 May 1974.
99. Cited *Nomination of Nathaniel Davis*. Hearings before the Committee on Foreign Relations Subcommittee on Africa, US Senate 1975, p. 39.
100. *The Times*, 7 November 1974.
101. Letter from Assistant Secretary for Defence, Near Eastern, African and South Asian Affairs to chairman of the Subcommittee on African Affairs, *Reviews of State Department Trip*, op. cit., pp. 174–5.

4. NATO AND WARSAW PACT INTERVENTION, 1970–78

1. Cited David Hall, 'Naval Diplomacy in West African Waters' in Stephen S. Kaplan (ed.) *The Diplomacy of Power: Soviet Armed Forces as a Political Instrument* (Washington DC: Brookings Institution, 1981).
2. Ibid. p. 551.
3. Elmo Zumwalt, *On Watch: A Memoir* (New York: Quadrangle, 1976) p. 332.
4. The first phrase is taken from Dr Kissinger's testimony before the Senate Subcommittee on African Affairs in January 1976 (*US Policy Towards Africa*. Hearings before the Subcommittee on Africa, Committee of Foreign Relations, US Senate, 94th Congress, 2nd Session, May 1976); the second from a speech delivered before the Economic Club of Detroit in November 1975 (Henry A. Kissinger, 'Building an Enduring Foreign Policy', *Department of State Bulletin*, 73:1903, 15 December 1975).
5. *The Guardian*, 24 March 1974.
6. Statement of Donald Easum, *Review of State Department Trip Through Southern and Central Africa*. Hearings before the Com-

mittee on Foreign Affairs, Subcommittee on Africa, 93rd Congress, 2nd Session, December 1974, p. 28.
7. K. Uralov, 'Angola: The Triumph of the Right Cause', *International Affairs*, No. 5, May 1976, p. 56.
8. Cited in Arthur J. Klinghoffer *The Angolan War: A Study in Soviet Policy in the Third World* (Boulder, Colorado: Westview Press, 1980) p. 20.
9. *The New York Times*, 20 December 1975.
10. The best account of the whole affair is Arthur Klinghoffer, *The Angolan War*.
11. *The New York Times*, 26 December 1975.
12. *The New York Times*, 17 December 1975.
13. *The New York Times*, 5 February 1976.
14. *The New York Times*, 7 February 1976.
15. Statement of John Reed, Director of Africa Regional Office of Assistant Secretary of Defence, *Disaster Assistance in Angola*. Hearings before the Subcommittee on Resources, Food and Energy Committee on International Relations, House of Representatives, 94th Congress, 2nd Session, 1976, p. 56.
16. *The New York Times*, 4 January 1976.
17. Ibid.
18. *The Guardian*, 13 December 1975.
19. *The Times*, 10 December 1975.
20. *Africa Research Bulletin* 13:2 March 1976, p. 3900.
21. *The New York Times*, 10 December 1975.
22. General George S. Brown, 'Current JCS Theater Appraisals: The Strategic Importance of Seven Vital International Areas', *Commanders Digest*, 20, March 1977 p. 21.
23. William H. Lewis, 'How a Defence Planner Looks at Africa' in Helen Kitchen (ed.) *Africa: From Mystery to Maze* (Lexington: Lexington Books, 1976) p. 295.
24. For the contrary view see Peter Vanneman, 'Soviet Intervention in Angola: Intentions and Implications' *Strategic Review*, Summer 1976 p. 97.
25. Cited Colin Legum, 'The Role of the Big Powers' in *After Angola: The War over Southern Africa* (New York: Africana, 1976) p. 12.
26. See Abram Shulsky, 'Coercive Diplomacy' in Bradford Dismukes/James McConnell, *Soviet Naval Diplomacy* (Oxford: Pergamon Press, 1979) pp. 144–53.
For a general discussion of the naval build-up, see Jiri

Valenta, 'The Soviet–Cuban Intervention in Angola', *US Naval Institute Proceedings*, April 1980, p. 55.
27. James McConnell/Bradford Dismukes (eds.), *Soviet Naval Diplomacy from the June War to Angola* (New York: Pergamon Press, 1979).
28. *The Times*, 8 November 1974.
29. R. C. Hiemstra, 'Containing Communism', *Africa Institute Bulletin*, 8:9 October 1969, p. 401.
30. Cited 'South Africa's Defence Strategy', UN Centre Against Apartheid, 2/76, January 1976.
31. *Notes on Africa* (Washington Office on Africa; February 1975).
32. Cited *Recent Developments in the Build-Up of the South African Military Forces*, Unit on Apartheid Notes and Documents 31/75, September 1975.
33. *Africa Confidential* 16:16, 15 August 1975.
34. *Africa Contemporary Record 1976–7* (ed.) Colin Legum (London: Rex Collings, 1977) p. A87.
35. *The Star*, 10 January 1976.
36. *The Sunday Telegraph*, 30 January 1977.
37. *The New York Times*, 29 March 1976.
38. *The New York Times*, 29 April 1976.
39. A. Castagno, 'A Neutral Somalia', *Africa Report*, 6 August 1961. See also Raymond Thurston, '*Détente* in the Horn', *Africa Report*, 24 February 1969.
40. *US Security Agreements and Commitments Abroad: Ethiopia*. Hearings before the Subcommittee on US Security Agreements and Commitments Abroad, Committee on Foreign Relations, House of Representatives, 91st Congress, 2nd Session, June 1970.
41. Brian Crozier, *The Soviet Presence in Somalia (Conflict Studies* 54), February 1975.
42. *The Soviet Union and the Third World: A Watershed in Great Power Policy*. Senior Specialist Division, Congressional Research Section, Library of Congress Report to Committee International Relations, House of Representatives, 1977.
43. Tom Farar, *Warclouds in the Horn of Africa* (N.Y.: Carnegie Endowment for Peace, 1979) p. 116.
44. *Africa* 74, October 1977.
45. Richard Remnek, *Soviet Policy in the Horn of Africa: The Decision to Intervene* (Alexandria, Virginia: Center for Naval Analyses, Professional Paper 270) p. 34.

46. *Africa* 78, February 1978.
47. *The New York Times*, 13 January 1978.
48. Cited *Africa Contemporary Record 1977-8* (London: Rex Collings, 1978, p. A98).
49. *Newsweek*, 26 September 1977.
50. For US decision, see Robert McGeehan, 'American Policy and the US–Soviet Relationship', *The World Today*, September 1978; for Soviet reaction, see FBIS-50V, 30 March 1978.
51. Alvin Cottrell/Frank Bay, *Military Forces in the Persian Gulf* (CSIS *Washington Papers* 6, 1978), p. 65.
52. *The Guardian*, 21 January 1978.
53. Ibid.
54. *International Herald Tribune*, 6 July 1978.
55. *Arab Report and Record*, 15 September 1978.
56. *The Times*, 21 January 1978. NATO already found it difficult to counter Soviet claims that the responsibility for the Ogaden invasion lay not with the Soviet Union for modernising the Somali armed forces after 1969, but the West for trying to divide the Arab and non-Arab states of the region by enticing Somalia into a Red Sea bloc (*Tass*, 20 March 1978).
57. *Africa* 84, August 1978.

5. FRANCE AND WESTERN SECURITY, 1974–83

1. Robert Ellsworth, 'New Imperatives for the Old Alliance', *Atlantic Community Quarterly*, 16:4, Winter 1978–79, pp. 421–2.
2. *Le Monde*, 4 June 1976.
3. *Le Monde*, 5 June 1976.
4. P. Gallois, 'French Defence Planning: The Future in the Past; *International Security*, Fall 1976, p. 28.
5. Dominique Moisi/Pierre Lellouche, 'French Policy in Africa: A Lonely Battle Against Destabilisation', *International Security*, Spring 1979, p. 121.
6. R. Luckham, 'Le Militarisme Français', *Politique Africaine*, 5, February 1982, p. 102.
7. Jacques Guillemin, 'L'intervention Exterieure dans la Politique Militaire de la France en Afrique Noire', *Revue Francaise d'Etudes Politiques Africaines*, July 1981.
8. C. R. Mitchell, 'External Involvement in Civil Strife: The Case of Chad', *Yearbook of World Affairs*, 1972, p. 157.

9. R. Pledge, 'Le Tchad ou la Theorie Francaise des Dominos Africaines', *Esprit*, February 1970, p. 377.
10. Colin Legum (ed.), *Africa Contemporary Record 1977–78* (London: Rex Collings, 1978) p. B544.
11. Colin Legum (ed.), *Africa Contemporary Record 1978–79* (London: Rex Collings , 1979) p. B535.
12. David Yost, 'French Policy in Chad and the Libyan Challenge', (unpublished paper, IISS, May 1982).
13. *The Guardian*, 19 August 1983.
14. *Le Monde*, 12 October 1982.
15. *Africa Confidential* 18:9, 29 April 1977.
16. Comment of Cyrus Vance, Secretary of State, 7 July 1977. *The New York Times*, 8 July 1977.
17. *New African*, July 1978, p. 27.
18. *Africa* 81, May 1978.
19. General Mery, 'L'avenir de nos armees', *Défense Nationale*, June 1978.
20. For references, see Pierre Lellouche and Dominique Moisi, 'French Policy in Africa: A Lonely Battle against Destabilisation', *International Security*, 3:4, Spring 1979, p. 108.
21. *The New York Times*, 1 June 1978.
22. Bruce Palmer, 'US Security Interests in Africa South of the Sahara' (*American Enterprise Institute Defense Review*, 2:6, 1978, pp. 39–40).
23. Cited Michael A. Samuel (ed.), *Africa and the West* (Boulder, Colorado: Westview Press, 1980) p. 96.
24. *The New York Times*, 1 June 1978.
25. *Africa* 69, May 1977.
26. *The New York Times*, 1 June 1978.
27. Peter Mangold, 'Shaba I and Shaba II', *Survival*, 21:3, May/June 1979, p. 113.
28. Charles Hernu, 'Répondre aux Defis d'un Monde Dangereux', *Défense Nationale*, December 1981, p. 9.
29. Charles Hernu, 'Sécurité Internationale et Développement, La France et L'Afrique', *Revue des Deux Mondes*, August 1982, p. 265.
30. Jean-Pierre Cot, 'Winning East–West in North–South', *Foreign Policy*, 46 Spring 1982, p. 6.
31. *Africa Confidential*, 25 August 1978.

6. NATO AND SOUTH AFRICA, 1974–83

1. Ian Greig, *The Communist Challenge to Africa* (London: Foreign Affairs Association, 1977) p. 35.
2. Memorandum to the Chairman of the Special Committee against Apartheid, 3 June 1975, A/AC 115/L 408.
3. Abdul Minty, 'Implementing the Arms Embargo Against South Africa', Excerpt from a statement before the UN Special Committee on Apartheid, 12 December 1977, *Objective Justice*, 9:4, Winter 1977/8.
4. *African Development*, September 1975.
5. Richard Bissell, *Southern Africa in the World: Autonomy or Independence* (Philadelphia: Foreign Policy Research Institute, 1978) p. 47.
6. Richard Bissell, *South Africa and the United States: The Erosion of an Influence Relationship* (New York: Praeger, 1982) p. 57.
7. *The New York Times*, 22 December 1975.
8. *Secret Collaboration of the West with South Africa* (Centre Against Apartheid: Notes and Documents, 32/78 September 1978).
9. Abdul Minty, 'Implementing the Arms Embargo', op. cit.
10. *The Star* (Johannesburg), 8 February 1975.
11. Summary record of 1st Part of 298th meeting of the Special Committee on Apartheid, 26 February 1975, UN Doc A/AC 115/SR 298, 26 March 1975, p. 4.
12. Cited Zdenek Cervenka/Barbara Rogers *The Nuclear Axis: Secret Collaboration Between West Germany and South Africa* (London: Julian Friedmann, 1978) p. 81.
13. *What have South Africa's Traditional Suppliers of Arms Done to Abide by the Mandatory Arms Embargo Against Apartheid South Africa?* (Centre Against Apartheid: Notes and Documents, 26/78, September 1978).
14. *Study Conference on Belgium and the Apartheid Regime*, 18/78, August 1978.
15. *Africa* 69, May 1977.
16. Zdenek Cervenka, 'The Two Germanies in African increase of Bonn's Aid and the GDR's Military Assistance', *Africa Contemporary Record 1981–2*, op. cit., p. A192.
17. Cited Barber, *South Africa's Foreign Policy*, op. cit., p. 82.
18. Cited Robert Jaster, *South Africa's Narrowing Security Options*, *Adelphi* 159 (London: IISS) p. 12.
19. Extract from a speech by R. F. Botha before the Swiss South

Africa Association, Zurich, 7 March 1979 (Republic of South Africa: Department of Foreign Affairs, 1979).
20. Samuel Nolutsunghu, *South Africa in Africa: A Study of Ideology and Foreign Policy* (Manchester University Press: 1975) p. 75.
21. Cited D. W. Kruger, *The Making of a Nation* (Pretoria, 1968) p. 303.
22. Cited Deon Geldenhuys, *The Neutral Option and Subcontinental Solidarity: A Consideration of P. Botha's Zurich Statement* (Johannesburg: South African Institute of International Affairs, 1979).
23. Cited 'Strategic Anchorages' *South African Panorama*, July 1980, p. 5.
24. Ibid.
25. *The Guardian*, 2 June 1982.
26. Bissell, *South Africa and the United States*, op. cit., p. 65.
27. A further development along these lines was the announcement in April 1979 that a marine corps was to be established with light patrol craft to protect harbour installations.
28. Cited Paul Gineiewski, 'South Africa and the Defence of the Cape Route', *NATO's 15 Nations*, 17:2, April–May 1972, p. 44.
29. Cited, *The Apartheid Warmachine: The Strength and Deployment of the South African Armed Forces* (International Defence and Aid Fund, 1980, Paper on Southern Africa 8), p. 33.
30. Notes taken by the International Defence Aid Fund Research and Information Department at a public meeting in London 27 October 1981, *Focus*, January–February 1982.
31. In fact, the number of Cuban troops fell from 30 000 in 1976 to 10 000 by the Autumn of 1981 (*The New York Times*, 8 January 1982).
32. *The Times*, 9 September 1981.
33. For a complete list see the two Angolan submissions to the International Mission of Jurists, June 1979–July 1980 and 1–9 October 1981 published by the Centre Against Apartheid UN Department of Political and Security Council Affairs, 2/81 and 12/82.
34. *The Guardian*, 29 July 1981.
35. *Report of the Peoples Republic of Angola to the Second Session of the International Commission of Enquiry into the Crimes of the Racist and Apartheid Regime in Southern Africa* (Centre Against Apartheid; Department of Political and Security Council Affairs 12/82, 1982).

36. *The New York Times*, 17 September 1981.
37. Communiqué issued by the Angolan Ministry of Defence, 17 August 1981.
38. See Peter Vanneman, *Soviet Foreign Policy in Southern Africa* (Pretoria: Africa Institute, 1982) pp. 43–44.
39. See David Martin and Phyllis Johnson, *The Struggle for Zimbabwe* (London: Faber and Faber, 1981) pp. 305–8.
40. The SADCC comprises Angola, Botswana, Swaziland, Lesotho, Mozambique, Malawi, Tanzania, Zambia and Zimbabwe.
41. John Edlin 'SADCC: Key to Southern Africa's Economic Independence', *Africa Report*, May–June 1983, p. 441.
42. See two articles on the MNR in *Africa Confidential*, 23:15, and 23:16.
43. Interim Report of the EEC-ACP Consultative Assembly fact finding mission to the Front Line States, 23 January 1982–1 February 1982.
44. *New African*, April 1981.
45. B. Tau, 'The Imperialist Threat to Africa', *African Communist*, 45, 1971, p. 45.
46. *The Star*, 5 December 1981.
47. *The Financial Mail*, 6 March 1982.
48. *Community Policy for the North–South dialogue* COM (81) 68, 7 May 1981.
49. *The Guardian*, 11 October 1982.
50. *Supplement to AIM Information Bulletin* 65, November 1981.
51. Cited Allen and Barbara Isaacman, 'Mozambique: In Pursuit of Non-Alignment', *Africa Report*, May/June 1983, p. 54.
52. Pierre Hassner, 'Superpower Rivalries, Conflict and Cooperation', *Diffusion of Power Part 2: Control and Conflict, Adelphi* 134 (London: IISS, 1977).

7. THE WARSAW PACT AND AFRICA, 1959–83

1. For two notable exceptions see David Albright, 'The USSR: Its Communist Allies and Southern Africa', *International Affairs Bulletin*, 4:3, 1980; and Melvin Croan, 'East Germany in Africa', in David Albright/Jiri Valenta, (eds.), *The Communist States in Africa* (Bloomington, Indiana: University of Indiana Press, 1982).

2. See for instance V. Baryshnikov, 'Raw Material Resources of Africa', *International Affairs*, (Moscow) December 1974; Dmitry Volsky, 'Southern Verison of NATO', *New Times*, 26 September 1976.
3. See the contributions of Marshall Goldman, Michael Dohan and Lawrence Theriot in *The Soviet Economy in a Time of Change* US Congress Joint Economic Committee (Washington DC: 1979).
4. *Zycie Gospodarcze*, 12 March 1961.
5. Arpad Orosz, 'Trade of African Developing Countries up to 1970 and Prognosis to 1980', *Studies on Developing Countries* No. 70 (Budapest: Institute for World Economics, 1975) p. 31.
6. Josef Nowicki, 'Mineral Economic Relations of Poland and the Developing Countries of Africa', *Studies on the Developing Countries* D. Morrison (ed.), No 2, 1972, p. 16.
7. B. Balkay, 'The Developing Countries and the Raw Material Supply of the World Aluminium Industry', *Economic Relations with the Socialist Countries* Vol I (Budapest: Institute for World Economics, 1978) pp. 106–7.
8. Vaclav Mondous, 'The Socialist Countries and Their Relations with the National Liberation Movement of the Colonial Countries', *Pravda* (Plzen) 4 July 1964. Cited Robert Lamberg, *Prag und die Dritte Welt* (Hanover: Verlag für Literatur und Zeitgeschehen, 1966) p. 27.
9. Milan Madr, 'Severoatlanticky Pakt a Afrika' (NATO and Africa), *Rude Pravo*, 21 October 1962.
10. *Narody Asii i Afriki*, (Moscow) No. 20, 1961.
11. See Raymond Vernon/Brian Levy, 'State Owned Enterprises in the World Economy: The Case of Iron Ore', in Leroy Jones (ed.), *Public Enterprise in Less Developed Countries: Multi-Disciplinary Perspectives* (Cambridge, Massachussetts: Harvard University Press, 1981).
12. Zuhayr Mikdashi, *The International Politics of National Resources* (Ithaca: Cornell University Press, 1976) p. 121.
13. For Polish economic works on Africa see Jerzy Prokopczvk, *The Third World in Search of a World to Develop* (Warsaw: 1973); Zbigniew Dobosiewicz, *Economic Integration of Less Developed Countries* (Warsaw: 1971); Michal Dobroczynski, *Africa and International Trade* (Warsaw: 1972).

14. Sandor Ausch, *Theory and Practice of CMEA Cooperation* (Budapest: Academiai Kiado, 1972) p. 59.
15. *Africa Economic Digest*, 6 February 1981.
16. Istvan Dobozi, 'Projected Trends of World Raw Material and Energy Markets until 2000', *Studies on Developing Countries*, No. 110 (Budapest: Institute for World Economics, 1982) p. 20.
17. R. Dietz, *Price Changes in Soviet Trade with CMEA and the Rest of the World Since 1975* (Joint Economic Committee of US Congress 1979). See also S. Rosfielde, 'Comparative Advantage and the Evolving Pattern of Soviet Commodity Specialisation' in S. Rosfielde (ed.), *Economic Welfare and the Economics of Soviet Socialism* (Cambridge: Cambridge University Press, 1981).
18. The Wharton Business School predicts that world market prices will grow by only $4\frac{1}{2}$ per cent between 1983–87. Nevertheless, even this growth rate may lead to a serious deterioration in the terms of trade for Eastern Europe and may demand greater Soviet financial assistance, a recycling of petroroubles earned from the export of oil, perhaps, in the form of low interest rate trade credits. See John Vanous, 'East European Economic Slowdown' *Problems of Communism*, 31:4, July/August 1982, p. 9.
19. *Scienteia*, 4 August 1978.
20. *Revista Economica*, 42, 12 November 1982, p. 54. Between 1975–80 trade with the West fell from 36 per cent to 30 per cent.
21. *The Lead and Zinc Industries in the Soviet Union* (US Central Intelligence Agency, March 1980) p. 10.
22. CIA figures cited, *Africa Contemporary Record 1980–81* (ed.) Colin Legum (London: Rex Collings, 1981) p. C135.
23. V. V. Strishkov, 'The Soviet Union', in *Mining Annual Review*, (1980) pp. 579–605.
24. *Non-Fuel Minerals Policy Review: Oversight Hearings before the Committee on Interior and Insular Affairs Subcommittee on Mines and Mining*, US Congress, 96th Congress, 2nd Session 1980 pp. 32–46.
25. *Soviet Economy in Time of Change*, op. cit.
26. Walter Labys, 'Role of the Soviet Union in the Metals Markets: A Case Study of Copper, Manganese and Chromite', paper presented at the Conference on the Soviet Union

in Commodity markets (Center for International Business Studies, University of Montreal, 8–9 October 1981). The measure of self-sufficiency in copper and lead deteriorated steadily throughout the life of the Tenth Five Year Plan. See Daniel Papp, 'Soviet Non-Fuel Mineral Resources: Surplus or Scarcity?' *Resources Policy*, 8:3, September 1982 and *The Non-Fuel Minerals Outlook for the USSR through 1990* (Washington DC: Bureau of Mines, 1981).
27. *Pravda*, 22 November 1979.
28. *Mining Journal*, 2 January 1981.
29. *Vneshniaia torgovlia*, (Foreign Trade) Percentages for 1973 and 1974 were 88 per cent and 79 per cent respectively.
30. Papp, 'Soviet Non-Fuel Mineral Resources', op. cit., p. 169.
31. Alan Smith, 'Economic Factors Affecting Relations in the 1980s' in Karen Dawisha/Philip Hanson (eds.), *Soviet–East European Dilemmas: Coercion, Competition and Consent* (London: Heinemann, 1981) p. 120.
32. Harriet Matejka, 'Soviet Coal Exports' paper presented at Conference on Soviet Union in Commodity Markets, Montreal, 8–9 October 1981 p. 13.
33. Marie Lavigne, 'The Problem of the Socialist Multinational Enterprise', *ACES Bulletin* 18:1, Summer 1975, pp. 33–62.
34. See Kalman Pecsi, *The Future of Socialist Integration* (New York: Sharpe, 1981); and Petro Pavlov, 'Problems of the Development and Improvement of the Mineral-Rich Material Complex of CMEA Countries', *Mezhdunarodni Otnosheniya*, 6, 1980, pp. 52–64.
35. Marie Lavigne, 'The Soviet Union inside COMECON', *Soviet Studies*, 35:2, April 1983, p. 147.
36. I. Dobozi, 'Raw Materials and Energy Policy Changes in CMEA Countries', *Kulgazdasag*, No 1, 1979, pp. 11–23.
37. For some standard criticisms by Hungarian economists see Andras Koves, 'East–West Trade and the Foreign Economic Strategy of CMEA Countries', *Kulgazdasag* 5 May 1982, pp. 3–15; Laszlo Csaba, 'World Economic Adjustment and Economic Development in Eastern Europe', *Kulgazdasag*, 4, 1982, pp. 12–29.
38. Laszlo Csaba, 'Some Problems of the International Socialist Monetary System', *Acta Oeconomica*, 23:1, 1979, pp. 17–37.
39. Laszlo Csaba, 'The Place of the CMEA in the World Economy of the 1980s', *Valosag*, July 1982, p. 5.

8. THE WARSAW PACT AND SOUTHERN AFRICA, 1974–83

1. *Kulpolitika* (Hungarian Institute of International Affairs) No 1, 1977, p. 132.
2. L. Zevin, 'New Concepts of Economic Development and International Cooperation in Third World Countries' *Voprosy Ekonomika*, 1978; See also *Multilateral Schemes of the Countries of the CMEA and Opportunities for Developing Countries in Trade and Economic Cooperation Resulting from the Implementation of these Schemes*, UNCTAD TD/B/AC 23/3, April 1977.
3. For a discussion see *Trade Relations between Countries having Different Economic and Social Systems*, UNCTAD TD/B/754, August 1979.
4. *Planovoje Khozjastvo* 2, 1977, p. 57.
5. *Trybuna Ludu* 1 May 1978.
6. F. Bartha, 'Some Ideas on the Creation of a Multilateral Clearing System among the CMEA', *Soviet and East European Foreign Trade*, Spring 1976.
7. Hans Siegfried Lamm/Siegfried Kupper, *DDR und die Dritte Welt* (Munich: 1976).
8. Anatoly Gromyko, 'Africa in the Strategy of Neo-colonialism', *International Affairs*, (Moscow) February 1978, p. 86.
9. Melvin Croan, *East Germany and the Soviet Connection* (Beverley Hills: Sage, 1976) p. 51.
10. See the testimony of Michael Keren in *East European Economies*, US Congress Joint Economic Committee (Washington, 1977) p. 722.
11. Tibor Kiss, (ed.), *The Market of Socialist Economic Integration: Selected Conference Papers* (Budapest: Academiai Kiado, 1973) p. 16.
12. G. Grabig/G. Brendel, *Commodity Market Relations in Socialist Economic Integration* (1975) p. 19.
13. Jochen Bethkenhagen, 'Energy Sector of the German Economy Faces Difficult Tasks', *Deutschland Archiv*, No 5, May 1981, pp. 505–6.
14. *African Economic Digest*, 3:39, October 1982.
15. Dieter Braun, *The Indian Ocean: Region of Conflict or Peace Zone?* (London: Hurst and Co., 1983) p. 8.

16. Dmitry Volsky, 'A Strategy without a Future', *New Times*, 3 August 1978.
17. Dmitry Volsky, 'Southern Version of NATO', *New Times*, 25, September 1978.
18. Donald Mitchell, *A History of Russian and Soviet Seapower* (London: Macmillan, 1974) p. 546.
19. Peter Janke, 'The Soviet Strategy of Mineral Denial', *Soviet Analyst*, 7:22 November 1978, p. 5.
20. *The Challenge of Soviet Shipping* (London: Aims of Industry, 1983) p. 9.
21. James Ellis, 'Expansion of the Soviet Merchant Fleet – Implications for the West', *NATO Review*, 3, 1979, pp. 22 (ref. 4).
22. S. Lukyanchenko, *Foreign Trade* No 1, 1977, p. 23.
23. Michael Davidchik/Robert Mahoney, 'Soviet Civil Fleets in the Third World', in Bradford Dismukes/James McConnel, *Soviet Naval Policy in the Third World* New York: Pergammon, 1979).
24. William Black, 'Soviet Fishery Agreements with Developing Countries', *Marine Policy*, 7:3, July 1983, p. 169.
25. *Wall St Journal (Europe)*, 26 July 1983.
26. Robert Athay, 'Perspectives on Soviet Merchant Shipping', in Michael McGwire (ed.), *Soviet Naval Developments* (New York: Praeger, 1973) p. 101.
27. David Scrivener, 'Merchant Marine in Soviet Naval Strategy', *Marine Policy* 7:2, April 1983, p. 119.
28. Anatoly Gromyko, 'Western Diplomacy versus Southern Africa', *International Affairs*, March 1979, p. 20.
29. Gromyko, 'Africa in the Strategy of Neo-colonialism', op. cit.
30. Friedel Trappen/Ulbricht Weishauft, 'Aktuelle Fragen des Kampfes un Nationale und Soziale befreung in sub-Saharischen Afrika', *Deutsche Aussenpolitik*, 24:2, February 1979.
31. *USSR and the Third World*, 1976, p. 155.
32. E. Tabarin, *The New Scramble for Africa*, (Moscow: Progress Publishers, 1974) p. 159.
33. Cited Stanley Uys, 'Namibia: The Socialist Dilemma', *African Affairs*, October 1982, p. 571.
34. *Kulpolitika*, 2 February 1978.
35. Peter Mandi, 'Trade Perspectives between European CMEA Countries and Africa and the Middle East', *Economic Relations*

of Africa with the Socialist Countries Vol. I: Hungarian Contributions (Budapest: Institute for World Economics, 1978) pp. 35–41.
36. I. Dobozi, 'Projected Trends of World Raw Material Markets', op. cit., 21.
37. Ibid.
38. *The Times*, 17 October 1979.
39. Anatoly Gromyko, 'African Realities and the "Conflict Strategy" Myth', *New Times*, 51, December 1978, p. 51.
40. *FBIS Monitoring*, 23 June 1978.
41. See, for example, Klaus Willerding, 'Zur Afrika-Politik der DDR', *Deutsche Aussenpolitik*, 29:8, August 1979.
42. *The Guardian*, 11 January 1981.
43. K. Uralov, 'The Acute Problem of Southern Africa', *International Affairs*, 1977, p. 112.

9. THE WARSAW PACT, EAST GERMANY AND THE THREAT OF WESTERN INTERVENTION

1. *Towards Improving US–Cuba Relations* 95th Congress, 1st Session Report of a Special Study Mission to Cuba, February 1977 (Washington DC: 1977) p. 15.
2. *The New York Times*, 12 June 1976.
3. *Suddeutsche Zeitung*, 9 February 1977.
4. *US Interests in Africa*, Hearings before the Subcommittee on Africa Committee on Foreign Affairs, House of Representatives 96th Congress 1st Session October/November 1979.
5. *ADN*, 24 February 1979.
6. *AFP*, 21 February 1979.
7. *Neues Deutschland*, 9 February 1972.
8. *Deutsche Aussenpolitik*, 25 November 1975.
9. *Die Vaterland*, 7 January 1976; *Windhoek Algemeine Zeitung*, 16 January 1976; *die Welt*, 21 November 1976.
10. *The Sunday Times*, 25 June 1978.
11. *International Herald Tribune*, 8 February 1979.
12. Hartmut Zimmerman 'The GDR in the 1970s', *Problems of Communism*, March–April 1978, pp. 11–12.
13. *Deutsche Aussenpolitik*, 17 August 1971.
14. Klaus Willerding, 'Die DDR und die nationalbefreiten staaten Asiens und Afrikans', *Asien, Afrika, Latinamerika*, 25, 1974.

15. *The Washington Post*, 12 December 1978.
16. *African Confidential*, 17 January 1979.
17. Cited Peter Janke, 'Marxist Statecraft in Africa: What Future? *Conflict Studies*, 95, May 1978, p. 6.
18. *African Development*, December 1976.
19. *The Times*, 2 September 1981.
20. *The Guardian*, 14 March 1981.
21. *Bundestag Publication*, 8/3463 4 December 1979.
22. *International Herald Tribune*, 24 July 1978.
23. *Volksarmee*, 5 June 1978.
24. *International Herald Tribune*, 24 July 1978.
25. *The Observer*, 21 May 1978.
26. *African Economic Digest*, 1:24 October 1980.
27. *African Economic Digest*, 3:36 September 1982.
28. Richard Lowenthal, *Model or Ally: The Communist Powers and the Developing Countries* (Oxford: Oxford University Press, 1977) pp. 359–76.
29. Opening address at the International Conference of Third World Groups, East Berlin October 1980. 'Joint struggle of the Working Class Movement and the National Liberation Movement against Imperialism', (Dresden: Verlag Zeit im Bild 1981) p. 19.
30. Cited *Africa Contemporary Record 1979–80*, op. cit. p. A167.
31. Ibid.
32. *Marches Tropicaux et Mediterranee* (Paris), 8 June 1979.
33. In 1981 SAM 6 missiles were sold to Angola; combined with an early warning system they represented the most advanced air defence system outside the Soviet bloc. After their destruction in a South African raid, however, they were not replaced.
34. *The Washington Post*, 20 October 1982.
35. For Soviet impressions of South Africa as a Western ally see A. Kislov/V. Vasilikov, 'The Current Stage of US Policy in Africa', *Asii i Afriki Segodnia*, 9 September 1978.
36. Cited Zdenek Cervenka, 'The Two Germanies and Africa during 1980', *Africa Contemporary Record 1980–1* op. cit., p. A148.
37. For a Polish view of this development see Leon Zurawicki, 'The Prospects of Tripartite Cooperation', *Intereconomics* (Hamburg), 7/8 1978, pp. 184–7.
38. *Business Europe*, 27 June 1980, p. 206.

39. *Karl Marx: Early Texts* (Oxford: Blackwells, 1971) p. 117.

10. AFRICA, THE WESTERN ALLIANCE AND THE SOVIET CHALLENGE, 1961–78

1. Many of the ties which bound the United Kingdom and Anglophone Africa had loosened considerably by the mid-1960s. When sterling was devalued in 1967 only two African countries followed suit. In Francophone Africa the story was somewhat different. When France devalued the franc in 1969 every African country in the franc zone devalued accordingly. Clearly military weakness is not the whole story.
2. Kwame Nkrumah, 'African Prospects', *Foreign Affairs*, 37:1, October 1958, p. 48.
3. Sylvanus Olympio, 'African Problems and the Cold War', *Foreign Affairs* 40:1, October 1961, p. 52.
4. Kwame Nkrumah, *Neo-colonialsm: the Last Stage of Imperialism* (London, 1965) p. xi.
5. For example, there was no great rush on the part of Eastern Europe to open up legations during the African independence wave of the 1960s. While relations were established relatively quickly with some states (notably Kenya, Guinea and Mali), others such as the Central African Republic, Gabon and Chad, it took from six to 16 years or longer. Poland established formal diplomatic links with Chad only in 1979.
6. Kenneth Kaunda. Opening address, third non-aligned conference, Lusaka 8–10 September, 1970, *Africa Contemporary Record 1970–1* (London: Rex Collings, 1971) p. C42.
7. Julius Nyerere. Opening address to preparatory meeting of non-aligned countries, Dar-es-Salaam, 13 April 1970, ibid.
8. R. M. Akwei, 'Brief on Ghana's Foreign Policy towards the Americas', *Conference Paper*, 19 1962, p. 201.
9. John Schlegel, *The Deceptive Ash: Bilingualism and Canadian Policy in Africa 1957–71* (University Press of America, 1978) p. 120.
10. Ibid., p. 327.
11. Cited Laurence Martin (ed.), *Neutralism and Non-Alignment: The New States in World Affairs* (New York: Praeger, 1962) p. 6.
12. Cited Special Committee on the Situation with Regard to the Implementation of the Declaration on the Granting of

Independence to Colonial Countries and People, 640th meeting, 30 September 1968, A/AC 109/SR 640 p. 16.
13. Cited Olajide Aluko, 'The Determinants of the Foreign Policies of African States', in O. Aluko (ed.), *The Foreign Policies of African States* (London: Hodder and Stoughton, 1977) p. 20, n. 36.
14. See in particular the Report of the ad hoc Committee on the Indian Ocean, UN General Assembly, 33rd Session, Supplement no. 29 (A/33ù29, 1978).
15. Statement of George Vest, Director of the Bureau of Politico–Military Affairs, Department of State, *Diego Garcia 1975: The Debate over the Base and the Island's Former Inhabitants*. Hearings before the Special Subcommittee on Investigations, Committee of International Relations, House of Representatives, 94th Congress, 1st Session, 1975, p. 4.
16. Special Committee on the Situation with Regard to the Implementation of the Declaration on the Granting of Independence to Colonial Countries and Peoples, AùAC 109ùSR 638, 1 October 1968.
17. Cited B. D. Hassan, 'Big Power Rivalry in the Indian Ocean: A Tanzanian View', *Africa Quarterly*, 15:3 1976, p. 82.
18. UN Doc A/AC 159/SR 139, 1 June 1981, p. 3.
19. Cited Philip Allen, 'The Indian Ocean: Very Much at Sea', *Africa Contemporary Record 1981–2* (London: Rex Collings 1982) p. A135.
20. *International Herald Tribune*, 5 July 1980.
21. Dieter Braun, *The Indian Ocean: Region of Conflict or Peace Zone?* (London: Hurst and Co., 1983) p. 45.
22. Isebill V. Gruhn, 'British Arms Sales to South Africa: The Limits of African Diplomacy', *Studies in Race and Nations*, 3 (Colorado: University of Denver, 1972).
23. Schlegel, *The Deceptive Ash*, op. cit., pp. 357–58.
24. 'Call for an end to all military cooperation with South Africa', Unit on Apartheid, *Notes and Documents*, 18/73, October 1973.
25. Survey of reports in *Africa Research Bulletin* compiled by *Africa Contemporary Record 1970–1*, op. cit., pp. C20–3.
26. See P. M. Allen, 'Rites of Passage in Madagascar', *Africa Report*, 17 February 1971.
27. As late as 1977, Sir Alec Douglas-Home reiterated his amazement that the Africans still did not understand the strategic importance of the Cape route, whatever their

feelings about South Africa. *Africa Confidential* 18:8, 15 April 1977.
28. Statement by Julius Nyerere, October 1970, cited *Africa Contemporary Record 1970–1*, op. cit., pp. C20–3.
29. Cited Rupert Emerson, *Africa and US Policy* (New Jersey: Prentice Hall, 1967) p. 73.
30. Julius Nyerere in *Africa Contemporary Record 1969–70* (London: Rex Collings, 1970) pp. C30–9.
31. Cited *Objective Justice* 4:2, April/May/June 1972.
32. Olave Stokke/Carl Widstrand (eds.), *The UN–OAU Conference on Southern Africa* (Uppsala: Scandinavian Institute of African Studies, 1973).
33. Ibid., pp. 69–71.
34. Michael Degnan, 'Mozambique's Three Wars', *Africa Report*, 18:5, September/October 1973, p. 13.
35. Stokke/Widstrand, *The UN–OAU Conference*, op. cit., p. 106.
36. James Dougherty, 'The Aswan Decision in Perspective', *Political Science Quarterly*, 74, March 1959, p. 32.
37. *The Guardian*, 8 June 1978.
38. Speech delivered by Samora Machel to 15th Summit Meeting of Heads of State and Government, OAU Khartoum 18/21 July 1978, reprinted *Africa Currents*, 12/13, Autumn/Winter 1978/9, p. 14.
39. *Newsweek*, 9 June 1978.
40. *Le Figaro* (Paris), 19 June 1978.
41. Speech delivered by Olusegun Obasanjo to 15th Summit Meeting of Heads of State and Government, OAU Khartoum, reprinted *Africa Currents*, op. cit., p. 9.
42. *Africa* 83, July 1978.
43. CM/Res 635, XXXI, 1978.
44. CM/Res 641, XXXI, 1978.
45. *International Herald Tribune*, 2 March 1979.
46. Cited Kenneth Adelman, *African Realities* (New York: Crane, Russak and Co., 1980) p. 139.
47. *The New York Times*, 28 January 1976.
48. *The New York Times*, 2 February 1976.
49. *The Washington Post*, 12 January 1976. Angostinho Neto made the same point in an interview with Rene Lefort in *Le Monde*, reprinted in *Africa Report*, January/February 1976.
50. *The Washington Post*, ibid.
51. *The New York Times*, 9 December 1976.

52. Julius Nyerere, 'America and Southern Africa', *Foreign Affairs*, 55:4, July 1977, p. 676.
53. Text of an address by Henry A. Kissinger to St. Louis World Affairs Council, 12 May 1975. *Department of State Bulletin*, 82:1875, 2 June 1975, p. 709.
54. *The Financial Times*, 5 February 1976.

11. CONCLUSION: NATO AND THE THREAT TO AFRICA

1. *General Report on Alliance Political Developments* (North Atlantic Assembly, October 1979) W145 PC(79)5.
2. *General Report on Alliance Political Developments* (North Atlantic Assembly 1978, V168 PC(78)5(27).
3. Cited Chester Crocker/A. Lewis, 'Missing Opportunities in Africa', *Foreign Policy*, 35, Summer 1979, pp. 151–2.
4. Ibid. pp. 151–2
5. *Newsweek*, 9 June 1978.
6. *The Guardian*, 29 October 1983.
7. Gérard Chaliand, *The Struggle for Africa: Conflict of the Great Powers* (London: Macmillan, 1982) p. 113.
8. Cited Manlio Brosio, 'Consultation and the Atlantic Alliance', *Survival*, 16:3 May/June 1974 p. 117.
9. *Summit Meetings and Collective Leadership in the 1980s* (Washington DC: Atlantic Council of the United States 1980).
10. NATO Press Communiqué H-1(81)5, 5 May 1981.
11. Leonard Taapori/T. A. Keenleyside 'The West and Southern Africa: Economic Involvement and Support for Liberation 1960–74', *Canadian Journal of African Studies*, 13:3 1980.
12. All quotations come from Mai Palmberg, 'Present Imperialist Policies in Southern Africa: The Case for Scandinavian Disassociation', in Douglas Anglin (ed.) *Canada: Scandinavia and Southern Africa* (Uppsala: Scandinavian Institute of African Studies, 1978) pp. 144–5.
13. John Killick, 'The East–West View from NATO', *World Issues*, December 1978.

Bibliography

PRIMARY SOURCES

Activities of Transnational Corporations in the Industrial, Mining and Military Sectors of Southern Africa (UN Centre on Transnational Corporations 1980).

Complex of US–Portuguese relations, Hearings before the Committee on Foreign Affairs, Subcommittee on Africa, House of Representatives, 93rd Congress, 2nd Session, 1974.

Contingency Plans for Chromium Utilisation (Washington DC: National Academy of Science: National Materials Advisory Board 1978).

Current JCS Theater Appraisals: The Strategic Importance of Seven Vital International Areas, Commanders Digest, 20 March 1977.

Diego Garcia: The Debate over the Base and the Island's Former Inhabitants, Hearings before the Special Subcommittee on Investigations, Committee on International Relations, House of Representatives, 94th Congress, 1st Session, 1975.

Ethiopia and the Horn of Africa, Hearings before the Committee on Foreign Relations, Subcommittee on African Affairs, US Senate, 1976.

European Security and Africa (Assembly of Western European Union: 23rd Ordinary Session (2nd Part) 3 November 1977).

European Security and the South Atlantic (Assembly of the Western European Union: 27th Ordinary Session (2nd Part) 26 October 1981).

Events Leading up to the Signature of the North Atlantic Treaty Cmnd 7692 (London: HMSO, 1950).

Executive Agreements with Portugal and Bahrein, Hearings before the Committee on Foreign Relations, US Senate, 92nd Congress, 2nd Session, February 1972.

General Report on Alliance Political Developments (North Atlantic Assembly, 1978).
General Report on Alliance Political Developments (North Atlantic Assembly, October 1979).
Hearings before the Special Subcommittee on North Atlantic Treaty Organisation Commitments, House of Representatives Committee on the Armed Services, 1972.
Implementation of the US Arms Embargo against Portugal and South Africa, Hearings before the Committee on Foreign Affairs, Subcommittee on Africa, 1973.
Indian Ocean's Political and Strategic Future, Hearings before the Committee on Foreign Affairs, Subcommittee on National Security Policy and Scientific Developments, July 1971.
Lead and Zinc Industries in the Soviet Union (US Central Intelligence Agency, March 1980).
Multilateral Schemes of the Countries of the CMEA and Opportunities for Developing Countries in Trade and Economic Cooperation Resulting from the Implementation of these Schemes (UNCTAD TD/B/AC 23/3 April 1977).
NATO Final Communiqués 1949–74 (Brussels: NATO Information Office, 1974).
Non-Fuel Minerals Policy Review: Oversight Hearings before the Committee on Interior and Insular Affairs, Subcommittee on mines and mining, US Congress, 96th Congress, 2nd Session, 1980.
Report of the People's Republic of Angola to the Second Session of the International Commission of Enquiry into the Crimes of the Racist and Apartheid Regime in Southern Africa (Centre Against Apartheid; Department of Political and Security Council Affairs 12/82 1982).
Report of the Security Council Special Mission to the Republic of Guinea Established under Resolution 289 (1970), UN Security Council Official Records, Special Supplement No 2, 1970.
Report of the Special Mission to Africa South and East of the Sahara, House of Representatives, Committee on Foreign Affairs, 84th Congress, 2nd Session, July 1956.
Resource Development in South Africa and US Policy, Hearings, US Congress, Committee on International Relations, Subcommittee on International Resources, Food and Energy, House of Representatives, 94th Congress, 2nd Session, May–June 1976.
Resources in Rhodesia: Implications for US Policy, Hearings, Committee on International Relations, Subcommittee on Inter-

national Resources, House of Representatives, 94th Congress, 2nd Session, 1976.
Special Study mission to Africa, South and East of the Sahara, Hearings before the Committee on Foreign Affairs, Subcommittee on Africa, House of Representatives, July 1965.
Towards Improving US–Cuba Relations, 95th Congress, 1st Session, Report of a Special Study Mission to Cuba, February 1977.
US Interests in Africa, Hearings before the Subcommittee on Africa, Committee on Foreign Affairs, House of Representatives, 96th Congress, 1st Session, October/November 1979.
US Minerals Dependence on South Africa, A Report to the Committee on Foreign Relations, US Senate 1982.
US Security Agreements and Commitments abroad: Ethiopia, Hearings before the Subcommittee on US Security Agreements and Commitments Abroad, Committee on Foreign Relations, House of Representatives, 91st Congress, 2nd Session, June 1970.
US Security Agreements and Commitments Abroad: Spain and Portugal, Hearings before the Committee on Foreign Relations, Subcommittee on US security agreements and commitments abroad, US Senate March/April 1969, July 1970, 91st Congress, 2nd Session.
Vandenburg Resolutions and the North Atlantic Treaty, Hearings held in Executive Session before the Committee on Foreign Relations, US Senate, 80th Congress, 2nd Session; 81st Congress, 1st Session, June 1948/9 (Historical Series: August 1973).
What have South Africa's Traditional Suppliers of Arms Done to Abide by the Mandatory Arms Embargo Against Apartheid South Africa? (Centre Against Apartheid: 26/78, September 1978).

SECONDARY SOURCES

I NATO and Africa

Adelman, K., *African Realities* (New York: Crane, Russak and Co., 1980).
Allen, P., 'Rites of Passage in Madagascar', *Africa Report*, 17 February 1971.
Allen and Isaacman, B., 'Mozambique: In Pursuit of Non-Alignment', *Africa Report*, May/June 1983.

Aluko, O. (ed.) *The Foreign Policies of African States* (London: Hodder and Stoughton, 1977).
Aron, R., 'Reflections on American Diplomacy', *Daedalus*, Fall 1962.
Attwood, W., *The Reds and the Blacks* (London: 1967).
Austin, D., *Britain and South Africa* (Oxford University Press, 1966).
Axel, L., 'La Congolisation de l'Afrique de l'Angola: Une grave menace pour l'Occident et pour l'OTAN', *Revue Militaire Generale*, October 1961.
Ball, G., *The Discipline of Power* (New York: Little and Brown and Co., 1968).
Barber, J., *South Africa's Foreign Policy 1945–70* (Oxford University Press, 1973).
——, *The West and South Africa* (London: Routledge and Kegan Paul, 1982).
——, *The Uneasy Relationship: Britain and South Africa* (London: Heinemann, 1983).
Bell, M., *Military Assistance to Independent African States*, Adelphi Paper 15 (London: IISS, 1964).
Bissell, R., *Southern Africa in the World: Autonomy or Independence* (Philadelphia: Foreign Policy Research Institute, 1978).
——, *South Africa and the United States: The Erosion of an Influence Relationship* (New York: Praeger, 1982).
Boateng, E., *A Political Geography of Africa* (Cambridge University Press, 1978).
Bosgra, S. and van Krimpen, C., 'Origin of Portuguese Military Equipment', *Portugal and NATO* (Amsterdam: Angola Comité, 1969).
Bosson, T. and Varon, B., *The Mining Industry and the Developing Countries* (Oxford University Press, 1977).
Braun, D., *The Indian Ocean: Region of Conflict or Peace Zone?* (London: Hurst and Co., 1983).
Brosio, M., 'Consultation and the Atlantic Alliance', *Survival*, 16:3 May–June 1974.
Bruce, N., *Portugal: the Last Empire* (New York: Wiley, 1975).
Buchan, A., *NATO in the 1960s: Implications of Inter-dependence* (London: Chatto and Windus, 1964).
Castagno, A., 'A Neutral Somalia', *Africa Report*, 6 August 1961.
Cervenka, Z. and Rogers B., *The Nuclear Axis: Secret Collaboration*

Between West Germany and South Africa (London: Julian Friedmann, 1978).
Chaliand, G., *The Struggle for Africa: Conflict of the Great Powers* (London: Macmillan, 1982).
Chichester, M., 'Whitehall Cover-up; Westminster Exposure', *Navy International*, July 1976.
Cleveland, H., *NATO: the Transatlantic Bargain* (New York: Praeger, 1970).
Connolly, R., 'Africa's Strategic Importance' in G. Haines (ed.) *Africa Today* (Baltimore: Johns Hopkins University Press, 1955).
Cot, J-P., 'Winning East–West in North–South', *Foreign Policy*, 46, Spring 1982.
Cottrell, A. and Dougherty, J., *The Politics of the Atlantic Alliance* (New York: Praeger, 1964).
——, *The Atlantic Alliance: a Short Practical Guide* (London: Pall Mall Press, 1964).
Crocker, C., 'France's Changing Military Interests', *Africa Report*, June 1968.
——, 'Military Dependence: The Colonial Legacy in Africa', *Journal of Modern African Studies*, 12:2, 1974.
—— and Lewis, A., 'Missing Opportunities in Africa', *Foreign Policy*, 35, Summer 1979.
Crozier, B., *The Soviet Presence in Somalia*, *Conflict Studies*, 54, February 1975.
Darby, P., *British Defence Policy East of Suez 1947–68* (Oxford University Press, 1973).
Debré, M., 'La France et sa Défense', *Revue de Défense Nationale*, January 1972.
Edlin, J., 'SADDC: Key to Southern Africa's Economic Independence', *Africa Report*, May–June 1983.
Ellsworth, R., 'New Imperatives for the Old Alliance', *Atlantic Community Quarterly*, 16:4, Winter 1978–9.
Emerson, R., 'The Atlantic Community and the Emerging Countries', *International Organisation*, 17:3, Summer 1963.
——, *Africa and US Policy* (New Jersey: Prentice Hall, 1967).
Farrar, T., *Warclouds in the Horn of Africa* (New York: Carnegie Endowment for Peace, 1979).
Fitzsimons, M., *The Foreign Policy of the British Labour Government 1945–51* (Notre Dame, Indiana: 1953).
Furniss, E., *France: Troubled Ally* (Oxford University Press, 1960).

Gallois, P., 'French Defence Planning: the Future in the Past', *International Security*, Fall 1976.

Geldenhuys, D., *The Neutral Option and Subcontinental Solidarity* (Johannesburg: South Africa Institute of International Affairs, 1979).

Gineiewski, P., 'South Africa and the Defence of the Cape Route', *NATO's Fifteen Nations*, 17:2, April–May 1972.

Govett, M., 'The Geographical Concentration of World Mineral Supplies', *Resources Policy*, December 1975.

Greig, I., *The Communist Challenge to Africa* (London: Foreign Affairs Association, 1977).

Grosser, A., *The Western Alliance* (New York: Continuum, 1980).

Gruhn, I., 'British Arms Sales to South Africa: the Limits of African Diplomacy', *Studies in Race and Nations* 3 (Colorado: University of Denver, 1972).

Grundy, K., 'We're Against Apartheid . . . But: Dutch Policy Towards South Africa', *Studies in Race and Nations*, 5:3, 1973–4.

Guelke, A., 'Southern Africa and the Superpowers', *International Affairs*, Autumn 1980.

Guillemin, J., 'L'intervention Exterieure dans la Politique Militaire de la France en Afrique Noire', *Revue Francaise d'Etudes Politiques Africaines*, July 1981.

——, 'L'Importance des Bases dans la Politique Militaire de la France en Afrique Noire Francophone et Madagascar', *Revue Francaise d'Etudes Politiques Africaines*, August–September 1981.

Gurtov, M., *The United States Versus the Third World: Anti-Nationalism and Intervention* (New York: Praeger, 1974).

Hahn, L., 'Last chance in North Africa', *Foreign Affairs*, 36:2, January 1958.

Hanrieder, W. and Auton, G., *The Foreign Policies of West Germany, France and Britain* (New Jersey: Prentice Hall, 1980).

Hassan, B., 'Big Power Rivalry in the Indian Ocean: a Tanzanian View', *Africa Quarterly*, 15:3, 1976.

Henderson, N., *The Birth of NATO* (London: Weidenfeld and Nicolson, 1982).

Hernu, C., 'Répondre aux Defis d'un Monde Dangereux', *Défense Nationale*, December 1981.

——, 'Sécurité Internationale et Développement: La France et L'Afrique', *Revue des Deux Mondes*, August 1982.

Hiemstra, R., 'Containing Communism', *Africa Institute Bulletin*, 8:9, October 1969.

Holmes, O., 'Portugal – Atlantic Pact Ally', *American Perspective*, 4:1, Winter 1950.
Jaster, R., *South Africa's Narrowing Security Options*, Adelphi Paper 159 (London: IISS, 1981).
Joire-Noulens, 'Quelle marine et pour quoi faire le temps de paix?', *Défense Nationale*, July 1976.
Killick, J., 'The East–West View from NATO', *World Issues*, December 1978.
Kissinger, H., *The Troubled Partnership: a Reappraisal of the Atlantic Alliance* (New York: Harper and Row, 1965).
Krasner, S., *Defending the National Interest: Raw Material Investment and US Foreign Policy*.
Laing, R., 'South Africa – A Bastion for an Oceanic Association', *Report from South Africa*, June 1969.
Laurie, G., 'The Simonstown agreement: South Africa, Britain and the Commonwealth', *South African Law Journal* 85:2, May 1968.
Legum, C., *The Fall of Haile Selassie's Empire* (London: 1975).
——, 'The Role of the Big Powers', in *After Angola: the War over Southern Africa*, (New York: Africana, 1976).
Lewis, W., 'How a Defence Planner Looks at Africa', in Helen Kitchen (ed.) *Africa: From Mystery to Maze* (Lexington: Lexington Books, 1976).
Ligot, M., 'La Cooperation Militaire dans les Accords Passes entre la France et les Etats Africains et Malgache d'Expression Francaise', *Revue Juridique et Politique*, 17, 1963.
Louis, W., *Imperialism at Bay: the United States and the Decolonisation of the British Empire 1941–5* (New York: Oxford University Press, 1978).
Luckham, R., 'Le Militarisme Français', *Politique Africaine*, 5, February 1982.
Mangold, P., 'Shaba I and Shaba II', *Survival*, 21:3, May–June 1979.
Marcum, J., *The Politics of Indifference: Portugal and Africa. A Case Study in American Foreign Policy* (Syracuse University: 1972).
——, *The Angolan Revolution 1950–62* Vol. I (Cambridge Massachusetts Institute of Technology Press, 1969).
——, *The Angolan Revolution. Exile Politics and Guerrilla Warfare 1962–76* Vol. II (Cambridge: Massachusetts Institute of Technology Press, 1978).

Martin, D. and Johnson, P., *The Struggle for Zimbabwe* (London: Faber and Faber, 1981).
Martin, L. (ed.) *Neutralism and Non-Alignment: The New States in World Affairs* (New York: Praeger, 1962).
——, *British Defence Policy: The Long Recessional*, Adelphi paper 61 (London: IISS, 1969).
——, 'The Cape Route', *Survival*, 12:10, October 1970.
Mayall, J., *Africa: The Cold war and After* (London: Elek Books, 1971).
Minter, W., *Portuguese Africa and the West* (London: Penguin Books, 1972).
Minty, A., 'Implementing the Arms Embargo Against South Africa', Excerpts from a statement before the UN Special Committee on Apartheid, 12 December 1977, *Objective Justice*, 9:4, Winter 1977/8.
——, 'International Action Against Apartheid in South Africa', *Objective Justice*, 5:3, July–August 1973.
Mitchell, C., 'External Involvement in Civil Strife: the Case of Chad', *Yearbook of World Affairs*, 1972.
Moisi, D. and Lellouche, P., 'French Policy in Africa: a Lonely Battle Against Destabilisation', *International Security*, 3:4, Spring 1979.
Moore, B., *NATO and the Future of Europe* (New York: Harper and Row, 1958).
Morris-Jones, W., *Decolonisation and After: The British and French Experience* (London: Frank Cass, 1980).
Müller-Ohlsen, L., 'Die Weltmetallwirtschaft im industriellen Entwicklungsprozess', *Kieler Studien*, 165 (Tübingen: 1981).
Nielsen, W., *The Great Powers and Africa* (London: Pall Mall, 1969).
Nkrumah, K., 'African Prospects', *Foreign Affairs*, 37:1, October 1958.
——, *Neo-capitalism: The Last Stage of Imperialism* (London: 1965).
Nolutsunghu, S., *South Africa in Africa: A Study of Ideology and Foreign Policy* (Manchester University Press, 1975).
Northedge, F., *Descent from Power: British Foreign Policy 1945–73* (London: George Allen and Unwin, 1974).
Nyerere, J., 'America and Southern Africa', *Foreign Affairs*, 55:4, July 1977.
Ojedokon, O., 'The Anglo-Nigerian Entente and its Demise 1960–2', *Journal of Commonwealth Political Studies*, 9:3, November 1971.

Olympio, S., 'African Problems and the Cold War', *Foreign Affairs*, 40:1, October 1961.
Osgood, R., *NATO: The Entangling Alliance* (Chicago: University of Chicago Press, 1962).
Ovendale, R., 'The South African policy of the British Labour government 1947–51', *International Affairs*, 59:1, Winter 1982–3.
Padelford, N., 'Political cooperation in the North Atlantic Comunity', *International Organisation*, II, Summer 1955.
Palmberg, M., 'Present Imperialist Policies in Southern Africa: The Case for Scandinavian Disassociation', in D. Anglin (ed.) *Canada, Scandinavia and Southern Africa* (Uppsala: Scandinavian Institute of African Studies, 1978).
Palmer, B., 'US Security Interests in Africa South of the Sahara' *American Enterprise Institute Defense Review*, 2:6, 1978.
Pledge, R., 'Le Tchad ou la Theorie Francaise des Dominos Africaines', *Esprit*, February 1970.
Reid, E., *Time of Fear and Hope: the Making of the North Atlantic Treaty* (Toronto: McLelland and Stewart, 1977).
Ripon, G., 'South Africa and Naval Strategy: The Importance of South Africa', *The Round Table*, 239, 1970.
Rivkin, A., 'Lost Goals in Africa', *Foreign Affairs*, 44:1, October 1965.
Samuel, M. (ed.) *Africa and the West* (Boulder, Colorado: Westview Press, 1980).
Sanger, C., 'What does Canada care about Africa?', *Africa Report*, 15:4, April 1970.
Schlegel, J., *The Deceptive Ash: Bilingualism and Canadian Policy in Africa 1957–71* (University Press of America, 1978).
Smart, I., 'The New Atlantic Charter', *The World Today*, June 1973.
Spence, J. E., *The Strategic Significance of Southern Africa* (London: Royal United Services Institute, 1972).
Spencer, J., *Ethiopia, the Horn of Africa and United States Policy* (Cambridge, Mass.: Institute for Foreign Policy Analysis, 1977).
Stokke, L. and Widstrand, C. (eds) *The UN–OAU Conference on Southern Africa* (Uppsala: Scandinavian Institute of African Studies, 1973).
Stransz-Hupe, R., *NATO at Thirty: Symposium on the Future of the Alliance* (Washington DC: Atlantic Council of the United States, 1979).

Touscouz, J., 'La Normalisation de la Cooperation Bilaterale de la France avec les Pays Africaines Francophones', *Etudes Internationales*, 2:2, June 1974.
Uys, S., 'Namibia: The Socialist Dilemma', *African Affairs*, October 1982.
Valenta, J., 'The Soviet–Cuban Intervention in Angola', *US Naval Institute Proceedings*, April 1980.
Vandenbosch, A., *South Africa and the World: the Foreign Policy of Apartheid* (Lexington: University of Kentucky Press, 1970).
Vernon, R. and Levy, B., 'State Owned Enterprises in the World Economy: The Case of Iron Ore', in L. Jones (ed.) *Public Enterprise in Less Developed Countries: Multi-Disciplinary Perspectives* (Cambridge, Mass.: Harvard University Press, 1981).
Vivekanandan, B., 'Naval power in the Indian Ocean', *The Round Table*, 257, January 1975.
Watt, D. C., 'The Continuing Strategic Importance of Simonstown', *US Naval Institute Proceedings*, October 1969.
——, 'Britain and the Indian Ocean: Diplomacy before Defence', *Political Quarterly*, 42:3, July–September 1971.
Wilson, H., *The Labour Government 1964–70* (London: Weidenfeld and Nicolson, 1971).
Wohlgemuth, P., 'The Portuguese Territories and the UN', *International Conciliation*, 545, November 1963.
Yost, D., 'French Policy in Chad and the Libyan Challenge' (unpublished paper, IISS, May 1982).
Zumwalt, E., *On Watch: A Memoir* (New York: Quadrangle, 1976).

II The Warsaw Pact and Africa

Albright, D., 'The USSR: Its Communist allies and Southern Africa', *International Affairs Bulletin*, 4:3, 1980.
Athay, R., 'Perspectives on Soviet Merchant Shipping' in M. MccGwire, (ed.) *Soviet Naval Developments* (New York: Praeger, 1973).
Ausch, S., *Theory and practice of CMEA cooperation* (Budapest: Academiai Kiado, 1972).
Balkay, B., 'The Developing Countries and the Raw Material Supply of the World Aluminium Industry', *Economic Relations with the Socialist Countries*, vol. I (Budapest: Institute for World Economics, 1978).
Bartha, F., 'Some Ideas on the Creation of a Multilateral Clearing

System among the CMEA', *Soviet and East European Foreign Trade*, Spring 1976.

Baryshnikov, V., 'Raw Material Resources of Africa', *International Affairs*, (Moscow) December 1974.

Bethkenhagen, J., 'Energy Sector of the German Economy Faces Difficult Tasks', *Deutschland Archiv*, No. 5, May 1981.

Black, W., 'Soviet Fishery Agreements with Developing Countries', *Marine Policy*, 7:3, July 1983.

Brzezinski, Z. (ed.) *Africa and the Communist World* (Stanford University Press, 1965).

Croan, M., *East Germany and the Soviet Connection* (Beverley Hills: Sage, 1976).

Csaba, L., 'Some Problems of the International Socialist Monetary System', *Acta Oeconomica*, 23:1, 1979.

——, 'The Place of the CMEA in the World Economy of the 1980s', *Valosag*, July 1982.

——, 'World Economic Adjustment and Economic Development in Eastern Europe', *Kulgazdasag*, 4, 1982.

Davidchik, M. and Mahoney, R., 'Soviet Civil Fleets in the Third World', in B. Dismukes and J. McConnel (eds) *Soviet Naval Policy in the Third World* (New York: Pergammon, 1979).

Dietz, R., *Price Changes in Soviet Trade with the CMEA and the Rest of the World since 1975* (Joint Economic Committee of US Congress, 1979).

Dobosiewicz, Z., *Economic Integration of Less Developed Countries* (Warsaw: 1971).

Dobozi, I., 'Projected Trends of World Raw Material and Energy Markets until 2000', *Studies on Developing Countries*, No. 110 (Budapest: Institute for World Economics, 1982).

Dobroczynski, M., *Africa and International Trade* (Warsaw: 1972).

Ellis, J., 'Expansion of the Soviet Merchant Fleet – Implications for the West', *NATO Review*, 3, 1979.

Goldman, M., Dohan, M. and Theriot, L., *The Soviet Economy in a Time of Change* (US Congress, Joint Economic Committee, 1979).

Grabig, G. and Brendel, G., *Commodity Market Relations in Socialist Economic Integration* (1975).

Gromyko, A., 'African Realities and the "Conflict Strategy" Myth', *New Times*, 51, December 1978.

——, 'Africa in the Strategy of Neo-colonialism', *International Affairs* (Moscow) February 1978.

Gromyko, A., 'Western Diplomacy Versus Southern Africa', *International Affairs* (Moscow) March 1979.
Kaplan, S. (ed.) *The Diplomacy of Power: Soviet Armed Forces as a Political Instrument* (Washington DC: Brookings Institution, 1981).
Keren, M., *East European Economies* (Washington: US Congress, Joint Economic Committee, 1977).
Kislov, A. and Vasilikov, V., 'The Current Stage of US Policy in Africa', *Asii i Afriki Segodnia*, 9 September 1978.
Kiss, T. (ed.) *The Market of Socialist Economic Integration: Selected Conference Papers* (Budapest: Academiai Kiado, 1973).
Klinghoffer, A., *The Angolan War: A Study in Soviet Policy in the Third World* (Boulder, Colorado: Westview Press, 1980).
Koves, A., 'East–West Trade and the Foreign Economic Strategy of CMEA Countries', *Kulgazdasag*, 5 May 1982.
Lavigne, M., 'The Problem of the Socialist Multinational Enterprise', *ACES Bulletin*, 18:1, Summer 1975.
———, 'The Soviet Union inside COMECON', *Soviet Studies*, 35:2, April 1973.
Lowenthal, R., *Model or Ally: the Communist Powers and the Developing Countries* (Oxford University Press, 1977).
Madr, M., 'Severoatlanticky Pakt a Afrika' (NATO and Africa) *Rude Pravo*, 21 October 1962.
Mandi, P., 'Trade Perspectives between European CMEA Countries and Africa and the Middle East', *Economic Relations of Africa with the Socialist Countries Vol. I: Hungarian Contributions* (Budapest: Institute for World Economics, 1978).
Mondous, V., 'The Socialist Countries and Their Relation with the National Liberation Movement of the Colonial Countries', *Pravda* (Plzen) 4 July 1964.
Morrison, D., 'Mineral Economic Relations of Poland and the Developing Countries of Africa', *Studies on Developing Countries*, 21, 1972.
Orosz, A., 'Trade of African Developing Countries up to 1970 and Prognosis to 1980', *Studies on the Developing Countries*, No. 70 (Budapest: Institute for World Economics, 1975).
———, 'Our economic relations with the developing countries', *Valosag*, March 1977.
Papp, D., 'Soviet Non-Fuel Mineral Resources: Surplus or Scarcity?', *Resources Policy*, 8:3, September 1982.

———, *The Non-Fuel Minerals Outlook for the USSR through 1990* (Washington DC: Bureau of Mines, 1981).

Pavlov, P., 'Problems of the Development and Improvement of the Mineral-Rich Material Complex of CMEA Countries', *Mezhdunarodni Otnosheniya*, 6, 1980.

Pechota, V., 'Czechoslovakia and the Third World', in M. Radu (ed.) *Eastern Europe and the Third World* (New York: Praeger, 1981).

Pecsi, K., *The Future of Socialist Integration* (New York: Sharpe, 1981).

Prokopczvk, J., *The Third World in Search of a World to Develop* (Warsaw: 1973).

Remnek, R., *Soviet Policy in the Horn of Africa: The Decision to Intervene* (Alexandria, Virginia: Center for Naval Analyses, Professional Paper 270).

Rosfielde, S. (ed.) *Economic Welfare and the Economics of Soviet Socialism* (Cambridge University Press, 1981).

Scrivener, D., 'Merchant Marine in Soviet Naval Strategy', *Marine Policy*, 7:2, April 1983.

Siegfried, H. and Kupper, S., *DDR und die Dritte Welt* (Munich: 1976).

Strishkov, V., 'The Soviet Union', in *Mining Annual Review* (1980).

Tabarin, E., *The New Scramble for Africa* (Moscow: Progress Publishers, 1974).

Tau, B., 'The Imperialist Threat to Africa', *African Communist*, 45, 1971.

Trappen, F. and Weischauft, U., 'Aktuelle Fragen des Kampfes un Nationale und Soziale Befreung in sub-Saharischen Afrika', *Deutsche Aussenpolitik*, 24:2, February 1979.

Uralov, K., 'Angola: The Triumph of the Right Cause', *International Affairs* (Moscow) No. 5, May 1976.

———, 'The Acute Problem of Southern Africa', *International Affairs*, 1977.

Vanneman, P., 'Soviet Intervention in Angola: Intentions and Implications', *Strategic Review*, Summer 1976.

Vanous, J., 'East European Economic Slowdown', *Problems of Communism*, 31:4, July–August 1982.

Volsky, D., 'Southern Version of NATO', *New Times*, 26 September 1976.

———, 'A Strategy without a Future', *New Times*, 3 August 1978.

Wiles, P. (ed.) *The New Communist Third World* (London: Croom Helm, 1982).

Willerding, K., 'Die DDR und die nationalbefreiten staaten Asiens und Afrikans', *Asien, Afrika, Latinamerika*, 25, 1974.

——, 'Zur Afrika-Politik der DDR', *Deutsche Aussenpolitik*, 29:8, August 1979.

Zevin, L., 'New Concepts of Economic Development and International Cooperation in the Third World Countries', *Voprosy Ekonomika*, 1978.

Zimmerman, H., 'The GDR in the 1970s', *Problems of Communism*, March – April 1978.

Zurawicki, L., 'The Prospects of Tripartite Cooperation', *Intereconomics* (Hamburg) 7/8, 1978.

Index

Acheson, D., 6, 63
Algerian war, 31–5, 121
Anglo-Nigerian Defence Treaty, 22, 212–4
Angola and NATO, 95–9, 101–2
  Soviet intervention, 235–40
Aron, R., 12, 242
Atlantic Pact, 3, 5–6, 248–54
Atlantic Policy Advisory Group, 113

BENELUX, 252–4
Brosio, M., 16

Caetano, M., 62, 65, 92, 229
Canada, 210–12, 223–4
Commonwealth Conference (1971), 25, 78, 222–7
Congo war, 4, 5, 10
Council for Mutual Economic Assistance (CMEA)
  Bulgaria and Romania as case studies, 162–4
  fuel/non-fuel shortages, 164–71
  and minerals, 158–62
Cuban missile crisis, 5, 10
Cubans in Angola, 94–7, 145–7, 190–2

Debré, M., 28, 37, 40
de Gaulle, C., 15, 33
Diego Garcia, 43–5, 55, 135, 217–22
Dulles, J. F., 10, 42

East of Suez, 24–9
Eisenhower Doctrine, 35
Ethiopia and Soviet intervention, 103–12
  NATO response, 108–12

French intervention, 29–40, 114f.
  Chad, 116–22
  since 1978, 129–33
  Zaire, 122–9, 230–5

GDR, 192–6
  and Warsaw Pact, 196–202
Guinea, 34, 56–9
  and USSR, 88–91

Heath, E., 25, 26, 227

Indian Ocean
  and France, 35–40
  and US, 43–7

Kagnew, 42, 103, 105
Kenya, 20–1
Kissinger, H., 12, 18, 101–3, 136–7, 172, 183, 238–9
Kolwezi, ix, 27, 232

Lajes, 63–4
Libya, 4, 21–2, 118–21

NATO Council, 9, 10, 13–14, 51
  and arms embargo against South Africa, 222–6
  and Portugal, 227–30
NATO Task Force, 28, 81
Nkrumah, K., 207–8
Nogueira, F., 52, 55
Non-alignment, 207–10, 212–22
Nyerere, J., ix, 210, 223–7, 234

Obasanjo, D., ix

Patricio, R., 58
Politique afrique, 20
Political committee (NATO), 241
Portugal, 11, 12
   and African colonies, 49–70
   and arms sales, 59–68
   and Canada, 66–8
   and defence of Europe, 50–2
   and public opinion, 68–71

SACLANT, 51, 54, 55
   and South Africa, 82–6
SADCC, 149–53
Salazar, A., 50, 52
SAN, 142–3
Silvermine, 134–6
Smuts, J., 5, 71
South Africa and arms embargo, 137–9

destabilisation, 143–53
NATO, 71–5
neutralism, 139–43
UK, 71, 73, 82
Soviet arms transfers, 243–8
Spaak, H., 8, 11

United Kingdom, 6, 119–29
United States, 40–7

Warsaw Pact
   Cape route, 177–82
   denial of minerals, 182–9
   Southern Africa, 176–89

WEU, 7
Wilson, H., 24

Zaire, 94–5, 122–9, 130